BEYOND
TOLERANCE

BEYOND TOLERANCE

Searching for
Interfaith Understanding
in America

Gustav Niebuhr

Viking

VIKING
Published by the Penguin Group
Penguin Group (USA) Inc., 375 Hudson Street, New York, New York 10014, U.S.A.
Penguin Group (Canada), 90 Eglinton Avenue East, Suite 700, Toronto, Ontario,
Canada M4P 2Y3 (a division of Pearson Penguin Canada Inc.)
Penguin Books Ltd, 80 Strand, London WC2R 0RL, England
Penguin Ireland, 25 St. Stephen's Green, Dublin 2, Ireland (a division of Penguin Books Ltd)
Penguin Books Australia Ltd, 250 Camberwell Road, Camberwell, Victoria 3124,
Australia (a division of Pearson Australia Group Pty Ltd)
Penguin Books India Pvt Ltd, 11 Community Centre, Panchsheel Park,
New Delhi – 100 017, India
Penguin Group (NZ), 67 Apollo Drive, Rosedale, North Shore 0632, New Zealand
(a division of Pearson New Zealand Ltd)
Penguin Books (South Africa) (Pty) Ltd, 24 Sturdee Avenue, Rosebank,
Johannesburg 2196, South Africa

Penguin Books Ltd, Registered Offices: 80 Strand, London WC2R 0RL, England

First published in 2008 by Viking Penguin, a member of Penguin Group (USA) Inc.

Copyright © Gustav Niebuhr, 2008
All rights reserved

ISBN-13: 978-1-60751-749-8

Printed in the United States of America

To Christopher and Jonathan

Contents

Preface

One weekend late last autumn, long after the leaves had fallen, I spent several hours hunting down small treasures in my parents' old home, one step ahead of the movers. Months earlier, my sister and I had helped move our mother and father from the suburban Boston house where they had lived for half a century, and where we had grown up. Now my mother had asked me to search especially for a small sugar bowl, a gift to her from a long-deceased aunt, who had pronounced it an ancient heirloom even when she—the aunt—had been a girl in the 1890s. Reaching around inside a mahogany cabinet, I felt pleased to locate the bowl. But I touched something else then, too, something with a feel both softer and more angular. Pulling it out, I found that I held a book of prayers, slightly larger than my own hand. Nearly sixty years old, it had a deeply worn navy blue cover and a spine cracked with use. Its place in my family became immediately apparent: On the flyleaf, I recognized my grandfather's handwriting. He had given the book as a gift to his mother on her birthday.

I mention it because this discovery explains something important about my family, and, perhaps, too, about how I came to write this book. As a child, I may well have seen my great grandmother with the prayer book. But I had neither cause nor curiosity to open it until that recent November day. What struck me this time was the sheer range—the catholicity—of its contents. Yes, to be sure, it was a Christian volume: After all, Lydia Niebuhr had been the daughter

and wife of Protestant ministers and the mother and grandmother
of theologians. But the book crossed all the usual boundaries, which
are so often fraught with specific disputations and a general hostility. Its prayers came from Puritan, Eastern Orthodox, Roman Catholic, and Anglican sources, among others. Here I held the words of
St. Augustine; Cardinal John Henry Newman, the famous English
convert to Catholicism; the Reverend Walter Rauschenbusch, the
great Baptist exponent of the Social Gospel. Here was a prayer from
the American Quaker and abolitionist John Woolman; here were
sections of the Greek and Coptic (Egyptian) liturgies. What united
this disparate collection? All the writings praised God.

I mention this because I come from a family that has, among its
traditions, a tendency to take religion seriously, by which I mean it
has been a part of our daily lives—not as a narrow, personal piety
(that is not part of our tradition), but instead as a way of understanding society and our relationship and responsibilities to it. I trace this
family tradition back four generations, to my great grandfather—
Lydia's husband—after whom I'm named. An immigrant, he ran
away from his German home as a teenager and made his way to the
American Midwest, where he quickly found work as a farmhand.
I've always admired his daring in making that move, but I've since
found far more in him to appreciate than that. Gustav Niebuhr un-
derwent a conversion experience not long after he arrived in the
United States, went to seminary and eventually emerged as a leading
figure in the old German Evangelical Synod of North America. He
worked for reconciliation and cooperation between Reformed
Protestants (his branch) and Lutherans. To outsiders, the differences
between such groups may seem obscure, even baffling. But they
were real and they remain so. The question is, how far apart should
they keep people? My great grandfather passed on his perspective to
two of his sons. My grandfather, H. Richard Niebuhr, a theologian
at Yale, worked successfully to unite denominations. His older
brother, my great-uncle, Reinhold Niebuhr, taught at Union Theo-

logical Seminary in New York and took the bold step in the 1930s in demanding Christians cease targeting Jews for conversion. Both men were committed Christians. But they had no use for legalistic literalism, for aggressive fundamentalism or its treacherous near-cousin, political militancy. As Reinhold would write, "Absolutism, in both religious and political idealism, is a splendid incentive to heroic action, but a dangerous guide in immediate and concrete situations. In religion, it permits absurdities and in politics cruelties, which fail to achieve justifying consequences because the inertia of human nature remains a nemesis to the absolute ideal. . . . The fanaticism which in the individual may appear in the guise of a harmless or pathetic vagary, when expressed in political policy, shuts the gates of mercy on mankind." These are sentences that I have always felt speak with enormous power and clarity as a check on human pretensions. He published those words in 1932. The previous year, my grandfather took his family to visit cousins in Germany. During the trip, he chanced to hear a speech by Hitler, then two years away from seizing political power. My grandfather, fluent in the German with which he had been raised, returned from that evil event so emotionally distraught that my father, then only five years old, could recall that day vividly more than six decades later. He told me the story and did so with a wonder that what his own father so readily perceived as utter malevolence should not have been obvious to all at the time.

My sister and I grew up in a home where our parents led us in grace at meals, prayers at bedtime, and to church on Sundays. They made sure we understood that we shared the world with a great variety of religious (and nonreligious) identities, all of which belonged to people who deserved as much respect as we ourselves would want. As a child and, later, as an adult, I've met people who share that perspective, people whom I would credit as possessing a genuine spaciousness with regard to others. I believe that quality works mightily to hold society together, even as prideful and angry individuals work to damage it. I have found myself often wishing such ordinary peacemakers were more publicly recognized. They are a larger group than the divisive and destructive among us. But with certain exceptions, their fame is fleeting—and their success is never guaranteed. Still, the risks they may take at times of crisis—risks on behalf of us all—can be breathtaking. As I write this, I think of those thousands of robed Buddhist monks who marched for democracy in Myanmar, risking beatings and bullets, on behalf of their fellow citizens in September 2007. Because of its generosity, as well as the danger involved, their action strikes me as far more emotionally involving, even riveting in its sense of dedication to shared ideals, than the threats and suicidal attacks by our era's terrorists.

Problem is, in the two professions in which I've spent my life—journalism and academia—the world I describe is little recognized. Religion itself is often conflated with a spiritual militancy (conservatism is *not* the right word). It is reduced to the status of a player in a zero-sum game, where its supposed opponent, secularism, is made to stand in for a host of freedoms and a base of knowledge that we Americans rightly hold dear. Such simplistic thinking, such an utterly unnuanced view of the universe sometimes strikes me as humorous. It has long made me wonder where I fit in, son of a woman who sang hymns in our home and also worked as a volunteer for George McGovern's presidential campaign?

I did my best as a journalist not to let my personal attachments intrude upon my writing. My ethics demanded a rigorous deference to the journalistic ideal of keeping oneself out of the picture. I tried to give everyone I spoke with the fair hearing he or she deserved and the dignity of being allowed to speak for him- or herself. But since I left that professional world, I've felt the freedom to shift somewhat—not toward partisanship—but toward my own formative past. It is from that perspective that this book springs.

In closing this section, I turn back to the prayer book, which sits beside me as I write, itself a demonstration of my conviction that the sacred and secular are never easily separated. Thus, Lydia's book contains prayers from people who were not ordained or sanctioned to write them by any church. Here's how one begins, written by Robert Louis Stevenson:

"We beseech Thee, Lord, to behold us with favor, folk of many families and nations gathered together in the peace of this roof, weak men and women subsisting under the covert of Thy patience. Be patient still; suffer us yet a while longer—with our broken purposes of good, with our idle endeavors against evil, suffer us a while longer to endure and (if it may be) help us to do better.... Amen."

INTRODUCTION

On Doubt and Conversion

On a restless night a few years back, William Swing came to a personal turning point—a conversion, he would call it. At the time, as bishop of the Episcopal Church's Diocese of California, he was one of the most prominent Christians in the nation's most populous state. His jurisdiction included a structural jewel, Grace Cathedral atop San Francisco's Nob Hill. The French Gothic building faces east, and above its grandly arched entryway rises a large and luminous rose window, flanked by two towers that root the cathedral into the soil of one of San Francisco's most picturesque locations. The event that preceded that night should have been exciting and gratifying. Hours earlier, Swing had received a call from the United Nations. An official there had rung up to request that the cathedral host a service commemorating the UN's upcoming fiftieth anniversary. In 1945, the organization's founding charter had been signed in a hotel on the very same block. The UN, the man told Swing, wanted to celebrate the date by bringing in ambassadors from nearly two hundred nations, along with representatives of the world's major religions—that was where the bishop would come in. "So we could have the nations and the religions together," Swing recalled him saying. The event would be purely symbolic. But it got Swing thinking—and now he couldn't sleep. An obvious irony lay in this idea, inviting representatives of the world's religions for an event emphasizing peace and unity. "There were forty wars going on in the world that night," Swing said, in a conversation we had years later. "Most of them fueled—not caused, but *fueled*—by religion."

That night happened in 1993—not that the year itself was unusual, given his basic point. A random check of headlines illustrates the grounds for Swing's dismay. Religious differences turn up repeatedly and prominently in stories describing devastating violence. In January, for example, investigators working for the European Community accused Serbian militiamen of using rape as a systematic weapon to terrorize Muslim women during the war in Bosnia. In May, in Sri Lanka, a suicide bomber murdered the president of that South Asian nation, adding a spectacular new chapter to a long-running civil war colored by ethnic, linguistic, and religious differences. A few months later, nine people perished in a fish and chips shop in Belfast, victims of a bomb planted by the Irish Republican Army. In every case, religious identities figured in the conflicts, such that each fight could be characterized as a lethal clash of spiritualities—Orthodox Christians versus Muslims in southeastern Europe, Hindus versus Buddhists in Sri Lanka, Roman Catholics versus Protestants in Northern Ireland.

Again, none of this made 1993 exceptional. Nonetheless, when Swing arose the next morning, he wanted to try to find some means to bring people with differing religious beliefs together, to find common ethical principles to bridge the volatile theological chasms that separated them, drawing on peaceful elements within their various traditions. As an idea, it insisted on the possibility of collaboration. To imagine such a long-term, collective process was an act of faith in human capability and far more strategically demanding than any one group's planning an act of divisiveness or violence. It meant taking a gamble on others, that they might act in kind. Swing felt a sense of mission that next morning. He had been forced to a turning point, as if he had undergone, in his words, "a conversion to how we're going to have to live together."

The world's major religions, in all their varying complexities, are essentially neutral systems in the way they affect human temperaments. The effect any one of them may have on an individual adherent defies prediction and is likely to be dependent on social, cultural, and personal factors. Thus, the Roman Catholic Church in the United States inspired Dorothy Day, once a passionate but rather unhappy bohemian, to emerge as a creative, nationally powerful force on behalf of the poor. Decades after her death, she continues to inspire; many American Catholics would plead her cause for sainthood. But then there is Day's near-contemporary, the Reverend Charles Coughlin, who used his great natural gift for oratory for poisonous purposes, broadcasting anti-Semitic and fascist-leaning diatribes in the 1930s until America's siding with the Allies finally forced him off the air. Similarly, South Asian Islam produced a Badshah Khan, an exponent of nonviolence and close associate of Mohandas Gandhi. But it also allowed for the emergence of an Osama bin Laden.

Here, let me say flatly, as a warning to the reader: This is not a book about the world's Coughlins or, worse, its Bin Ladens. To be sure, I will mention incidents of religious hatred and religiously in- spired destruction, but only as inevitable reference points to an- other, quite different subject. I'm well aware of the way in which religious ideas have been, are, and will be used to sow contempt for entire populations and to bring about their oppression, injury, or even death. That's a subject on which others have written amply and insightfully. In the library at the university where I teach, books by the shelfful explore ways religious faith is manipulated by indi- viduals hell-bent on civil society's destruction, be they political demagogues, guerrilla leaders, or terrorist chiefs. The scholars and journalists who write these works, who have studied the perpetra- tors of religious violence, visiting them at their headquarters or in their jail cells, know that today's extremists share an essential quality with the most notorious of their recent, ideological counterparts—Stalin, Mao, and Pol Pot. They freely discount the basic humanity of entire populations of people whom they depict with terrifying stereotypes. Who suffers the consequences when such broad slanders are made? The European Community report estimated that twenty thousand Muslim women had been raped, saying sexual violence had become a tool of warfare, "usually perpetrated with the conscious intention of demoralizing and terrorizing communities," in order to drive them from their homes.

Neither is this a book about religious fundamentalism, an elastic term lately stretched to cover a vast variety of militant tendencies, including violence. Originally, "fundamentalist" served as a label for only the most theologically conservative of American Protestants, adherents of "The Fundamentals," a series of early twentieth-century pamphlets that argued the Bible's literal truth as a guide to history—the creation of the world and its inhabitants, the story of ancient Israel, the virgin birth, miracles, and the bodily resurrection of Jesus. But in recent years the word has leaped the banks of its theological origins and has become shorthand for rigorously exclusive, sometimes dangerous movements within all the world's major religions. Fundamentalism is a well-studied subject. For more than a dozen years, the University of Chicago Press published a series of books on fundamentalist expressions of religion worldwide, volumes principally edited by the scholars Martin Marty and R. Scott Appleby. Fundamentalism, with its unnuanced view of the world, its tendency to reduce everything to a struggle between cosmic good and evil, provides great fascination for the news media: Its proponents are often eminently quotable. But it is the province of a small, if significant, minority. Of necessity, I will refer occasionally to fundamentalism's most extreme forms and the political violence they produce, but they are not my main focus.

Instead, I have a different interest to explore—ironically, one that happens to be neatly identified in a book about religious terror, written by the sociologist Mark Juergensmeyer. At one point, he writes, "It is difficult to belittle and kill a person whom one knows and for whom one has no personal antipathy." The key phrases are *"whom one knows"* and *"no personal antipathy,"* six words that point toward a markedly different type of interaction among people in a world in which violence seems so dominant. (For example, we are approaching the centenary of World War I's famous "Christmas Truce," when British and German soldiers, entrenched against each other in Belgium on December 24, 1914, ceased shooting, joined in singing Christmas carols across no-man's-land, and eventually emerged to greet each other on that brutalized landscape to exchange gifts of chocolate, tobacco, and whiskey.) What interests me in writing this book is the idea that some people choose to build networks that deliberately cross boundaries in an era in which religious differences are so explosive. Call it a quiet countertrend: It directly challenges violence in God's name, even if it does not replace it. At its heart, it's a grassroots educational process in which the goal is to gain knowledge about individuals and their beliefs in a way that lessens fear. It is a new activity in the world, an entirely new phenomenon in our history. It is a social good, a basis for hope, and a tendency that ought to be nurtured and cultivated.

This book is based on visits and conversations with some of the people who have participated in this countertrend, my effort to learn what they were up to and why. They are not celebrities, but rather mostly people who move and work beneath the public radar—although the same could be said about their opposite numbers, the religious extremists, until one of the latter blows himself up. Nevertheless, I have been struck by how often these individuals cite recent, heroic figures as their true inspiration: Day, founder of the Catholic Worker Movement; Gandhi; the Reverend Dr. Martin Luther King, Jr.; Pope John Paul II; the fourteenth Dalai Lama of Tibet; Nelson Mandela; Malcolm X in his final years as an orthodox Muslim, having journeyed beyond insular black nationalism.

These figures stand among the most influential of the twentieth century. Their work endures despite the brutality, even outright genocide, through which they lived. Indeed, they remain far better known and more widely influential than their detractors. To get a sense of their enduring power, especially among the people about whom I write, their words are worth rereading, like this from King: "We are caught in an inescapable network of mutuality, tied in a single garment of destiny. Whatever affects one directly, affects all indirectly." He wrote that in his letter from a Birmingham, Alabama, jail on April 16, 1963. Who remembers the eight white clergymen to whom it was ostensibly addressed, who had first written King, deploring his nonviolent civil disobedience and urging "our own Negro community" not to support King?

Why does such language matter now, especially? For one, we live in an era in which religion cannot be excluded from public discussion—and increasingly it isn't. In the United States, as in much of the world, religious belief is often central to people's lives—a direct contradiction of expectations created by the Enlightenment three centuries ago. Despite the complaints of its most ardent despisers, religion is not going away. And given that, it seems a simple proposition to state that ignorance of religious differences can be perilous, for the obvious reason that what one does not know about other people can provide a blank slate on which demagogues can write with great, destructive effect. If some prominent person declares that Judaism equals Zionism equals racism, or describes Islam as evil or labels Christians as bloodthirsty "Crusaders" (all of which statements are made, with some regularity), the negative effect is likely to be all the greater among people who know no Jews or Muslims or Christians, regardless of how good their basic intentions might be. In the face of such ruthless stereotypes, there can be no substantive counterargument without personal experience. In 2007, Stephen Prothero, a Boston University professor, eloquently argued that basic education about religions ought to be requisite in our schools.

Most certainly not for proselytizing, but for creating an informed generation of future citizens. I would say that based on my experiences, knowledge is gained most effectively—not always, but often—through direct contact with other living, breathing believers. My argument here is for communication among people. It doesn't point toward utopia—there's no silver bullet. But such efforts can work against stereotyping. They can mitigate corrosive social fears that work to isolate entire groups of innocent people. And we can hardly discount the possibility that a single individual emerging from an encounter with someone of a different faith convinced that they share a common humanity might make a difference. Occasionally, one person can stop a mob.

I began this project a few months after 9/11, but not as a response to the terrorist attacks that day. The mass murders in New York and Washington, D.C., serve as a harrowing reference point by which we can measure the enormity of violence linked with religion. I worked at *The New York Times* on the day itself, an experience I will describe later. I have a vivid memory of stepping from the *Times* building on West Forty-third Street that night and finding bright yellow tape, strung by the police across Times Square's southern end, shutting off miles of Manhattan to all but emergency vehicles and pedestrians. The southern end of the city had become a vast, no-go zone, capped by burning ruins.

My interest in this other idea, counterintuitive as it is—that religious differences might be used as a basis for forging peace rather than inspiring hatred—had been building for a much longer period. By 9/11, I had spent two decades working as a newspaper journalist, the majority of that time covering religion in the United States and the world. The longer I did so, the more I encountered two emerging realities: one, that a new degree of religious diversity was becoming obvious in the United States and Europe; the other, much more subtle, was that more people wanted to use this diversity constructively. After 9/11, that second trend accelerated, pressed by a new sense of urgency to encourage peaceful encounters across religious lines.

My career as a religion reporter began in 1986 at *The Atlanta Journal/Constitution,* an assignment primarily focused on covering Southern Baptists, the dominant religious group in the South and one then undergoing something close to a schism between two warring, yet essentially conservative, factions, one commonly identified as "the moderates," the other as "the fundamentalists." Family fights tend to be particularly bitter; here, the Baptist fundamentalists triumphed. But beyond that fight lay a story at least as compelling, that the Bible Belt landscape was undergoing a tectonic shift in its religious character. Catholics, once a small minority in Georgia, had emerged as the state's third-largest religious group and one of its fastest growing. Job-seekers had moved in from the North, as well as from Mexico and Central America. In some Atlanta parishes, it had become difficult to find a space in the pew during Mass. The seismic shift in the state's Christian population pointed toward a growing spiritual complexity. By 1989, I counted four mosques downtown, and a sufficient number of Hindu families had immigrated to the area to begin plans for a temple designed in traditional, South Indian style. None of this made Atlanta unique. Muslim, Buddhist, Hindu, and Sikh communities were emerging across the nation, a trend later described in detail by Harvard scholar Diana L. Eck. Less obvious were the efforts of individuals to reach out collaboratively to their counterparts across theological dividing lines. But by the 1990s, this trend was fully engaged.

"The greatest factor," said the Reverend Bud Heckman, "is the growing sense of awareness that we have religious diversity in our midst." By the time I spoke with him, long after I had left Atlanta, Heckman, a United Methodist minister, was serving as executive director of Religions for Peace-USA, a nonprofit organization that works to create cooperative efforts among people of different faiths. In 2004, he and his staff attempted to count the number of organizations involved in activities that deliberately sought to bring people together across religious lines. They came up with about one thousand—many of them local efforts whose members often focused on a single cause, like helping people infected with HIV-AIDS or championing environmental conservation. Heckman's research also included more ambitious enterprises, like Bishop Swing's United Religions Initiative. After years of planning and consultation with various religious leaders and organizational strategists, Swing got his program off the ground in 2000. Its plan was a decentralized but global one, inviting people into local "cooperation circles." Each circle would include members of at least three different faiths. "Some are working on the environment, some are working on AIDS, some are working on literature for children that doesn't demonize other religions," Swing told me. By 2006, he counted 320 circles in sixty-five nations; the budget at the organization's San Francisco headquarters stood at $1.3 million.

One of the late-twentieth-century figures who took note of this trend was a man with a keen appreciation of the appalling destruction that could be wreaked through the violence erupting from a group with a dangerously distorted idea of itself and its place in history. John Paul II, elected pope in 1978, had come of age in Nazi-occupied Poland, whose German rulers unleashed terror against one of the largest Jewish populations in Europe. More than five decades after that era, in a speech in Assisi, Italy, the pope praised cooperation among people of different religious faiths. Speaking before a crowd that included representatives of twenty different religious traditions, he called it a "sign of hope" at the turn of the twenty-first century. He didn't dwell on the dangers of religiously inspired violence—he didn't need to. But a subtle urgency pervaded his speech, as if in choosing to address such a spiritually mixed audience, he was telling them that if they wanted to be peacemakers, they would be going head-to-head with fanatics for the world's future. Make no mistake, this is a war of ideas under way, as important as the long struggle of democratic ideals against crushing authoritarianism.

John Paul's presence at Assisi is notable in another way. Call it dialogue, call it collaboration, but work across religious lines tends to worry some people, including well-meaning people, who fear that conversation among believers in different traditions inevitably leads to a wearing down of important differences—the unique teachings that comprise Christianity or Judaism, for example. Yet the best of this work, it seems to me, is not about erasing differences but trying to understand and allow for them. "This isn't about meeting in the middle," a rabbi who specialized in Christian-Jewish relations has remarked. In other words, if you're a Christian, you don't deal authentically with other religious people by muzzling your affirmation of Jesus' divinity. Likewise, a real Muslim who wants to speak as such with Christians and Jews can't be expected to declare Muhammad just another prophet. The "hopeful sign" that John Paul discerned at the dawn of the millennium had nothing to do with creating some new religion or attempting to meld the existing ones. Yes, new faiths arise all the time—and as often die out—but their inspiration comes from individuals who claim divine revelation, not from some group effort to create a spiritual Esperanto. I have never personally had much time for people who want to start up a new religion or for those who would try to blend old ones in search of an elusive spiritual common denominator. Claims to new revelation or efforts at syncretism have never interested me, except perhaps as a news story or the focus of academic study. Certainly, that's not what this book is about.

The sign of hope has to do with the willingness of people to take one another seriously, to acknowledge the vitality of the beliefs that separate adherents of different faiths rather than their lethal potential. As one Catholic theologian put it succinctly to me: "Can one admit differences without being adversarial? Now, that's a radical thing in the world—that you're not me, and I'm not you, but that doesn't mean a threat." Radical it is, indeed. It cuts directly against tribalism, an impulse to which most of us are prey. It is about living in the world, which we are repeatedly told is globalized and globalizing, throwing us daily into ever-widening contact with people who would have been unknown to our grandparents and perhaps our parents as well. We might quote Ralph Waldo Emerson: "He has not learned the lesson of life who does not every day surmount a fear." In dealing with religious differences, that's our charge. There is nothing easy about it.

Why write about this subject now? To speak today about peace across religious lines seems counterintuitive. As we are repeatedly told by government officials who claim special access to privileged information, we are engaged in a "war on terror," a struggle against enemies (who often identify themselves as Muslim) on which the future of our civilization rests. That's the public narrative of our post-9/11 lives. No rational person can fail to take seriously the deadly challenge raised by groups like Bin Laden's al-Qaeda, which mix religion and politics for the purpose of wholesale destruction. But the efficacy of fear has its limits, and the idea of a war against terror works only so far as it is possible to regard humanity as existing utterly without nuance, divided with stark permanence into two warring camps. Us-versus-them 'til time's end.

War must never replace or exclude other efforts to construct a civil society. Consider the example of Franklin D. Roosevelt, as he prepared Americans for the country's eventual entry into World War II. He delivered a national speech describing the ideals for which the nation should necessarily strive. His "Four Freedoms" address—lifting up the ideals of freedom of speech and of worship, along with freedom from want and from fear—offered a vision of community amidst violence, a vision that implicitly included a respect for religious diversity. The discovery of common interests, which lies at the heart of democracy, cannot be forced by polarization, especially when religious differences are involved. Societies are nurtured through people willing to claim a role as citizens, working together. In any case, violent extremists comprise only a sliver of the world's population. Despite the risk involved, it is imperative to bring together as many people as possible in order to forge a community with a hope for the future. "When bad men combine," Edmund Burke, the eighteenth-century statesman, wrote, "the good must associate, else they will fall one by one, an unpitied sacrifice in a contemptible struggle." To be sure, not everyone's going to join. But the effort, if it builds constructive relations, is not misplaced. This isn't about tolerance—essentially, living and letting live. Mere toleration of differences can be a wonderful alternative to mayhem. But it is not a stopping point in human relations. It does little to educate people about one another. That's an activity that demands a greater, more committed effort.

And yet the drama involved is necessarily subtle. One autumn day, I received an invitation from a Catholic nun to sit in on a discussion between Christians and Muslims about the essentials of their respective faiths. It took place at the headquarters of the Islamic Society of North America, an umbrella organization for local mosques nationwide. The building, whose red brick surface appears to glow in the sunshine of a late midwestern afternoon, occupies a small hill in suburban Indianapolis. I had visited once years before and found the field out front deep in ripening corn, creating a visual impression of Islam come to heartland America. But that image seemed less significant than what I saw on this second visit. The meeting I attended brought together two dozen Catholics and Muslims, prominent people in their communities throughout the Midwest. A few years earlier, the group had been put together by John Borelli, a veteran interreligious organizer then working for the United States Catholic Conference, the American bishops' social policy organization. The project involved creating an educational pamphlet for congregations to use; the idea was to tell Catholics what Muslims believe and Muslims what Christianity teaches. I arrived late in the process, as participants were doing a line-by-line edit. The discussions, friendly and detailed, lasted through the day. In late afternoon, the Catholics adjourned for prayers on the building's first floor. The Muslims came and stood quietly beside them. Afterward, the Muslims moved into the carpeted space that functioned as the building's mosque to bow and kneel in their evening prayer. The Catholics sat quietly outside the area and looked on.

I sensed an attitude of mutual respect in the meeting and during prayers. These people had come to know one another. I was not witnessing mere courtesy: What transpired had nothing to do with being "nice." Instead, the meeting offered an example of vitality within a functioning civil society, the creation of networks that reach beyond obvious boundaries. And in that sense, it seemed to echo the insight King had articulated in his Letter from a Birmingham Jail. We live in an era not simply of religious violence, but one in which bitter divisions are painfully evident and often gratuitously cultivated. That's especially true in national politics, in which rhetoric is often suffused with partisan rage. Public debate seems laced with poison—in Congress, and even more so on cable television and the Internet. Such rough trade in raw insult denies the possibility that we might share anything like a common life. In such circumstances, it is remarkable that some people would try to use religion—or rather different religions—to create not explosive divisions, but rather a sense of community.

Religion, more than government, is something that matters deeply to many Americans in a way that sets us apart from other postindustrialized countries. In terms of the esteem we accord religious belief and the regularity with which we say we practice it, Americans are more like people in the developing nations of Africa and South Asia than those in France or Canada. Moreover, religion is no longer a "private matter" (if indeed it ever was). Like other once-taboo topics—sex, money, politics—it is very much a public subject, explored in best-selling books, movies, popular music, and on television talk programs. Celebrities freely talk about their religious lives and politicians feel compelled to do likewise, even those who would clearly prefer not to. Religion is a source of public identity to many Americans. And because of that, religion cannot be ignored. It is natural that what people believe and practice be a source of curiosity, a topic that lies open to honest and civil discussion. To put it another way, differences in personal identity can be grounds for fear, or they can serve as an opportunity for learning. To return again to King, his leadership of the civil rights movement relied on a broad public understanding of a moral and spiritual cause that crossed racial, ethnic, and religious lines. A climatic moment for African American civil rights came in March 1965, when the movement's marchers attempted to cross the Edmund Pettis Bridge in Selma, Alabama, on the way to the state capitol in Montgomery. Those who walked—and suffered the injuries and terror resulting from police efforts to turn them back—included not simply King's fellow Baptists, but Unitarians, Catholics, Jews, and atheists. In an essay he would write two years later, King said the various technological advances of the mid-twentieth century had brought all of humanity into a state of such proximity that it could best be described as living in a "world house." Gifted at articulating vivid images of the human condition, King struck upon an especially potent one. People who live in the same house are vulnerable one to another: If trouble breaks out, everyone is affected.

Real discussion of religious differences, even if undertaken in the cause of peace, is not going to appeal to everyone. Engagement of this type involves risk taking, if only because the ground on which one treads is so deeply scored by unavoidable—and vital—theological differences. The major world religions hold truth claims that privilege their own believers. Christians cite the New Testament to ground their belief in Jesus as God's son as the only way to heaven. Jews have biblical authority to testify to their status as God's chosen. Muslims believe the Qur'an is God's ultimate revelation, faultlessly delivered through Muhammad as God's final prophet. For Buddhists, the ultimate goal is achieving enlightenment, reached by following the Eightfold Path taught by the Buddha twenty-six hundred years ago. An adherent of any one of these traditions faces a fundamental question: Given such statements, how am I to relate to people of other faiths? Does Jesus' unique, saving status or Muhammad's prophetic finality mean the divine is utterly lacking—or perhaps fatally obscured—within others' beliefs? There are certainly people for whom the answer will be yes. But my professional experience, along with others' research that I have read, suggests that the people who see absolute darkness outside their own religions are in the minority, and not just in the United States. Protestant theologian Paul Tillich made such an observation half a century ago, noting critically that many people assumed that Christianity held "an exclusively negative attitude toward other faiths." But, Tillich said, such a flat rejection could not be further from the truth. "In this assumption a confusion frequently takes place between the attitude of Christian churches toward the Christian heretics, especially in the later Middle Ages, and the attitude toward members of other religions." The churches' campaigns against heretics (the Cathars in southern France, for example) were characterized by "demonic cruelty." By contrast, Christianity's approach to other religions has always been more complicated, nuanced, and uneven, he said.

Besides, there are a great many people for whom the sum of being religious is not reduced to a single, dogmatic principle that disallows respect for others as humans with some contact with the divine. In that case, religious identity may be something more than a declarative signpost on a one-way street. The world contains a very large number of religious "moderates"—to use the news media term that distinguishes the vast majority of believers from the militants. In 2006, theologian Rowan Williams, Archbishop of Canterbury, declared that while Christians must think of their faith as uniquely fulfilling, that should not prevent them from recognizing that other faiths may contain elements of ultimate truth. Nor should Christians' distinctive beliefs keep them from listening carefully and respectfully to others and collaborating with them. Williams delivered his remarks to the World Council of Churches, an association of 330 Orthodox and Protestant churches.

One doesn't need to possess Williams's status to reach a conclusion that works similarly in practice, even if it is not the same in theory. The individual religious imagination can be a subtle and nuanced thing; most people do not move in lockstep with a literal understanding of dogma. Personal experience plays a vital role in how individuals understand themselves and the world around them, including the way in which they see others. Thus, as one Christian theologian told me, his sister's view of Hindus and Muslims comes from having them as suburban neighbors, people whom she and her husband like. It is possible, too, to draw a similarly broad conclusion from reading one's own sacred texts. The biblical account of Genesis says all people are created in God's image. That was sufficient for a Catholic priest I met in Los Angeles to conclude that he should extend a respect to other believers, even sharing a platform with them, offering prayers alongside Jews and Muslims and Buddhists in special services that brought everyone together in an expression of a common civic destiny. His position might be restated as a question: Are you willing to respect others, even work with them, because you believe that is what God wants? That's a radically different trajectory to follow than the path upon which Bin Laden and his ilk urge their young followers.

Here's a passage I believe illustrates the principle: "The religious sense of the absolute qualifies the will-to-live and the will-to-power by bringing them under subjection to an absolute will, and by imparting transcendent value to other human beings, whose life and needs thus achieve a higher claim upon the self." The statement comes from my great-uncle, Reinhold Niebuhr. I quoted him in the preface and I do so again, evidence of how his words have inspired

me. Because he died in 1971, he lived to see only the beginning of
an era of interreligious dialogue and collaboration. But he thought
about the experience of and demands made by religious pluralism.
In 1944, he wrote that there could be a religious approach to accommodate the challenge posed by religious diversity. "The solu-
tion requires a very high form of religious commitment. It demands
that each religion, or each version of a single faith, seek to proclaim
its highest insights while yet preserving a humble and contrite recognition of the fact that all actual expressions of religious faith are
subject to historical contingency and relativity." It is his call to
humility—an acknowledgment that even when one professes an
adherence to religious truth, one doesn't fully know God's mind.
But as he certainly knew, humility is an elusive quality in individuals, as it is even more so in nations and organized religions. It is
continually challenged by pride.

I bring to this subject my observations and reflections. I recognize that others have made this work their entire lives, organizing
conferences, launching organizations, preparing courses, and writing
theological books. I cannot pretend to such accomplishments. Nevertheless, the decade and a half I spent as a journalist speaking to
people across a very wide religious spectrum left me with a lasting
awareness of what may result from the serious crossing of religious
borders. I occasionally found my experiences deeply unsettling—
they could be nothing else—as when I spent a day among adherents
of the Christian Identity movement, which regards Jews as demonic
and African Americans as subhuman. But such encounters with raw
bigotry and latent violence were rare indeed. Yes, I met people who
presented their faith or lack of it in a way I found to be intolerant,
arrogant, or shallow. But more often—and of far greater value to
me as an American, heir to a founding idea of religious pluralism—
I visited and revisited serious and articulate people whom I might
not have known otherwise. They emerged from within the undif-
ferentiated mass of their own group as particular individuals. There-

after, I often winced inwardly when I heard friends or acquaintances make sweeping generalizations about groups like conservative Protestants, Mormons, Orthodox Jews, Buddhist converts, immigrant Muslims, secular humanists, or anyone else who lived beyond their own frame of reference. I was dismayed when such negative images were served up raw and unexamined. I had gotten to know some of those people through extensive conversations, eating at their tables, and visiting places they considered holy or meaningful. No, that certainly didn't mean I sacrificed my own values. I had no desire to join another faith, even on those rare occasions when an individual politely offered to help me do so. My great grandfather passed to his descendants—three of his four children and at least one grandchild, my father—an openness to a calling to preach or teach. I credit my mother, too, with helping form my religious identity. A southerner with a great gift for music, she spent many evenings at the piano, playing old American folk tunes and favorite hymns of hers, including African American spirituals. She sang the latter with such pleasure that I hear her voice when the lyrics come to mind— "Were you there when they crucified my Lord? Oh! Sometimes it causes me to tremble, tremble, tremble. . . ."

Music, sung or simply heard, provides a deeply sensory experience. It can seep into a person's being. When I hear the hymns with which I grew up, they impart to me a feeling of spiritual pleasure—a type of pleasure I rarely hear spoken of, but one I firmly believe others share from within their own personal experiences. Some years ago, a deacon in an eastern rite Catholic church described to me how he felt the sacred engulf him when he entered a church vivid with icons and redolent of incense. Similarly, the Zen Buddhist monk Thich Nhat Hanh once told me he felt that his own practice of meditative mindfulness could be compared with the Christian experience of taking communion ("If you are mindful, you can eat the bread and the bread represents the whole cosmos") or the Jewish experience of preparing food for a holy day ("You set the table, you lay the food in the presence of God. Mindfulness is the awareness that shines on every act in every moment"). The point here is the common appreciation of what we find deep within our own experiences that link us as humans, spiritually attuned and grateful for it, despite the differences that give vitality and durability to our various traditions.

Years later, my travels as a journalist gave me a thorough, lasting sense of how truly diverse American society is, how wide the breadth of human experience, and how varied its grapplings with ultimate meaning. Spend time meeting with people across the spiritual spectrum and it will render impractical a zero-sum way of regarding the world, of us-versus-them. My experience may be unusual in that it was so tied to my profession, but a growing, visible religious diversity makes such encounters far more likely for a great many people.

Sometimes the extraordinary can happen when you cross these boundaries, not in fear but with a sense of expansive possibility in meeting and knowing someone shaped by another, radically different tradition. Thus, three years after writing his Letter from the Birmingham Jail, Martin Luther King, Jr., met and befriended Thich Nhat Hanh, then early into his exile from Vietnam, where he had advocated a new way to peace in his divided homeland, to ending the war between the U.S.-supported South and the Communist North. In their mutual commitment to nonviolence, King found inspiration to oppose American involvement in the war. In a memorable sermon he preached at Riverside Church in April 1967, he quoted Vietnamese Buddhists and went to call for "a genuine revolution of values" that would place love of neighbor above tribe, race, and nation. "When I speak of love I am not speaking of some sentimental and weak response. . . . I am speaking of that force which all of the great religions have seen as the supreme unifying principle of life. Love is somehow the key that unlocks the door which leads to ultimate reality." He described it as "this Hindu-Moslem-Christian-Jewish-Buddhist belief," which he saw reflected in the New Testament's First Letter of John: "Let us love one another: for love is of God, and every one that loveth is born of God, and knoweth God." King was remarkable. But his discovery was hardly unique.

To be sure, there are cautionary tales about interfaith encounters. How could there not be? I remember reading one about a well-meaning midwestern Muslim who took a copy of the Qur'an to an inquiring Protestant minister right after 9/11. The Muslim wanted to share what it is that he and others so value and revere. But the minister found reading it such an offensive experience he felt moved to preach against Islam itself. His sermon title, posted on a sign outside the church, identified the religion as America's principal enemy. Meeting individuals of another faith, reading their sacred texts, won't always yield constructive results. Still, one can't avoid the question: Is that a reason not to do it?

Similarly, I'm quite aware of how the idea of fostering constructive engagement among people of different faiths has its detractors. Some suspect it can never be more than superficial. Others fear that any meaningful contact with people across religious lines will risk undermining their own faith—or, far worse, their children's, if the latter are also involved. There is a phrase that sums up the dismissive attitude toward multireligious encounters. The critics say, "It's holding hands in a circle and singing, 'Kum by Yah.'" What an odd choice for a put-down! "Kum by Yah" is a modern Christian hymn, most likely of African American provenance. Researchers believe it arose among descendants of slaves living on the islands off the South Atlantic coast. They speak Gullah, a part-English, part-African dialect. (The hymn's first line, "Kum by yah, O Lord," translates as "Come by here, O Lord.") Civil rights marchers sang it with gusto in the 1960s, quite probably holding hands as they supported one another in truly fearsome circumstances, amidst the hatred of southern police forces and the Ku Klux Klan. From there, the hymn spilled over to youth groups at campfire gatherings in the 1970s. Its simplicity, its three-chord melody, no doubt enhanced its popularity. But somewhere along the way, it became a "mocking metaphor" for almost any communitarian endeavor, to borrow a phrase from a reporter for *The Dallas Morning News* who wrote about the song in 2006. I have heard "Kum by Yah" sung by Christian youth groups (although not recently), but I've never encountered it in an intentionally multireligious gathering. And I have not seen people circled and holding hands in such settings either. That's not to say it cannot be done. The great Trappist monk Thomas Merton, speaking at a conference of Catholic and Buddhist monastics in Calcutta in 1968, asked his fellow monks to take one another's hands as he prayed aloud, "You have made us one with You. You have taught us that if we are open to one another, You dwell in us. Help us to preserve this openness and to fight for it with all our hearts. Help us to realize that there can be no understanding where there is mutual rejection."

Frankly, when I began this project, I expected I would provide more space in these pages to those to whom Merton refers in passing as the "mutual rejectionists"—those individuals whose regard for their own ultimate truth is such that they will enter no religious discussions with anyone unless it is for the purpose of converting that other person. I have met those people, individually and in groups, and recognize their right to their position. I respect individuals who are clear and, better still, clearly knowledgeable about their faith—there is much to be learned from them. But people who engage in monologues are another matter. And increasingly, I felt as if their story was being told elsewhere and at length—in the news media, which values aggressive clarity, and in academic studies like the Fundamentalism Project. By contrast, the story of interreligious dialogue goes largely untold—again, especially by the news media—and as I did my research, I found myself intrigued by the personal stories that those involved brought to it. Some reached way back to recall the message imparted to them by their parents about "other people"; some came to their commitments as adults, as a result of a friendship they developed, or even because of a realization about the state of the world.

Nevertheless, I think I understand some of the doubt that efforts at positive, interreligious contact can produce. As I researched this book, I wound up occasionally in situations where I felt little was actually being accomplished: The group involved seemed too small, the talk too limited, sometimes less than real conversation, as when those individuals present seemed more interested in speaking than listening. I could recount some of those incidents, but I am not convinced that would accomplish much. They are easy to imagine. Doubt itself is natural, a human quality that exists to protect us from credulity. Ideally, we learn from our experiences. To return to Merton in Calcutta: In a separate, informal talk there, he said that faith did not mean suppressing doubt. "It is the overcoming of doubt, and you overcome doubt by going through it. The man of faith who has never experienced doubt is not a man of faith." He spoke then about faith in God, but he could as easily have been speaking about faith in human beings. I suppose, too, for all those times I felt doubtful about the value of dialogue and common action, I found my doubts mitigated by two thoughts. One is that even in the midst of the most superficial of exchanges among people, there exists the possibility of someone hearing something for the first time—"an old story, unless you've never heard it," to borrow a terse and meaningful phrase. Sometimes people stumble across something they come to consider of real value, to explore and build on, which everyone else seems to know about. I have been in that position, where I have heard something—a supposition, an idea, a fact—that stopped me cold. "You didn't know that?" I have been asked incredulously.

The other thought has to do with the wider world. In this decade, we've learned an entirely new vocabulary of activities and place-names that describe how the United States lives in the world, and how we as Americans responsible for our government live in it. It's the language of contemporary battle and all related to it—everything from preemptive warfare to troop surges, to extraordinary rendition, waterboarding, and profiling, to insidious acronyms, like elusive WMDs and ever-present IEDs that harm and kill our troops. Increasingly, we hear too that the tools we've adopted and named are never quite enough. Even the generals say that weapons, artful surveillance, and reams of barbed wire are not sufficient for the security we want to achieve. Of course, we hope that such assets have a deterrent effect on truly dangerous individuals and groups. But security forces and new laws may do little to help with the task of sustaining civil societies. Can war be fought without some realization that ultimately you need a vision for peace? I don't mean the initial vision that everyone has, that everything will turn out just the way the war planners expected. We might recall what Lincoln said in his second inaugural address, delivered nearly four years after the fall of Fort Sumter: Each side had "looked for an easier triumph, and a result less fundamental and astounding." Those last three words remind us of what is at stake in all-out wars. By extension, those words put me in mind of the warning once delivered by a Sri Lankan Buddhist monk, in a speech he gave to Christians and Buddhists at Merton's former monastery: "The only alternative to talking is the building up of resentment and anger, which in time must inevitably become open hostility and conflict."

One spring afternoon a couple of years ago, I traveled to an interreligious conference in Los Angeles. A session took place at the Hsi Lai Temple, a thirty-million-dollar monastic complex that rises across a fifteen-acre hillside. Its architectural plans had originally unnerved neighbors, who fretted about the traffic and noise it might bring. But temple authorities calmed the situation by opening the place to all comers, offering tours, open houses, and adult education classes. At the temple, I happened to meet Judith Simmer-Brown, a professor at Naropa University in Boulder, Colorado, and a prominent figure among American Buddhists. During our conversation, she recalled a Buddhist-Christian meeting she attended some years back at which the Dalai Lama and prominent Catholic monks were also present. They spent days together, discussing aspects of each other's religious practices and setting aside time for prayer and meditation. The occasion allowed those participating to meet one another as spiritually serious individuals. And that, Simmer-Brown said, meant not conversion to another faith but something richer, "conversion to another person." Individuals had communicated their basic humanity to one another, in the process striking a blow for a common life, with important and lasting differences.

ONE

Under the Pillar of Smoke

About the time hijackers flew the first of two commercial jets into the World Trade Center on September 11, 2001, the Reverend Frank A. Hubbard was setting up folding chairs in his church's front room in South Brunswick, New Jersey. Hubbard, who described himself as an evangelical, held a weekly Bible study each Tuesday at St. Barnabas Episcopal Church. A few minutes after 9 A.M., one of his parishioners rushed in, distraught. Tearfully, she told him she'd heard on the radio that a passenger jet had slammed into the Trade Center. As he listened to her, Hubbard felt an initial incredulity, swiftly replaced with a rising sense of outrage. Some radio shock jock, he suspected, had decided to perpetrate an extraordinarily tasteless hoax on innocent listeners. After all, years earlier, the area had been the subject of a similar broadcast scare. St. Barnabas sits a few miles north of Grover's Mill, the hamlet that Orson Welles identified in 1938 as the landing place of invaders from Mars. Welles's broadcast set off a panic; New Jerseyans took to the roads in flight. As Hubbard hurried out to his car to listen to the news, he began to hope the story was only that—a hoax. Moments later, of course, he learned otherwise.

When the priest returned to the church, he found the phone ringing. The local school superintendent told him to come to an emergency meeting of community leaders. The terrorists' attack would be felt locally. South Brunswick lies an hour from Manhattan, making it highly likely that some of its commuting residents worked in the center's towers. But before he rang off, the superintendent asked Hubbard whom else he should call. Phone the two local Roman Catholic priests, Hubbard replied. And, he added, the head of the local mosque, Hamad Chebli, the Lebanese-born imam who served as spiritual leader at the Islamic Society of Central Jersey. Hubbard then drove to the school board offices, where city officials were gathering. On the way, he began to fear that the Islamic Society, a green and white building with a distinctive dome and a large, identifying sign, might pose an inviting target for someone— "some idiot," he would say—to vent his rage. So when Hubbard spotted South Brunswick's police chief, he rushed over and said, "You need to get cruisers down to the mosque." When the chief replied that he had already sent police to protect the building, Hubbard let out his breath. And he offered a silent prayer: "Thank you, Lord, for this community."

His prayer, brief though it was, encapsulated a vital and important truth: that in the United States, community can extend beyond religious boundaries, incorporating people whose fundamental views of the universe are sharply different one from another. If not the prayer itself, then that idea of community was on the minds of an untold number of Americans that same day and many of them acted decisively to preserve it. As they did so, they acted to keep alive the civil society that is necessary to our most basic freedoms. I had no idea that such work was going on that day.

I did not meet Hubbard until months later, but on September 11, 2001, I shared his initial apprehension. One of the questions raised by violent acts is the degree to which innocent bystanders will be made to pay for them. I worked then as a reporter at *The New York Times,* and on that day I thought it entirely possible that the terrorism would be closely followed by a backlash—random attacks against American Muslims and their property by people who wanted to get even. I'd encountered this response before, in circumstances less terrifying (from my standpoint), as when American and allied forces fought Iraq in the first Persian Gulf War in 1991. "There's been a backlash after every major international crisis involving the Middle East," the director of an American Muslim public policy organization told me. At the *Times,* I and other reporters prepared to write that story. And I was partially right; we would not lack for material.

Within thirty-six hours of the attacks, Long Island police arrested a man attempting to run down a Pakistani immigrant woman with his car; he shouted that he was "doing this for my country," police said. On the following Saturday, someone gunned down another immigrant in his store in Dallas, Texas. The dead man, also a native of Pakistan, had recently moved to Texas from New Jersey to open a grocery called Mom's. Hundreds of miles away the same night, another man died in his workplace, a Chevron station in Mesa, Arizona, when someone opened fire on him. The victim, the county attorney would say, "was killed for no other apparent reason than that he was dark-skinned and wore a turban." In other words, the victim shared two superficial characteristics with Osama bin Laden. But the deceased was a Sikh, adherent of a religion separate from Islam; his turban was of a different cut and worn for a different purpose than Bin Laden's headcovering. Sikhs, like Christians, Jews, and Muslims, worship one God. But although Sikhism is five hundred years old, and its American population stands at 250,000 and growing, it is barely known in the United States. Devout Sikh men do not cut their hair; the turban serves as its covering.

Elsewhere after 9/11, vandals targeted mosques. A firebomb struck one in Denton, Texas. A driver rammed his Ford Mustang into another near Cleveland. In the latter incident, late at night, the car barreled through the mosque's front doors, with speed sufficient to land atop a marble fountain inside. Conveniently for the police, who crunched across glass strewn throughout the mosque's lobby, the crash's force pinned the driver inside his car.

As these scattered acts of destruction took place across the country, the 9/11 attacks had created an appalling symbol over New York that served to keep the shock of the atrocity alive and vivid. Its twin towers fallen, the World Trade Center burned for days on end, throwing a pillar of smoke high above Manhattan into the radiant, late summer sky. If you commuted into the city from New Jersey, as I did then, you saw it every morning. For any Jew or Christian with a biblical imagination, the sight might seem a demonic inversion of the story in Exodus, in which God appears by day as a pillar of smoke, leading the Israelites to freedom. But the smoke hanging over New York Harbor rose from the fires of cremation. On the commuter trains, conversations would wither as it came into view. In Manhattan, people built shrines to the dead in the train stations, an inherently religious act whether or not they recognized it as such. Flyers with photographs of missing family members were taped to the walls at Grand Central and Pennsylvania stations. Many of the pictures showed happy moments, a man or woman enrobed at graduation, dancing at a wedding, or holding a toddler aloft. Commuters would break stride and stop. Some left bouquets. Others scrawled messages, promising never to forget.

Acts of violence possess a vivid fearsomeness that works deeply on the human imagination. They are easy to picture. Violence has a quality too that makes it a natural fit for news reports. That is, its effects can be quantified—so many people dead, so many injured, so much damage in dollar amounts. By day's end, the costs can be counted up, or at least the immediate ones. Transmitted through the news media, such a reckoning makes for compelling reading, listening, or viewing. But violence never comprises the full story. It did not in the case of how individuals responded to 9/11. I wish I had known at the time about Hubbard's other reaction—his concern for Chebli and for an Islamic house of worship. I wish I had known because the priest was by no means alone in expressing such feelings on that terrible day. That suggested another force was at work amid the horror—a constructive force, alive at the grass roots, defined by neighborliness and an active commitment to the preservation of peace and the safety and rights of vulnerable people. It makes a far more interesting story about contemporary America than I had imagined.

I only began to make this discovery months later, to piece together the other, purposefully nonviolent response to 9/11. In so doing, I began to feel drawn back to my curiosity to know better the desire shown by some people to take America's emerging religious diversity and create a community of it. In this sense, I had my eyes opened during an impromptu stop I made at the Islamic School of Seattle in January 2002. I had not planned to go there. It was a couple miles east of downtown, where I had come to attend a conference. But someone suggested I visit, that it might be useful to some other research I was doing at the time. After an initial phone call, I drove over late one afternoon, pulling up in front of a modest, two-story brick building in a residential neighborhood. Hardly an arresting sight, it had once housed a Jewish day school. Now, it had an enrollment of about seventy students, elementary school age and one in four on financial assistance. The point was that as an Islamic institution in the heart of a non-Muslim neighborhood, the school became the focus of drama on and after 9/11. The morning of the attacks, the school's small staff discovered their neighbors were watching. That sounds ominous—but in this case, it proved quite the opposite. Some people placed bouquets at the building's entrances. There were handwritten letters, too. "They said things like, 'Not all Americans blame all Muslims,'" Ann El-Moslimany told me. She was one of the school's founders and she worked there, keeping it going. A gracious, older woman who wore a headscarf in keeping with Muslim injunctions toward modesty, she recalled her surprise at the neighbors' response. Still, as a precaution, the school was shut down for a week. When it reopened, teenagers from a nearby alternative high school, along with their teachers and parents, greeted the returning Muslim students with flowers. "Welcome back!" declared one banner. That week, El-Moslimany got a call from the Church Council of Greater Seattle, an ecumenical Christian organization. Would the school like to have volunteers come out to keep an eye on things, to guard against possible vandalism? A few days earlier, a man with a gun had attempted to set fire to cars in a local mosque's parking lot. So El-Moslimany told the caller, yes, let them come. For months thereafter, when she arrived for work, she found people standing outside the school, walking up and down the sidewalks. The volunteers had signed up for a program called "Watchful Eyes," created by the church council shortly after 9/11. Alice Woldt, the council's interim director, said after news of the attacks broke, the organization began getting calls from worried citizens. "People think of us as first-responders," Woldt said. The callers were not concerned about their personal safety. Rather, they feared an imminent backlash. Most didn't know Muslims personally, but they knew Muslims lived in Seattle and they wanted to head off violence, particularly anything that might endanger children. Volunteers served around the clock. Local congregations got involved. And for the first time, a lot of people got to speak with one another—Christian to Muslim and Jew to Muslim—about their religious differences. "I think," Woldt said, "there's too little thought given to creating opportunities to understand one another." I could hardly disagree.

What happened in Seattle (and elsewhere, as I will soon describe) points to a rarely discussed strength in America, and one highly relevant to appreciating a society in which religious differences exist and are increasingly apparent. Yes, we celebrate individualism as a guiding principle in our culture, but some Americans put another interest on public display in 9/11's aftermath—that is, their concern with maintaining a humane community. Some felt impelled to reach beyond themselves, to incorporate others across volatile boundaries of religious differences—even while those lines seemed so fraught with peril. In the very week when the nation suffered a grievous injury from a stateless criminal gang that identified itself by its members' religion—as Muslims—some Americans chose to express concern and friendship toward their Muslim neighbors.

What occurred was a demonstration by citizens of American values—not the "values" so casually cited by politicians bent on their own electoral aggrandizement. Not "values" as code for hostility to gay people or undocumented immigrants or whatever other social demon can be conjured up amid the demagoguery of election times. Instead, the fact that some people chose to reach out in the wake of 9/11 suggests that an essential idea of community—and of individual responsibility to maintaining that idea—remains alive in our nation. It may be difficult to discern except in times of crisis, and to acknowledge it certainly cuts against the grain of almost everything we are told about the American character—that success belongs to the single-minded individualists, going it alone, true descendants of Daniel Boone, but now prepared to hack a way not through the forest but up an ever-ascending economic ladder.

In retrospect, what makes these post-9/11 actions even more significant is how they differed from the militant rhetoric increasingly used by the American government since 9/11. The Bush administration declares the United States to be waging a war on terror, a global campaign against an elusive and unconventional enemy who might be found almost anywhere. Of course, al-Qaeda and like-minded organizations pose a deadly threat whose ruthlessness has been made appallingly apparent in its attacks in New York, Washington, Madrid, Bali, and London. But war on terror—is that what we're all about? The phrase makes for a grand narrative, one that would define our era, even our national purpose. But it's also a radically simplistic one, distinguished by a stark dualism that cuts against the essential complexities of how human beings live together and interact. In his speeches, President Bush has portrayed the United States as a warrior nation engaged in an epic struggle to rid the world of "evil." That is, of course, a theological term with great resonance among major religious traditions, even if it is casually used by politicians these days. (One might add that the president is no stranger to potent theological imagery. In a nationally broadcast speech he made against the backdrop of the Statue of Liberty, on 9/11's first anniversary, Bush concluded by saying, "This ideal of America is the hope of all mankind. That hope drew millions to this harbor. That hope still lights our way. And the light shines in the darkness and the darkness will not overcome it." His final sentence closely paraphrased John's Gospel, which uses that very language about light in darkness to describe God.) So, the narrative declares, we are embarked on a cosmic struggle, the situation necessarily polarized. When evil is the standard against which you fight, you don't think of persuading other people, of considering their concerns, of giving them a hearing in order to rally them to your side. You simply expect them to fall into line, because there's an enemy out there who is beyond redemption and who might act at any moment, at any time.

It is fortunate that, for the most part, Americans did not try to apply this line of thinking—the war on terror model—to their towns and neighborhoods immediately after 9/11. In some instances, a completely different approach prevailed, in which citizens responded to the attempt to terrorize them by emphasizing community. The people who rallied outside mosques and Islamic schools drew no line, issued no challenge, and refrained from asking, "Whose side are you on? Are you with us or against us?" Instead, their acts conveyed a different message—no doubt at times a risky one—implicitly stating, "You're with us and we're in this together." These were acts that involved a faith in the idea of a common life, even in the midst of wartime. As such, they served as a direct response to terror. And terror, as others have pointed out, is an idea. If you confront it with the sword, you can only pursue its practitioners (with no guarantee they will not first pass their lethal methods, their plans for terrorist acts, to others). Any fight against terror ought to recognize that its potency exceeds its physical effects: It is a social and psychological weapon. And as such, it demands as much a social and intellectual response—a challengingly hopeful response—as it does a military one. People die in terrorist attacks, but the perpetrators mean for their idea to claim a far wider number of victims. They want to disrupt many more lives. They want to create a state of fear, to make people suspicious of one another, to break up friendships, to make even coexistence difficult, ultimately to break society apart. They do not fear backlashes against the innocent. Indeed, they may welcome them as a means further to divide people one from another. Even if Osama bin Laden knew enough about America's religious complexity to understand that the nation is home to a substantial Muslim minority, it is impossible to believe he would have been dissuaded from attacking the country out of concern that American Muslims might suffer at their neighbors' hands. Instead, it would have served his interests. In attacking the symbols of American economic and military power, he was, he said, fighting "Crusaders." A backlash against Muslims would serve to illustrate his images of the enemy—as if to say, this is what they can do to people living among them.

A healthy capacity to feel fear may be necessary to an individual life, but fear as a continual, cultural state is deeply corrosive to society as a whole. It leads to an atomization of society in which individuals are easily manipulated. It was not for nothing that Al Capone was reputed to have said that fear was the foundation upon which he built his criminal enterprise.

The "antibacklash" incidents that followed 9/11 in the United States—those acts of protecting mosques and schools that some people took on behalf of Muslims—fit an important but underreported pattern. They were, in essence, part of an alternative idea to terror, a potent and highly important one. Each act overtly valued civil society by effectively declaring it would involve people across religious lines. Each of those acts was remarkable because it ran counter to the simple division of the world into God-ordained good and Satanic evil. It takes more than a book of laws and an able police force to hold society together. It takes the social and intellectual capital derived from the voluntary effort of citizens to cooperate, to be ready to act on the proposition in times of enormous stress that violence need not be the only response to violence. The people who rallied around an Islamic school after 9/11 emphatically rejected not just al-Qaeda's methods but the fundamental idea of terrorism. Theirs was an act of peace, in the face of radical, lethal exclusivity.

This did not just go on in New Brunswick and Seattle. In Denver, volunteers linked arms to cast a symbolic "ring of protection" around a mosque there. And in northern Virginia, neighbors let Muslims there know they cared. That came after vandals desecrated a mosque in Herndon, Virginia, the night of September 11, defacing its walls with slogans like "Kill the Muslims" and spray painting vulgarities onto an outdoor sign that identified some land as the mosque's future home. But once word of the vandalism spread, neighbors called and offered to help clean up. "We experienced a level of love and support we had never felt before," a member of that mosque told me later. "We received letters, flowers, cards, e-mails, and phone calls of support from the local community." A Jewish neighbor offered to buy the mosque a new sign. The original sign became a symbol: People left flowers beneath it and lit candles at night. Someone who left a message, signed, "Your Christian neighbor," actually pledged to protect it.

And there was more. Some women, inspired by an idea posted on an Internet site, began wearing headscarves as a gesture of friendship and support for Muslims. By August 2002, when the Council on American–Islamic Relations, an advocacy organization in Washington, D.C., surveyed 945 of its members, four-fifths said that they "had experienced kindness or support from friends or colleagues of other faiths." The council reported: "Neighbors visited Muslims in their homes and volunteered to help do grocery shopping or to accompany them on shopping trips. Members of other faith groups showed up at Friday prayer services at their mosques to express solidarity. Colleagues at work challenged rude and negative remarks about Muslims. Supervisors told Muslim employees to report any offensive behavior, as it would not be tolerated."

In Washington and New York, multifaith services were held—at the National Cathedral and Yankee Stadium, respectively. Protestants, Catholics, Jews, Muslims, and others shared the same stage. And after one of these events, Cardinal Theodore E. McCarrick, then Catholic archbishop of Washington, said, "It's important that we pray with our Muslim brothers and sisters. There are some people who are really starting to take the wrong attitude, and looking at them as lesser or hateful people. I think it's important we put our arms around our Muslim brothers and sisters right now, and they know we love them, and they know we care." Years later, it remains a striking statement, one that speaks to the kind of people we can be. Yes, these were the words of just one man. But he also happened to be one of the most publicly visible and influential Roman Catholics in America, and as such, a leader in the single largest religious body in the nation. Washington's archbishop is expected to serve as someone who can speak for his church when needed, particularly on American foreign policy. Gregarious, direct, and possessed of an outspoken concern with global human rights, McCarrick had recently arrived in Washington, after spending fourteen years as archbishop of Newark, New Jersey. Nine months before the 9/11 attacks, Pope John Paul II had elevated him to the rank of cardinal, a status traditionally reserved for fewer than a dozen American prelates. When he spoke of "our Muslim brothers and sisters," he indicated three factors at work in American society. Most obviously, for those words to have more than symbolic meaning, there had to be a significant population of Muslims in the United States. Second, the cardinal's statement suggested that at least some of those Muslims were public figures—they would be there for his embrace, as they had been willing to engage him and other neighbors in dialogue and cooperative civic projects. Third, for a priest to utter those words indicated a subtle but highly important change had taken place within Christianity in recent years—or at least a substantial segment of Christianity. Other faiths were no longer widely understood as merely human creations, devoid of God, but instead as meaningful systems that incorporated aspects of the divine and so deserved a measure of respect that would also be extended to their adherents as believers.

The roots of these three factors lie in the 1960s, that most colorful and misunderstood of decades. The sixties changed America in ways we still may not fully grasp, but it had particular importance for the nation's religious landscape. The decade's midpoint witnessed the cresting of the civil rights movement, a reform of immigration law, and a decision by the world's Catholic bishops about other religious faiths—all of which affected the expression of religion in the United States and diversified the relationships possible among religious people.

But the religious changes that occurred in the sixties rest on older foundations in America, including the reality that the country has always been religiously diverse—even if the idea of such diversity has been understood quite differently in earlier eras. During and immediately after the American Revolution, for example, the country's political leaders had a keen sense of a nation in which important religious differences were obvious. To be sure, the overall population at the time—the white population, whose property-holding male members had access to political power—was overwhelmingly Protestant But people did not mistake that fact for religious uniformity, not when there were Congregationalists, Anglicans, Presbyterians, and Baptists, and perhaps 10 percent of the population was Quaker. In our era, those distinctions may carry little weight. But two hundred years ago, they appeared significant. In 1774, members of the Continental Congress protested the idea of appointing a chaplain to lead them in prayer, because they said they "were so divided in religious sentiment" that they could not "join in the same act of worship."

What did that mean? We can look to a discussion of the subject by James Madison, who once had studied theology at Princeton. In 1784, legislators in the Commonwealth of Virginia began considering a bill that would use tax revenues to pay people to teach Christianity. As a member of the Virginia House, Madison led the fight against the bill. If such a thing became law, how, he asked, would a judge ever be able to define what constituted authentic Christianity? What version of the Bible, what liturgy, what baptismal practice? Madison had the full support of Thomas Jefferson, American ambassador to France at the time. The legislative battle took two years, at the end of which the bill went down to defeat, partly because some Protestant groups in Virginia—notably, Baptists—realized that Madison was right. In 1788, Madison drew a fundamental conclusion about an inherent diversity in religion in America and how that worked to benefit everyone. "Freedom," he said, "arises from a multiplicity of sects, which pervades America, and which is the best and only security for religious liberty in any society. For where there is such a variety of sects, there cannot be a majority of any one sect to oppress and persecute the rest. . . ." It boils down to a simple equation: Religious diversity equals religious liberty. It is crucial that Madison understood that; the very next year, he began writing the text that would become the First Amendment, with its guarantees of religious freedom.

Madison's insight about Christianity in America remains valid today. On one hand, the majority of the American population describes itself as Christian, which is enough for some to refer to the United States as a "Christian nation." But the label continues to function as a very big tent. In 2001, researchers at the City University of New York's Graduate Center published one of the most extensive polls ever conducted on religion in America. Telephone surveyors randomly contacted more than fifty thousand adults; their findings, published as the "American Religious Identification Survey," showed that 77 percent of Americans identified themselves as Christians. But then it got interesting. When the graduate center's pollsters asked people with which branch of Christianity they identified, the pollsters drew more than three dozen responses, from Roman Catholic to Baptist, Presbyterian to Mormon, Nazarene to Eastern Orthodox, Quaker to Jehovah's Witnesses, and way beyond. It was hardly an exhaustive list of possibilities, but to read it is to hear James Madison anew, asking what Bible, what liturgy, what baptismal practice truly defines Christianity. The answers would be many.

For more than two hundred years, the American religious landscape has been dynamic, shaped by immigrants who brought their faiths with them and also by spiritual innovators who created new religious organizations, adding to the wide range of choices Americans faced. In the mid- and late nineteenth century, right up through the 1920s, the United States became a great destination for millions of Roman Catholics and Jews, whose populations rose with enormous rapidity relative to their original numbers here. At the time of the American Revolution, there were about forty thousand Catholics living in English-speaking America—equivalent to about 1 percent of the population. By the 1840s, thanks largely to immigration, Catholics had emerged as the largest single religious group in America, a status they have never lost. Again, going back to the American Revolution, Jews numbered about two thousand Americans in all—a truly tiny minority. Less than a century later, their population had increased more than one hundred times to a quarter million people. Within less than half a century, the Jewish population grew tenfold, to about three million. In the period between

1820 and 1920, nearly one quarter of Europe's Jewish population moved to the United States. Today, by most estimates, the American Jewish population numbers close to six million.

Visitors to the early United States, among them Alexis de Tocqueville, remarked on American religious diversity and how it differed from anything they had encountered in Europe. Tocqueville once asked one of his hosts—a New York state legislator and future federal cabinet officer named John Spencer—how the members of the various churches managed to get along. Spencer replied that it was in the interest of each church, a minority in itself, to be tolerant of the others. Still, as a formula for social accord, the spirit of toleration proved superficial, prone to breaking down in periods of stress. The high rate of immigration by Catholics triggered occasional violent backlashes by Protestant groups, who claimed to discern in rising Catholic numbers the workings of a papal plot against American democracy. In one famous incident, rioters destroyed a Catholic convent in Boston; in a far more devastating eruption, mobs killed Catholics during an antiimmigrant uprising in Kentucky. For decades, Catholics and Jews suffered social and legal limitations on where they could work, go to school, and live.

Against this background, the 1960s mark a watershed. The election of John F. Kennedy as president, at the beginning of the decade, is usually taken as a triumph for religious "outsiders," symbolizing the rise to cultural and political acceptance of Catholics in Protestant America. But even more profound changes in the American religious experience lay just ahead. In particular, a series of events in 1965—including an American law and a Vatican declaration—helped create conditions in which a greater engagement among people of different faiths could occur. To return to Cardinal McCarrick's statement about embracing "Muslim brothers and sisters," these three events worked to permit Muslims to come to the United States in significant numbers, to identify themselves publicly as Muslims, and finally, to be recognized as faithful people by many Christians.

It's long been common for politicians and commentators alike to disparage the sixties as a dark, chaotic time. In the melodramatic narrative, a decade marked by both creativity and violence is simply reduced to a witch's brew of illegal drugs, sexual promiscuity, and riotous civil disobedience. It's a stereotype short on real history. In the summer of 1965, Congress passed the Voting Rights Act, which banned the sort of special tests used in southern states to deny blacks' access to the ballot box. The law, which owed its success to the civic consciousness aroused by the Reverend Dr. Martin Luther King, Jr., and others in the civil rights movement, was a signal contribution to American democracy. It was among the movement's greatest achievements. In the three decades following, the proportion of African Americans registered to vote doubled in some southeastern states, tripled in others, and in one case—Mississippi—increased more than ten times. The movement for African American civil rights has had a long-term, if indirect, effect in making religious diversity more visible in the United States. The movement inspired among blacks a greater sense of pride in their racial heritage; by the mid-1960s, some had begun wearing clothing whose particular cut and design provided a symbolic link with Africa. Their willingness to assert a distinct public identity would effectively grant a permission to other racial, ethnic, and religious groups to proclaim their own uniqueness through the wearing of cultural or sacred symbols. Black pride made it much easier for future residents of the United States to dress as they felt religiously called to do—for Sikh men to wear turbans and Muslim women to put on *hijab,* covering their hair with a headscarf. I heard a vivid example of this process from a rabbi prominent in a fervently Orthodox Jewish organization. As a teenager, he felt self-conscious being seen wearing tzitzis, the knotted threads that hang from the tallis, the four-cornered shawl that strictly observant Orthodox

Jews wear in adherence to a biblical injunction. These fringes truly marked him as a member of a distinct minority in an overwhelmingly gentile society. But everything changed for him after a chance encounter he had with a black man wearing a dashiki, a tunic modeled on African tribal garments. Simple as it may sound now, the future rabbi realized that obvious differences could be a source of pride. Thereafter, he wanted people to take note of who he was religiously. "I made sure people could see my yarmulke," he said, referring to the skullcaps worn throughout the day by observant Jews. The Orthodox, he said, "got a lot of security out of the black liberation movement of the 1960s." But for such a cultural message to have a wider effect, other religious minorities would have to take advantage of it. And this became possible later that year, through a sweeping reform of the nation's immigration statutes.

When I worked as a journalist, people often asked me how many Muslims live in the United States. There's no precise figure—the census does not ask people to identify themselves by religion. Still, scholars who study American Muslims have often estimated roughly between four million and six million live in the nation. Such numbers would likely have been unimaginable to President Lyndon B. Johnson at the time he signed the Immigration and Naturalization Act into law on October 4, 1965, thirty-five years earlier. Johnson in so doing scrapped a four-decade-old system that had heavily favored western Europeans and Canadians while sharply limiting entry into the United States by Asians and Africans. From then on, there was a far greater opening to would-be immigrants from beyond Europe and North America. Johnson, with the document spread out before him on a table at the base of the Statue of Liberty, underestimated the impact of what he was about to sign. The legislation before him was "not a revolutionary bill," he said. "It does not affect the lives of millions." He must have been relying on what he had heard said during the congressional debates on the bill. No one who testified in Congress on behalf of immigration reform seemed to understand how much this idea might alter the nation's ethnic composition—and thus its religious landscape. Secretary of State Dean Rusk predicted that "based upon the best information we can get," no more than eight thousand Indians would move to the United States between 1965 and 1970. But by the year 2000, census takers counted more than one million Americans who claimed to have been born in India—more than double the total counted only a decade earlier. Together with their American-born children, Asian Indians numbered nearly two million in 2000. While this meant a sharp rise in the number of Hindus and Sikhs in the United States, it also contributed to the growth of America's Islamic communities. India's largest religious minority is Muslim. Indeed, research has shown that Muslims from India and neighboring Pakistan together form the largest single component among the dozens of ethnic groups that comprise America's Muslim population. All three religious groups—Muslims, Hindus, and Sikhs—have become increasingly visible throughout the United States as they have constructed new houses of worship in city, suburb, and rural landscape alike. By 2007, researchers at Harvard University's Pluralism Project estimated there were nearly 1,600 mosques, more than 700 Hindu temples, and almost 250 Sikh gurdwaras in the United States.

Some of these sites have become known as places where a minister, a priest, or a rabbi might find someone willing to speak with his or her congregation about Islam or Hinduism or Sikhism. The individuals who have become presidents or board members of the new American mosques and temples represent an important facet of the post-1965 immigration, one that in some instances has helped Americans adjust to a changing religious landscape. As a journalist, I encountered many such people who had accepted leadership positions in these houses of worship. Typically, they were male—although there were notable exceptions—and often held white-collar day jobs as physicians, engineers, or accountants. They had become spokespeople for their faiths. They included prayer leaders, too, like Imam Sayid Hassan al-Qazwini, spiritual leader of the Islamic Center of America in suburban Detroit. When I met him in the spring of 2002, seven months had passed since the 9/11 attacks, but he was still on the receiving end of a steady volume of invitations from non-Muslims to come explain Islam to them. "I have been to over eighty-five churches, colleges, schools, public places, speaking about Islam," he said. The fact that the invitations had been issued at all was as interesting as Qazwini's willingness to accept them. These non-Muslim audiences demonstrated a widespread hunger among Americans for information about Islam in the wake of the 9/11 attacks, a response vastly different from the backlash attacks I had reported on at the *Times*. Members of those religious and civic groups in Detroit had wanted to meet with, hear, and speak to a Muslim. Any one of these groups could have simply ordered a textbook and organized a study session on Islam—or they might simply have hunkered down and ignored the religious diversity around them. Instead, they wanted to meet a Muslim, preferring their information from a living source.

The mosque Qazwini served stands in Dearborn, Michigan, a place internationally famous as home to the Ford Motor Company's corporate headquarters. The Islamic Center is a seventy thousand-square-foot, granite-faced octagon perched on an embankment above busy Ford Road. The building is capped by a gold-colored dome and flanked by a pair of ten-story minarets. Even when I first saw it, long before construction was completed in 2005, it possessed enough visual impact to make me want to pull off the road and simply stare. Built at a cost of fourteen million dollars, it works as a symbol of the strength and ambition of a particular religious presence, in much the same way as a cathedral can make a similar statement about Christianity. Inside, the prayer hall contains space for one thousand people—seven hundred men on the first floor and

three hundred women in a separate gallery upstairs. Although Muslims in America come from all over the world, many in Dearborn
are of Arab ancestry, particularly from Lebanon and Iraq. Immigration by Arabs (including Christian Arabs) goes back at least a century,
to the opening of the city's Ford manufacturing plants, where many
Arab immigrants found work. In 2000, the U.S. Census Bureau reported that nearly 3 percent of the 2 million people living in Wayne
County, where Dearborn is located, claimed Arab ancestry. The census also reported that the number of Americans claiming Arab descent rose by nearly 40 percent nationwide between 1990 and 2000,
to 1.2 million. Half of those people lived in five states—Michigan,
California, Florida, New Jersey, and New York.

The Islamic Center is by no means the only mosque in the area.
An academic study in 2000 counted twenty-seven others in surrounding Wayne County and two adjacent counties. Three years
later, another study located five more, indicating continuing growth
among Muslims in metropolitan Detroit. Some of the mosques, like
the Islamic Center, were conscious of their non-Muslim neighbors
and were willing to get in touch with them. In 2004, a survey of
Muslims who attended mosques in the Detroit area, by a researcher
at the University of Kentucky, reported that about half of the
mosques had joined with non-Muslims in sponsoring dialogues or
social service projects.

But the Islamic Center's size, location, and its identification as a
place of worship for Shi'a Muslims make it distinct. For years, the
center had been housed in an unremarkable, rectangular building
on a nearby commercial strip. By contrast, the new building stands
squarely amidst a row of large Christian churches on a small street
adjacent to Ford Road. The place is called Altar Road, an allusion
to the dominant (and once exclusive) Christian identity of the
buildings there. The Shi'a, members of the smaller of Islam's two
major branches, trace their theological roots to the tensions that
erupted in the early Muslim community after the death of the

Prophet Muhammad in the year 632. The question arose of who should hold political and spiritual authority over the new community. The Shi'a emerged as partisans of the prophet's son-in-law, Ali, who died violently during the struggle. In many parts of the world, Shi'ites have suffered oppression from Islam's other branch, the Sunni—including in Saddam Hussein's Iraq, where Shi'ites form the popular majority. Qazwini has served as the Dearborn mosque's spiritual leader since 1997. A member of a family of Iraqi religious scholars, he is a tall man with a serious manner who wears the black turban that among the Shi'a distinguishes a religious leader as a descendant of Muhammad. Born in Karbala, Iraq, a city considered holy by Shi'ites, he fled Iraq as a teenager with his family, escaping Saddam Hussein, and spent a dozen years as a seminary student in Iran before immigrating to the United States in 1992, following his father, who had established a mosque and school in Southern California. By the time I met him, he was emerging as a national figure among Muslims. He had been a guest at the White House, invited with other religious leaders. In 2003, he would offer prayers to open a session of Congress, and, in 2006, meet with Pope Benedict XVI, whom he asked to promote a dialogue between Christians and Muslims. In April of that year, he also attended a gathering called the International Prayer for Peace at Georgetown University. It's worth noting, if only because of its varied guest list and the paper trail it left behind. Organized in part by Georgetown and the Washington Archdiocese, the gathering carried a high-level imprimatur. One of the cardinals came from the Vatican, two from the United States, and a fourth from Africa. The head bishop of the German Lutheran church attended, as did the chief rabbi of Haifa, Israel, and the archbishop of the Greek Orthodox Church in America. Several prominent American Protestants (mainline and evangelical) attended, as did nine Muslims from the United States, Africa, and Asia. The event closed with a declaration that denounced the use of violence in the name of religion. And in a nice turn of phrase, it criticized religious fundamentalism as "the childhood disease of all religions and cultures." Finally, the statement helpfully explained the purpose of such meetings, that they are directly meant to promote communication and lead to knowledge. "Dialogue is an art. It is not the choice of the fearful, of those who give way to evil without fighting. . . . Dialogue challenges all men and women to see the best in others and to be rooted in the best of themselves." Afterward, Qazwini posted a photograph of the event on his Web site; in it, he walks beside Cardinal McCarrick.

It's fair to assume that the primary texts and traditions of any major religion make for exclusivity—that is, among their basic principles are those that create boundaries that distinguish that religion's adherents from their neighbors. You are a Muslim if you affirm that Muhammad is God's final prophet. Or if you describe the Adi Granth—the fourteen-hundred-page book of hymns compiled in north India four centuries ago—as your guru, or religious teacher, you are telling the world you are a Sikh. Religious exclusivity in this sense is not violence; it's simply identity, functioning as nationality or ethnicity can. Affirming who you are religiously does not prevent your entering into respectful conversation with people of other faiths and seeking common ethical ground with them. That's the message that came out of Georgetown. It is not unique.

In recent years, an outpouring of documents from within various faith groups—ranging from official declarations and the formal statements of religious leaders to the reflections of individual theologians—has encouraged a wide range of believers to cooperate with adherents of different traditions. In effect, they have laid down a paper trail of spiritual and intellectual resources that point the way toward peaceful relations among different believers. For Catholics like McCarrick, the statement at Georgetown built on a far more influential document written by their church leaders four decades earlier, one now widely influential among Christians

worldwide. The Vatican published "The Declaration on the Relation of the Church to Non-Christian Religions" in October 1965,
three weeks after the revision of American immigration laws. The
declaration formed another crucial element that year in leading
to major changes within the nation's religious landscape. With the
assent of its bishops worldwide, the Catholic church—the world's
largest Christian organization—decisively declared that other major faiths were not to be seen as mere competitors or as dry reposi-
tories of merely human ideas. Instead, they would be viewed as
living traditions with some connection to God. The document did
not directly address the question of whether these other faiths possessed an element of saving grace (thereby suggesting their members might enter heaven as Christians understand it). Instead,
Catholics were encouraged to get to know other religious
believers. These days, the declaration is typically known by its ecclesiastical shorthand—*Nostra Aetate*—Latin for the phrase with
which it opens, "In our time...." It was among the last of sixteen
documents crafted by the twenty-six hundred bishops who met in
Rome, off and on, between 1962 and 1965. Collectively, their sessions were called the Second Vatican Council, an event that
amounted to a legislative reform summit for the entire church. Its
decisions would profoundly affect the religious experience of ordinary Catholics and, equally, the relationship of their church to the
world. Some Catholic scholars consider the council to have been
the single most significant event within Christianity in the half millennium since the Protestant Reformation. The bishops decided
that the Mass would no longer be celebrated in Latin, but rather in
the languages spoken by the people who filled the pews. They recognized the crucial importance of laypeople to the church. The
bishops also formally embraced the idea of religious liberty, describing freedom of conscience as a fundamental part of human
dignity. That made it clear that the Catholic church did not expect

secular governments to grant it a privileged status at the expense of other churches and faiths (a philosophy long justified on the principle that "error has no rights"). The declaration on relations with non-Christians, released a few weeks before the council concluded, said the Catholic church regarded serious, cooperative contact with non-Christians to be a social good.

Catholics have never formed a majority in the United States. But they have been the nation's largest single religious institution since the mid-nineteenth century and these days comprise about a quarter of the American population (the proportion runs well above 40 percent in some northeastern and upper midwestern states). The church is influential not simply because of numbers, but also because of its hierarchical nature. The declaration on relations with non-Christians is a binding statement of a church council—an exceptionally rare event, as there have been only two in the last four hundred years. It is most unlikely that any priest has passed through seminary in the last forty years without the expectation that he would familiarize himself with the documents of Vatican II, including the declaration. Furthermore, the council launched a new era of cooperation between Catholics and Protestants, and because of this, too, the declaration has proven influential across church boundaries. Although the declaration is most often cited for its role in helping establish a new, far more constructive relationship between the church and the world's Jews (a subject that will be dealt with in a later chapter), anyone who reads it will discover that it treats other faiths with respect, too—it names Hinduism and Buddhism as well as Islam. "The Catholic church rejects nothing that is true and holy in these religions," the declaration states. "She regards with sincere reverence those ways of conduct and of life, those precepts and teachings which, though differing in many aspects from the ones she holds and sets forth, nonetheless often reflect a ray of that Truth that enlightens all men."

Specifically, on the question of relations with Muslims, the declaration demands a new reading in the midst of a highly contentious era in which violent Islamic groups have so damaged their faith's image in the eyes of so many Europeans and Americans. The declaration calls on Christians and Muslims to put aside historic enmities and instead "to work sincerely for mutual understanding and to preserve as well as to promote together for the benefit of all mankind social justice and moral welfare, as well as peace and freedom." The declaration goes further, finding aspects of Islamic belief and practice to admire from a Christian point of view. Muslims, it says, "adore the one God . . . ; merciful and all-powerful, the Creator of heaven and earth." No, they do not recognize Jesus as the Messiah, the document acknowledges, but "they revere Him as a prophet. They also honor Mary, His virgin Mother; at times they even call on her with devotion. . . ." It credits Muslims with valuing "the moral life"—a statement, coming as it does from Christians, that packs more punch today than when it was written.

Nonetheless, it's important to recognize that the declaration does not equate any other faith with Christianity—only there, the document says, lies the full path to salvation. But in place of an outright claim to Christianity having an exclusive hold on *all* religious truth, the declaration takes a more nuanced position, that elements of God's truth may be revealed in other faiths. To be sure, Muslims, Buddhists, and others would not recognize themselves within such constricted space. But in going as far as they did theologically, the bishops in the council opened wide the possibility of serious dialogue between Catholics and others. To get a sense of how this has worked, I asked Paul J. Knitter, a Catholic theologian who recently joined the faculty of Union Theological Seminary in New York (after a long career at Xavier University), what effect the declaration has had in the forty years since its publication. That the council had gone on record recognizing "truth and grace" in other faiths,

Knitter said, remained remarkable and fostered continuing conversations between Catholics and others that the bishops may never
have envisioned or even necessarily desired. "Now, what are the
theological implications of this? That's what we're wrestling with
now," he said. Some who have participated in serious religious discussions with non-Christians "have realized they are coming to a
deeper understanding of spirituality and God and God's workings
in the world. While it does not contradict what they have known
about God through Christ, these are understandings, insights, they
never would have had if they had not entered into dialogue."

"The practice of dialogue has produced results that are way
ahead of the theology," Knitter added. "That's usually the case isn't
it? Our experience exceeds our understanding." But while such
discussions might go on at a high level—within the context of formal meetings—a similar process has been taking place at a much
more popular level with a great deal more spontaneity. That is,
more Americans are meeting people in their own neighborhoods
who are religiously unlike them and this, too, has had its own effect,
quite apart from official theological reflection. Knitter's sister and
her family, he said, live in a Chicago suburb in a neighborhood they
share with Hindu and Muslim families. "My sister and her husband
love to spend time with them. No way can you say these people are
not connected to God when they're your good friends." Knitter's
remark called to my mind an autobiographical reflection once offered by Pope John Paul II, who showed a great sensitivity toward
the world's Jews during his long pontificate. In response to a question posed by an Italian journalist—one of several in an extensive
interview that would later be published as a book—the pope reminisced about the Poland of his boyhood, before the Nazi Holocaust
decimated its Jewish population. One fourth of the students in his
elementary school in Wadowice were Jewish. (He was particularly
close to one boy who happened to survive the Holocaust.) "I can
vividly remember the Jews who gathered every Saturday at the

synagogue behind our school. Both religious groups, Catholics and Jews, were united, I presume, by the awareness that they prayed to the same God."

Drawing on the spirit of the Vatican Council's declaration, John Paul spoke about shared efforts among believers—cutting across nationalities, ethnicities, and even theologies—on behalf of peace, justice, and human freedom. During his pontificate, he traveled to Vatican-organized conferences at Assisi, Italy, that brought together representatives of different faith groups. Speaking in 1999 at one such meeting, which included men and women from twenty different religious faiths, John Paul called it hopeful "that in many parts of the world interreligious associations have been established to promote joint reflection and action. In some places, religious leaders have been instrumental in mediating between warring parties. I am convinced that the increased interest in dialogue between religions is one of the signs of hope present in the last part of this century." He called on his audience to go further, toward "coordinated common action on behalf of the human family."

It's more than coincidence that the year John Paul spoke in Assisi, the National Council of Churches of Christ in the U.S.A. published a policy statement on interfaith relations, calling on its member churches to "initiate conversations with people and organizations of other religious traditions in the United States." The document encouraged such dialogue for the purpose of promoting "peace and justice around the globe." As such, it represented another basic idea—that the way to a constructive common life is through conversation and collaboration among people of different religious faiths. As the involvement of bishops, popes, and church councils makes clear, this conviction doesn't reside on the margins, but instead represents an important current within religious life. Militant exclusivity, particularly in its violent forms, may command the headlines. But serious thinking about and encouragement for respectful dialogue among believers has been going on for years, and in the twenty-first century, it is a competitor with religiously based extremism in a global battle of ideas.

No one would argue that the National Council of Churches possesses the influence of the Vatican. For one thing, the council lacks the power to command; for another, some of its key Protestant members are far less important in the religious landscape than they were in 1950 when the organization was founded. Yet the council serves as an unusual umbrella organization, including about three dozen independent Protestant and Eastern Orthodox churches. Their combined memberships account for about forty-five million Americans. Some of those churches are well known, such as the Episcopal Church, the Presbyterian Church (USA), the African Methodist Episcopal Church, and the Greek Orthodox Archdiocese of America. But the council's ranks include others much less widely familiar, such as the Hungarian Reformed Church in America. Because each is independent, the council's statements are purely advisory; for the most part, they are obscure to many people in the pews. Still, leaders of the member churches approved the document, "Interfaith Relations and the Churches," in a rare consensus. It is far longer than *Nostra Aetate,* and arguably makes for less felicitous reading. But in it, the council refers appreciatively to the Catholic declaration. And like the bishops in 1965, the document's authors make it clear they are not theological radicals. They offer no attempt to equate Christianity with any other religion: "It is our conviction that reconciliation among people and with the world cannot be separated from the reconciliation offered in Jesus Christ." But they place themselves behind the concept of collaborative action across faith lines: "If we meet others as they are, then we must accept their right to determine and define their own identity. We also must remain faithful to who we are; only as Christians can we be present with integrity." It's an argument for the peaceful retention of differences, but also an invitation to gain from knowing others.

When the council composed the document, the Reverend Jay Rock served as its officer in charge of interfaith relations and was involved, step by step, in its writing. Years later, he described it to me as a theological argument that Christians need to build up a sense of community where they live. "Relating to neighbors of other faiths is part of Christian discipleship. That's the basic argument—that to be a faithful Christian should include establishing relationships of respect and understanding with neighbors who are not Christians," Rock said. The statement did not say that religious diversity is God's will. But, he said, "it makes the argument that religious diversity is the reality in which we live and has always been from the very beginning of the church." Indeed, in much of the world where Christians can be found—in Iraq, India, and Indonesia, for example—they live as minorities in religiously diverse cultures.

Rock eventually left the National Council and took a similar position in charge of interfaith relations at the Presbyterian Church (USA). Presbyterians, who account for slightly upward of 2.5 million people, may offer as good a cross section of Protestant America, past and present, as anyone. Ronald Reagan was a Presbyterian, as was Woodrow Wilson and Andrew Jackson. So is Condoleezza Rice, President George W. Bush's secretary of state. And so too is Sally Ride, the first female astronaut. Rock's work involves visiting its congregations nationwide. I asked him how he understood Presbyterians to be dealing with religious diversity around them. A good many admit they lack information about people of other faiths, he said, and that frustrates them, because they feel they ought to know. "People realize they don't really understand who these Muslims are, or they don't understand who the Sikhs are, or they don't understand who the Hindus are. They realize they need to understand something they don't understand." Rock said he hears people wonder aloud how they are to make sense of news reports that focus on "Muslim violence" in the Middle East or describe some intertwining of religion and nationalism like the militant Hindu organizations in India that want laws to keep individual Indians from converting to Christianity. For people who know little or nothing about the faiths in question, those reports lack context, leaving them with more questions than answers. But there are other concerns as well, Rock said. He met Presbyterians trying to figure out how to arrange a wedding for a son or daughter marrying a Jew or a Muslim. He encountered hospital workers who wanted to know what they might do to accommodate patients who were Buddhists or Sikhs. These were basic questions—and no less urgent for being just that—emerging at the local level, where Americans increasingly experience religious diversity.

Finally, Rock said he hears from people who worry that the non-Christians in their neighborhood or workplace, the people among whom they lived, risk eternal damnation if they die without a belief in Jesus as the Messiah. Shouldn't they as Christians try to reach out to try to convert those people—to "witness" to them— with the message of the Gospel, they ask him. "I'm the coordinator for interfaith relations, but what I really do is teach theology," Rock said. "I go around having theological conversations about what salvation means." To that group, he said, he asks questions in return that emphasize the need to get to know other believers as individuals: "Can you make a witness to this person or that group without having a relationship to them? Don't you need to respect them before you make a witness that will be heard?" He said he would never try to talk people out of wanting to proclaim their faith— that concept is embedded within Christianity. "But I do a lot of talking to people about how you do that," he said, "and the role of respect and openness and relationship in that process."

Of course, not everyone who devoutly believes in his or her own faith feels the need to convert others. But those who do—who feel so deeply persuaded by the truth of their own faith to care about the eternal future of others—may well also regard others as something more than objects to be converted or despised. Instead, it is possible through theological conversations to come to regard others—if one does not do so already—as full human beings, precious in God's sight as people who deserve to be known as the individuals they are. And in such interaction can lie the basis for real cooperation. "There are certainly people around our table who are convinced theirs is the way to salvation," said the Reverend Clark Lobenstine, executive director of the Interfaith Conference of Metropolitan Washington, D.C. The organization, founded in 1978, includes representatives of eleven religious groups—from Baha'is and Buddhists and Catholics to Jews and Sikhs and Zoroastrians—and, among other things, runs a speakers' bureau, making representatives of different faith groups available to talk to local congregations. Regardless of whether its members believed their own faith contained truth more fully than others, Lobenstine added, "they certainly recognize the importance of being with people of shared values. We come together out of the integrity of our own traditions." That they did so, he said, reflected their awareness of religious globalization. "In our very religiously and culturally diverse communities and world, we have no choice but to get to know our neighbors who are different from us," he said. "If we do not, we hide ourselves in a shelter of false security that we can just be by ourselves, that we can just be with the people who are like us, and that's enough to protect us." In other words, a wider web of relationships awaited those who would take the risk to engage people across religious lines.

Lobenstine's remark about getting to know the neighbors brings me back to the story of Frank Hubbard, the Episcopal priest in New Brunswick, New Jersey. I met him after I saw a notice announcing a memorial service for the World Trade Center's dead a year after the attacks. It was to be held at the Islamic Society of Central Jersey—the mosque he'd feared might be vandalized on September 11. That evening, the imam, Hamad Chebli, spoke, saying that two Muslims who regularly attended Friday prayers there had been among the Trade Center workers who perished that day. Others spoke, too—the mayor, a couple of city councilors, the police chief, as well as several Christian clergy, a rabbi, and a Hindu priest. I counted 150 people present, the folding chairs spread wall to wall in the prayer room. It was the full neighborhood, in its civic and religious dimensions. Over lunch several days later, I asked Hubbard why he'd thought it important, that morning a year before when many people felt overwhelmed by the singular horror of the terrorist attacks, to worry about the welfare of local Muslims. He responded that he had had two thoughts in mind. He feared the terrorist attacks might simply be a beginning, albeit an extraordinary one, and that destruction could ripple outward, shredding the country's social fabric. A line had to be drawn, he said, explaining that if vandals vented their rage against the mosque, with spray paint, rocks, or guns, that meant "a further spiral of violence that's going to make the situation more difficult." In that sense, reaching out across faith lines meant trying to stabilize the situation on behalf of a common good whose loss could be exceptionally dangerous. But he also said he had another reason: He had gotten to know Chebli and to appreciate him as a thoughtful and hospitable man. "There was a face on the mosque," Hubbard said. "There was my friend Hamad. It wasn't just this foreign building that you pass on route one. The fact that it's personal makes a difference."

He had gotten to know the imam the day he and some other ministers stopped by the mosque to pay a courtesy call on Chebli, whom Hubbard had not met. Unexpectedly, they arrived at an intimate moment in the Islamic Center's life, with the imam engaged in preparations for a funeral. But rather than excusing himself, he invited his visitors to stay and observe how he as a Muslim dealt with this rite of passage. "At first I was rather startled," Hubbard said. "I thought, 'Well, that's very gracious—what do we do?'" He ended up shedding his shoes, taking a seat in the back of the prayer room, and watching. He decided that the imam's invitation was "part of his educational outreach to us," non-Muslims who were his local colleagues. Chebli had indeed been gracious. The imam told the family of the dead man that the other clergy present were his friends.

Later, Chebli told me he intended the invitation to help lay a common foundation. His visitors, who themselves conducted funerals, would get to see him do the same; religious people would observe a religious rite. "I don't consider it a sadness issue," he said. "Let us be familiar with each other." That sort of familiarity was still a relatively new concept for Chebli. He had briefly served in New Orleans before coming to New Jersey. But prior to that, his experience was of Lebanon, a nation riven by civil war in the 1970s, in which religious divisions—between Christians and Muslims, as well as between Sunni Muslims and Shi'ite Muslims—were amply apparent. There, he had taken no part in interreligious ventures: He'd never set foot inside a Christian church nor had he ever seen clergy of different faiths share a platform. But in New Jersey, he had been invited by the Catholic Archdiocese of New York to take part in discussions between Roman Catholics and Muslims, a process he remembered fondly. Along the way, he had met the late Cardinal John O'Connor, and at one point, camera in hand, had asked permission to photograph the cardinal as he stood between two other imams, one a Sunni, the other a Shi'ite—representing the two major branches of Islam whose relations have often been very tense, as in present-day Iraq. To Chebli, that particular moment felt like a watershed. The Catholics had passed on an idea, and Chebli, a newcomer from the Middle East, had picked it up. After 9/11, the imam received an invitation to speak in Princeton Theological Seminary's chapel, the first Muslim to be so honored. That day, he presented a copy of the Qur'an to the seminary's president. He had concluded that such interactions were a blessing on America. "I consider it good in the eyes of God what we have achieved in this society." He was describing himself as a participant in the process. As if on cue, while he and I sat talking in his Spartan office, his fax machine began to hum and click. We paused for a moment as it dispensed a letter from a Bible college an hour or so away, thanking Chebli for agreeing to host twenty-four students from a world religions class that coming Saturday. The imam turned back to me. "All of us are on the same boat," he said. "We pay the same tax, we share the same sewers, we use the same water, breathe the same air."

That's one way of putting it. But it seemed to me that something larger is at work here, something more than a willingness simply to live and let live that makes for peaceful coexistence. As I left the mosque knowing that the Bible college students would be there shortly, I realized it was eminently possible some would want to meet a Muslim simply to figure out how to proselytize one eventually. That would certainly be their right in a nation that embraces religious liberty. But it might equally be true that meeting Chebli, a single, believing Muslim, might introduce some of them to the world into which they would graduate, in which they would live with billions of people who sincerely held beliefs different from their own. As the National Council's statement said, "Today the spectrum of religious tradition and practice in the United States is wider and more complex than ever before. Islam, Buddhism, Judaism, Hinduism, Sikhism, Native American traditions, Baha'i, and other faiths are now part of the American landscape." The council's statement also identified a way for Christians to discern a common denominator among these groups: As it says in Genesis's first chapter, everyone is made in God's image. "When we meet a human being, no matter what her or his religion, we are meeting a unique creation of the living God." In one way or another, that realization was acted out by people in various places in the United States in the immediate wake of 9/11. One can read a theological meaning

into it, or one can simply identify its civic value—those constructive acts demonstrated a belief in a common society that incorporates differences, that values life by valuing individual lives. It's a
belief that rejects utterly the means and goals of fearmongers, especially the terrorists who attacked the United States. It is also a more
subtle and inspiring (and, one hopes, more durable) approach to the
world than one that sets up a contested realm of us-versus-them.

TWO

Beyond Toleration

A danger of declaring an open-ended war on terror lies in propelling an entire nation into a metaphysical battle whose specific enemy is so vaguely defined that it can easily shift shapes. The description, such as it is, fits innocent bystanders as well as terrorists. It makes it easy, in such circumstances, for individuals to make grave mistakes when they take the battle into their own hands. In central New York one night two months after 9/11, a group of adolescents attacked a house of worship and burned it to ashes. The people who practiced their faith there had nothing whatsoever to do with Osama bin Laden or with militant Islam. They were not even Muslims, but Sikhs, adherents of a monotheistic faith developed in the Punjab region of South Asia five hundred years ago and since grown to twenty million followers. Devout Sikh men wear turbans to bind up their hair, which they keep uncut, as one of the five principles of dress that distinguish themselves spiritually. Sikhs have been no less immune than other religious and ethnic minorities to the tides of immigration, so it should be no surprise that some should end up living in upstate New York or that one particular organization, following advice from its India-based leader, should buy a rural farmhouse and convert it to a place for worship.

The Sikhs named it Gobind Sadan U.S.A., the first name a reference to one of Sikhism's early teachers, Guru Gobind Singh, who is credited with creating the specifically Sikh appearance that includes the uncut hair and turban. But who knew that in Oswego County,

New York, and specifically in the town of Palermo, where the converted farmhouse stood, drawing in worshipers from upstate New
York and lower Ontario, Canada? All the young people knew—the
ones who would torch the building on November 18, 2001—was
that at least one of them had seen "men in turbans" standing in the
building's driveway. Not only that, the assailants misread the sign:
Gobind Sadan looked to them like, "Go, bin Laden!"—an insidious
cheer on behalf of the nation's new archenemy.

   Much later, after local police had solved the crime and its authors had been sentenced to various degrees of punishment, the local school board president tried to put the event into its political
context for me. "You know during that time, we were being told by
our leaders, 'Watch your back. Look behind you. Look out for terrorists,'" said Mark Lichtenstein. The message had been received
with little nuance among some people in Oswego County; some
adolescents believed terrorists might come speedboating across Lake
Ontario and slip, lethally armed, into the woods. By the time we
spoke, Lichtenstein had become deeply involved in trying to set
matters right. He had become closely acquainted with the local
Sikhs, helped introduce them to the schools, listened as they publicly forgave the arsonists, and then traveled with them to the main
Gobind Sadan community outside Delhi, India, at his own expense,
where he offered an apology for the destruction on behalf of Palermo. "I also tried to explain to them," Lichtenstein said, referring
to his hosts, what had happened in the United States after 9/11—
"the fear, and how fear evolves into anger." He had taken photographs of Sikhs in India, especially of men in turbans. When he
came back, he showed them at the local high school. "I've spoken
to a lot of kids' groups, done a lot of Power Point presentations,"
he told me. "Shown pictures from India, talked about turbans and
really had some frank discussions with kids about 'ragheads' and
'towelheads,' and what it means when you say those types of words."
He tried to explain the differences between a Sikh turban and the

headgear worn by Osama bin Laden. It wasn't easy. "To people who don't know, it's the same thing. Sikhism—I don't think anybody knew what that was in my area, certainly not the kids."

It's easy to find labels for the arson incident. It might be called a hate crime or, at the very least, an act of intolerance, of a particularly virulent kind. But how do we label its spiritual opposite—the work of deliberately constructive relations between groups? We must search to find language capable of bearing such a positive meaning. There is a story of another building—also a house of worship set back from a rural road in the Northeast—but one whose history tells of a remarkably different relationship between religious groups. The building began life as a church, in Falmouth, Massachusetts. Clad in gray shingles, its walls are punctuated with enough windows that on a cloudless day the sunlight can play about the Puritan-influenced interior—the rows of straightbacked, wooden pews, each with its own little door separating it from the adjacent aisle. Architecturally, the building neatly reflects Cape Cod's traditional style. Local Congregationalists built it in 1797, and it served them for nearly two centuries. But then it passed to a group of Jewish families for their use as a synagogue, but not by way of a sale.

Rabbi Elias Lieberman explained to me how the building and its new congregation came to be linked. I met him one morning at a weekend retreat well away from the Cape. The gathering had been arranged as a study session, bringing together priests, ministers, and rabbis for the purpose of discussing how Christians and Jews can read the same biblical texts, but with often very different meanings. Early on, as people stood to introduce themselves, Lieberman identified himself as the rabbi from Cape Cod, a designation that seemed to elicit a sigh of envy among others present. Later, he told me that organized Jewish life on the Upper Cape began in 1981, after recently arrived families met to found the Falmouth congregation. For about a year, they met in borrowed space, until something unexpected occurred—the Congregationalists gave their building, its surrounding land, and an endowment fund to the Jewish families in Falmouth. By then, the heirs of the church's founders had dwindled sharply in numbers; they were not getting the use out of the building they once had. They gave it over without strings attached, other than a pledge that the Jewish families preserve the building and keep up the old cemetery behind it. Lieberman was not the rabbi then, but arrived a few years later. He had inherited the story and seemed eager to share it.

Later, he sent me some material about the synagogue. Among the papers was a single news clipping—a local paper noting the gift as it might any other real estate transaction in which an old structure is put to new use. The rabbi also included a copy of an official proclamation, issued by the town's selectmen celebrating the building's two hundredth anniversary. In it, they hailed the gift of the building, saying it reflected the spirit of America. As such, they said, it exemplified religious "tolerance."

But did it really? Consider what occurred here: Through this transaction, one religious group affirmed the identity of another. A group of Christians had given a Jewish congregation a building, land, and money to maintain the property. Between people of different faiths, such a gesture is unusual indeed, signifying not only financial but theological generosity. The gift would seem to say, we respect you as believers and we want you to live and thrive. Put that up against the long history of Jewish-Christian relations, a story that often makes for dark reading, and it becomes even more significant. If the relationship between Christians and Jews has improved in many western nations, it's happened only recently, the greatest changes taking place in the last half century. Falmouth's officials did not mean to say that Jews were merely "tolerated" in their town. The gift of the building showed something more meaningful. But, again, how does one describe it?

The challenge here goes beyond semantics. Often, when people speak of tolerance, the word becomes a sort of umbrella, fit to cover a wide range of human interactions. To some, it simply means keeping the peace—my fist stopping short of your nose. Others use the word to signify varying degrees of positive activity. The problem is that tolerance, boiled down to its essential meaning, does not bear the good intentions with which some would invest it. For that reason, calls to tolerance do little to point the way toward the sort of constructive actions we're capable of when we deal with people unlike us. In its most common definition, tolerance means forbearance. Doctors typically speak of what a patient can tolerate medically, by which they mean "endure." In a social sense, a state of mutual toleration signals the peaceful coexistence of groups that differ from one another, perhaps uncomfortably so. Where there is a danger that groups within society are threatened by bigotry, oppression, and outright violence, efforts to promote tolerance are clearly worthy, even important. But why stop there? Is tolerance a means or an end, a floor or a ceiling?

Public officials, when faced with outbreaks of social tension—especially at times of verbal or physical attacks against a specific group—typically call on everyone to show "tolerance." It's like asking people to calm down. But often enough, the hope expressed goes beyond that. To call for tolerance in such circumstances means to call for coexistence. But that can be a shallow foundation on which to construct a community. If I am asked to tolerate someone, I hear it as a call to leave that person alone, unhindered to pursue his or her own way. Tolerance is often a low bar to clear. It does not suggest people might learn about—and possibly from—one another. Toleration serves as a basis for a cease-fire, but it does not offer a vision for what might follow. One of the best-known recent instances of that very situation took place under the unblinking glare of television lights on May 1, 1992. Rioting had engulfed Los Angeles, threatening entire neighborhoods. "Can we all get along?" plaintively asked Rodney King, a twenty-seven-year-old African

American, as he appeared with city officials that day. Large sections of Los Angeles had collapsed into mayhem. Looters and arsonists roamed the streets; people armed themselves. The city had begun to tear itself asunder along racial and ethnic lines. Standing before the cameras, King seemed frightened, yet city officials must have known his would be the most resonant voice that day. Fourteen months earlier, he had been a deeply obscure figure. But in March 1991, law enforcement officers arrested him after a lengthy, high-speed chase—and subjected him to a prolonged beating. An on-looker captured part of the confrontation on videotape, subsequently broadcast worldwide on television. The scene provoked widespread outrage, particularly among Los Angeles's African American com-munities, which had long complained of police harassment and brutality. The officers involved said they believed King to be resist-ing arrest, even threatening them. In April 1992, a jury acquitted them of assaulting him. In the midst of the rioting, King pleaded for order. Had people heeded him, it would have been grounds for celebration—but not without the attendant question of what might follow that return to peace. Might there be more to sharing the city beyond citizens tolerating one another?

Sometimes, hints of that broad landscape beyond toleration can be discerned beneath the surface of public events. California is home not only to King; at the other end of fortune's spectrum, Arnold Schwarzenegger participated in another public event in-volving a call to "tolerance" a dozen years later. In the spring of 2004, the recently elected governor traveled to Israel on an official visit, using the occasion to promote what he called a personal, global mission. As an international film star, Schwarzenegger has a crowd-drawing power that other politicians can only envy. But this trip held a particular fascination in its own right, given his status as an immigrant to the United States, the son of an Austrian who fought for the Nazis. His father's wartime activities, which report-edly included serving as a storm trooper, had been discussed during

Schwarzenegger's political campaign the previous year, a public airing that lent his visit to Israel an added emotional power. In a speech set against a backdrop of memorials to the Holocaust, Schwarzenegger acknowledged Austrians' participation in the genocide. He loved his birth country, he said, but recognized its citizens' complicity in the destruction of Europe's Jews. In Austria, "intolerance and ignorance led to atrocities and heartache," Schwarzenegger said. And so, he added, "I want to do whatever I can to promote tolerance around the world."

Let's be clear: When set against the memory of the Holocaust, his goal was laudable. And he did have an obvious source for his choice of language—in Jerusalem, he helped dedicate a new Museum of Tolerance, a branch of the Simon Wiesenthal Center, a Jewish human rights organization. (The center, based in Los Angeles, runs a Museum of Tolerance, which guidebooks point out is really about intolerance, focusing as it does on the dangers of bigotry and the coming of the Holocaust. What I have appreciated is the museum's insistence, in its exhibits, that public speech is never without consequences.) But Schwarzenegger's statements did carry a bit of irony; he later acknowledged his support of the Wiesenthal Center, which predated his political career. By 2003, he had given it at least $750,000 and directed fund-raising events that generated millions of dollars more. His Hollywood work in films had made him a very wealthy man. But the level of his financial generosity indicated a relationship with Jewish institutions beyond the merely tolerant.

What about Schwarzenegger's linking ignorance with intolerance? It is eminently reasonable to suggest that if you know nothing about a group of people, you're more likely to fall prey to dangerous rumors and untruths about them. Wasn't that why a worldwide outcry ensued when a Saudi Arabian newspaper, in 2002, published an opinion column whose author claimed Jews used blood from Christian or Muslim children to flavor holiday pastries? The U.S. State

Department complained to the Saudi government about this recrudescence of the old blood libel against the Jews. In turn, the paper's editor (who had been away at the time) apologized, fired the columnist, and published a statement that said, "We have full respect for all religions." Simply tolerating people is not likely to make you know them any better. Coexistence is hardly a recipe for the acquisition of knowledge, although it may make possible an interaction that leads in that direction. To reach beyond tolerance is to open oneself to getting to know others, to appreciate their role in the world. In that sense, it's an activity that involves recognizing (with some humility) that one can actually learn from others. "One should always understand another man's point of view," said Cardinal Agustin Bea, a German Catholic scholar who played a leading role during the Second Vatican Council. Bea went on: "This means putting oneself in his place and seeing things from the position from which he sees them." The cardinal said he spoke from concern for truth. If one professed to love the idea of truth, he said, one had "to bear in mind the limitations of our knowledge and also to recognize the aspect of truth which others see." Putting it another way, individuals and groups perceive one another dimly, even as they pridefully believe in the clarity of their own personal vision. Bea, it should be clear, wasn't suggesting that people could come to consensus on inherently divisive issues like theological differences, but that they might instead consider a more respectful and attentive attitude toward one another. When it comes to religious differences, basic knowledge of what another person believes can be helpful, if only to humanize him and separate him from gross stereotypes.

And gross stereotyping is inevitable, a human failing without end. The real question is, how ought one respond to such slanders, beyond simply declaring, "That's wrong"? In 2002, months after the United States had declared its war on terror, a handful of very prominent Protestant ministers began to identify Islam itself as the enemy—effectively describing the United States as caught in a religious war. Franklin Graham called the faith of Muslims "evil," and Jerry Falwell described Islam's Prophet Muhammad as a "terrorist"—a remark for which he later apologized, after news of it generated lethal riots in South Asia. The danger, of course, is that such talk from influential sources may serve as virtually the only information many people are likely to have about another faith— and they may be far more likely to hear the original insult rather than the ensuing apology, if there is one. (Hence, the international concern about the Saudi opinion column.) But often, in instances like these, the people who may be the best informed on such matters mix their denunciations of the insult with a call for tolerance. In effect, they seek a verbal cease-fire, where it would be much better to work to create occasions for people to meet and talk with each other, Christian to Muslim, Muslim to Jew, and so on.

Besides, simple calls for tolerance can be rejected as attempts to foster "political correctness" (a much-used canard) or, worse, to muffle free speech. Aha! The thought police are at it again, says the person who has been called upon to be tolerant. Now the original speaker becomes the aggrieved party, laying claim to the mantle of victimhood while nobly defending a constitutional right. Colleges and corporations have tried to develop policies to keep students or employees from attacking groups and individuals based on their ethnicity, faith, or sexual orientation. But such attempts to keep the peace on campus or in the corporate workplace do not always fare well in court. In 1942, the Supreme Court ruled in a case called *Chaplinsky v. New Hampshire* that "fighting words" that "inflict injury or tend to incite an immediate breach of the peace" are not protected. But the Court's ruling has been applied narrowly— evidence of its high regard for First Amendment guarantees. In 2006, the *Los Angeles Times* reported that some conservative Protestants had begun filing lawsuits to declare a right *to be intolerant,* on free speech grounds. The story described a student at a southern university who had filed suit against the institution for its official efforts to keep her from criticizing gay students. The university, the article noted, had a "tolerance policy."

In any case, such codes offer very low bars to clear in human relations. One illustration might be the statements President Bush began making in 2003, as he publicly established his position against gay marriage. He pointedly avoided using harsh language against gays. We're all sinners, the president said, when asked his opinion of homosexual activity. In so saying, he staked out a theological position that regarded gay behavior as wrong in God's eyes, but not uniquely wrong. The day the president gave his news conference, a Yale Law professor described Bush's position as expressing a toleration that was "not gay friendly," but that nonetheless rejected "outright persecution or criminalization of gay activity." In other words, the professor said, "Bush is trying to situate himself as tolerant, which he defines as not persecuting people, but not anything more." In that sense, Bush could be described as following the basic idea of tolerance laid down by the English philosopher John Locke for religious differences. Locke's argument, in his book *A Letter on Toleration*, published in 1689, was a singular achievement for the time, offering an alternative to the traditional practice of governments' enforcing religious uniformity. "If Christians are to be warned to abstain from revenge, when provoked by repeated injuries, even until seventy times seven, how much more ought they, who have suffered nothing at another's hand, to forbear from all anger and hostility, take the greatest care to avoid doing any kind of harm to those from whom they have received none." (The mathematical formula that Locke cites—seventy times seven—comes straight out of the Gospels, when Jesus answers Peter's question about whether he ought to forgive personal injustices seven times over: "I say unto thee not seven times, but seventy times seven.") Locke continues the argument: "Above all they should take care not to injure those who only mind their own business, and are solicitous for nothing but that, whatever men think of them, they may worship God in the manner which they believe will be most acceptable to him, and embrace the religion which afford them the greatest hope of eternal salvation." Locke was advancing a revolutionary idea, that religion is a matter of individual choice, not beholden to the state or the community. You don't approve of your neighbors' beliefs? Well, let them live in peace and society will actually benefit. It's a sort of Hippocratic oath: First, do no harm. When governments put this idea into official policy, it's often been seen as a social advance. In the 1780s, the Austrian emperor Joseph II promulgated a law granting free worship to Lutherans and Calvinists. They received a status nearly equal with the Roman Catholic Church; henceforth, they counted themselves as tolerable and tolerated.

But Americans ought to know (and rejoice in the fact) that even as it gained ground in Europe, toleration—as an official policy—was weighed and found sorely lacking on their side of the Atlantic. It carried the taint of condescension, as if it were a benefit bestowed by the powerful on the barely worthy. Toleration could be granted, and just as easily it could be removed, Thomas Paine argued. He's best remembered as author of *Common Sense*, the 1776 pamphlet that bluntly made the case for American independence from Great Britain. Fifteen years later, he wrote *The Rights of Man*, a book sympathetic to the French Revolution and a best seller in its time. In it, he criticized the idea of official toleration, which he declared was "not the *opposite* of Intolerance, but is the *counterfeit* of it. Both are despotisms. The one assumes to itself the right of withholding Liberty of Conscience, and the other of granting it." Paine dedicated the book to George Washington, who happened to agree with him on that subject.

Washington doesn't hold a reputation as a political philosopher. We remember him for his military leadership and as a civic role model, the man who defined the unscripted office of president. But his words of greeting to a delegation of American Jews are relevant here and eminently worth repeating. He told them religious minorities were not going to be officially tolerated in the United States, because another superior idea would prevail: religious liberty. "It is now no more that toleration is spoken of," Washington wrote to the Jewish congregation of Newport, Rhode Island, "as if it was by the indulgence of one class of people, that another enjoyed the exercise of their inherent national gifts." He sounds like Paine in this instance, although Washington wrote those words years before Paine published his. In his letter, he spoke directly to the new nation's smallest minority of free citizens. Jews in Newport formed a fraction of a population numbering no more than two thousand people scattered between New England and Georgia, this in a nation of four million. But they were not newcomers. They traced their American roots to 1654, when two dozen refugees from Recife, Brazil, landed in Manhattan aboard the ship *St. Cathrien*. After a period of Dutch control, Recife had passed into the hands of the Portuguese, which left its Jews unguarded against harassment by the Inquisition—the Catholic legal tribunal whose official mandate to root out heretics often involved it in wider, brutal operations against Jews, Muslims, and Protestants. In Manhattan, the settlers first had to withstand efforts to oust them by an anti-Semite, the colonial governor, Peter Stuyvesant. They succeeded. Within the same decade, a few ventured to Rhode Island, founded by the Puritan dissident Roger Williams, who had established a colony with a spacious view of religious freedom. For that very quality, the Dutch in Manhattan called Rhode Island a latrine. But in his letter to the Jewish congregation, Washington essentially said Roger Williams had been right all along.

Today, a small, elegant building stands to remind visitors of that moment. Touro Synagogue sits above Newport's harbor, the design of Peter Harrison, a renowned eighteenth-century architect who so placed the structure that worshipers within face toward Jerusalem. Local Jews dedicated the building during Hanukah in 1763. When Washington came ashore on his first official visit to Rhode

Island on August 17, 1790, he met Moses Seixas, the congregation's warden, its top official in the absence of a permanent rabbi. And in the letter in which he responded to Seixas's written greetings, Washington extolled freedom of conscience. "The citizens of the United States of America have a right to applaud themselves for having given to mankind examples of an enlarged and liberal policy: a policy worthy of imitation. All possess alike liberty of conscience and immunities of citizenship." In other words, Jews (and by extension other religious minorities) would find themselves on a level playing field in the United States, all faiths regarded as equal before the secular government. This equality implies a basic respect for all religions and an understanding that they have a role to play in the nation. None will be privileged, none will be demeaned.

How might this idea play out today, more than two centuries later, as individuals make their own choices about how to acknowledge a particular religious group? There's a subtle illustration that arose in very polarized circumstances, during a nearly global uproar over the publication of cartoons depicting the Prophet Muhammad in 2006. That controversy began after a newspaper in Denmark commissioned, then published twelve mostly derogatory cartoons, one portraying the Prophet as a suicide bomber, an ignited explosive stuck in his turban. For the most part, the images played to the worst stereotypes that have flourished about Muslims of late—that they are murderous fanatics with no concern for the lives, never mind the liberties, of anyone else. If the Danish editors did not actually know that Muslims consider any portrayal of Muhammad to be offensive, other European editors who reprinted the cartoons after the controversy got going certainly did. They could have read almost any Muslim commentary on the subject. Or they could have watched the broadcast news as rioting broke out in several Middle Eastern and South Asian cities. That violence was flatly inexcusable, just as it nicely reinforced the very stereotypes some of the cartoons portrayed.

But what added meaning to the controversy was the response to the furor among American news media—or at least the major organizations that tend to be called mainstream. In the United States, editors and broadcasters largely resisted the argument that the controversy was purely about free speech, such that not to publish the cartoons meant giving in to intimidation. For the most part, newspapers and broadcasters chose to describe the cartoons verbally. Unless one is sufficiently paranoid to buy into the idea of a giant media conspiracy, then one has to recognize that the actions resulted from many individual decisions made in newsrooms across America. One at *The Boston Globe,* the largest newspaper in New England, is worth noting. When interviewed in February 2006 on National Public Radio, the newpaper's editor, Martin Baron, explained why the *Globe* chose not to run the cartoons: "We are often confronted with images or phrases that are considered to be grossly offensive to a religious group or a racial group or an ethnic group. Our standard policy is not to publish those images or phrases that are considered to be offensive." He said he did not regard the decision as undermining free speech. Instead, it was a matter of editorial judgment. "It comes up all the time. This is not an exception. This is, in fact, the general rule."

Implicit in his statement is that the *Globe* recognized Muslims as a religious group—one among many—that carried a basic dignity, such that the newspaper would not *gratuitously* offend them. Muslims existed within the *Globe*'s understanding of its community, just as did other religious groups. They were not simply "people over there"—the exotic, the unstable, the dangerous—but a population that included people in New England of which the newspaper might reasonably take account. It is a position that goes beyond mere forbearance in that it affords Muslims a recognition as a religious group on an equal footing with other religious groups in the community. This is important because it involves a crucial issue of identity—how it is formed, how it is sustained. Until very recently,

Muslims have been a blank slate to most Americans. Until the first oil embargo in the early 1970s, they might as well have simply been the "other guys" in the Crusades, or exotic figures in *Arabian Nights*. Anything that separates "Islam" as a rich, ancient, and varied system, a living, universal faith, from the narrow and frightening word "terrorist" is beneficial all around. As the philosopher Charles Taylor argues, individuals and groups do not come to understand who they are entirely on their own. Rather, he says, a sense of identity develops through an ongoing series of social interactions, a process that for individuals begins at birth with their parents and continues lifelong, with friends, coworkers, strangers, and everyone else one is likely to meet. Discovering your own identity, Taylor says, does not mean working it out in isolation, but negotiating it "through dialogue, partly overt, partly internal, with others."

The key word there is "dialogue." That does not mean shouting and it does not mean forcing a group of people to confront the worst stereotypes about themselves (i.e., that they are *all* dangerous), such that they feel they have to fight to defend their very reason to be. Furthermore, dialogue is an activity that represents a state of relations going well beyond tolerance. To put it simply, you can coexist with people without ever having to speak meaningfully with them. What holds society together is not just people who will tolerate others, but people who will actually go beyond that, to provide the glue that nourishes social relationships.

Let's consider another example, drawing on the same controversy. A relative exception among American newspapers, *The Philadelphia Inquirer*, decided to print one of the Danish cartoons. But the basis for the decision—and the way in which the newspaper's editor followed it up—contrasted sharply with the behavior of many European media. The *Inquirer* ran one of the cartoons inside its news pages, along with a note to the paper's readers, informing them that the editors had discussed the issue and concluded that the story was too important and the image too powerful not to display. On the day the *Inquirer* printed the cartoon, two dozen picketers showed up outside the newspaper's offices in protest. The editor, Amanda Bennett, went outside and met with them. "I assured them," she told an interviewer later, "that neither the paper nor I had any interest in being disrespectful to them or their religion, and I was actually proud of them exercising their freedom of speech to protest in front of my building." That amounted to an exercise in professional explanation (the cartoon printed as news, not to insult), as well as a seeking of common political ground. We're all Americans here, she effectively declared, peacefully exercising our First Amendment rights.

Does such an incident signify agreement? No. But that people will be willing to speak seriously with and listen to one another is the hope of education. It allows for a very wide range of speech that can certainly involve disagreement, but not defamation. In it, people will articulate differences, some very strongly held without resorting to the sort of divisive rhetoric in which they question each other's intelligence, patriotism, moral worth, or right to be. As Amy Gutmann, president of the University of Pennsylvania, has written, "A multicultural society is bound to include a wide range of such respectable moral disagreements, which offers us the opportunity to defend our views before morally serious people with whom we disagree and thereby learn from our differences."

A constructive appreciation of differences can occur even when what divides people seems particularly fraught with social anxiety, as in differences over what is appropriate in human sexuality. I had a direct experience of that possibility when I worked as a reporter covering the Presbyterian Church (USA) while an internal debate raged over whether the denomination might ordain gay people. That issue has obsessed and deeply divided the nation's major Protestant denominations since the 1970s; by 2007, the relative success of the supporters of gay ordination within the Episcopal Church had prompted such a backlash among their opponents worldwide that the denomination faced an official loss of status within its global association, the Anglican Communion. Despite the enormous contention the issue aroused, at one annual meeting of Presbyterians I covered, I happened upon two organizations in the exhibition hall that proclaimed radically different messages but whose booths stood in proximity to each other. One advocated "biblical marriage," heterosexual unions—one man–one woman, period. The other urged greater inclusion of actively gay men and lesbians within the church. The two, obviously, had very different understandings of what was possible and morally right in human relationships, but calm prevailed between them during the days I was there. They were not calling each other names. But there was something else, too. I remember one of the biblical marriage people told me that he firmly disagreed with the gay organization, but he had looked into their message and realized he could respect the theological argument they were making. In retrospect, it seems his choice of verb—respect—had everything to do with the situation. He indicated he had given thought to someone else's ideas and was willing to acknowledge the effort that had gone into articulating them. In other words, his response was not simply one of abstaining from name-calling—that is, of being merely tolerant. Instead, he chose to extend a basic recognition to his neighbors, to weigh their opinions, and even to accord them a moral status.

Commitment to individual rights and commitment to the idea of a common life are not mutually exclusive. We've seldom heard this idea in recent years, but it has been enunciated in America's past, perhaps most memorably in January 1941, as the United States prepared to enter a global war. Speaking to Congress fully eleven months before Pearl Harbor, President Roosevelt called on the United States to build up its military might for the struggle he so presciently foresaw against demonic fascism. Yet the address he delivered concerned much more than that. It was a visionary statement, which became known as the Four Freedoms speech. At its conclusion Roosevelt briefly described four principles that utterly distinguish democracy from tyranny. They are freedom of speech, freedom of worship, freedom from want (especially hunger), and freedom from fear, which he said could be achieved by an eventual reduction in world armaments. What makes the list so compelling still is the way that he linked two ideas that we typically understand as individual rights (free speech and worship) with two others that are societal goals, vast projects intended for the betterment of humanity. Roosevelt put them together, in effect joining the individual with the community. The four principles served as the basis for "a moral order" and a "good society," he said. "Freedom means the supremacy of human rights everywhere." You cannot truly be concerned about human rights unless you believe that each individual has an inherent worth and dignity. And to assume that is to do more than simply tolerate people. It is to extend to them a recognition of their uniqueness—an idea articulated with particular eloquence by the twentieth-century Jewish philosopher Martin Buber.

After the United States entered the life-or-death struggle of the World War, the illustrator Norman Rockwell took up the challenge of visually depicting Roosevelt's four principles. It may seem strange now that it would be Rockwell who would do so, as much of his work comes across as sentimental. But Rockwell, like Roosevelt, possessed an enormous gift of being able to reach people. And naïve art does have the power to move us. At least two of the paintings succeed in the task. Rockwell's *Freedom of Worship* preserves James Madison's basic insight about American religious diversity—and goes well beyond it. The painting shows the faces of eight individuals, each person immersed in an act of prayer. They are men and women, racially and ethnically diverse and—in a way more hinted at than displayed—religiously diverse as well. Rockwell boldly painted a phrase into the picture itself: "Each according to the dictates of his own conscience," a motto found in several state constitutions. While the painting portrays an individual right, guaranteed in the United States by law, what makes the work memorable is its underlying suggestion of a community here. The eight people occupy an equal plane and they face (more or less) in the same direction, toward the painting's left, the source of the painter's light, which illuminates their faces. What goes on here is not something we do entirely alone; there are others, different from us, who do it too, and they are persons of worth and dignity.

As a journalist—and one who lived for a while in the Berkshire Hills, where Rockwell practiced—I've long had a certain admiration for one of the other paintings in this series. Titled *Freedom of Speech,* it shows a young man standing among and speaking to a crowd of people inside a building. The setting is a New England town meeting—that's obvious because the young man and two others are holding copies of a document marked as a town's annual report. (Rockwell was not subtle.) The speaker wears an old jacket over a work shirt, suggesting he's just come in from the fields or from beneath a vehicle in an automotive shop. By contrast, the two men seated closest to him are older and wear coats and ties. Yet from their expressions, we know that these wiser, more experienced individuals are listening carefully, weighing the younger man's words with respect. What I've come to like about the painting is not just its portrayal of a constitutional right, but the context in which it occurs. People are shown paying attention. Presumably, they will have an opportunity to talk too, and the current speaker will then give them his attention. There are two intrinsically related activities going on here—speaking and listening. This isn't a picture of people tolerating one another, simply allowing one another space. The implicit message here is that free speech is at its most valuable in a democracy when it is not simply about individual expression, but involves the community.

Speaking and listening are vital activities that build civil society. They are activities that should be sufficiently wide to include space for ideas rooted in many different perspectives, including differing theological understandings of how the world works. This is hardly easy. To go beyond tolerating someone amounts to a civic discipline. It is something that belongs to a world in which people regard themselves as citizens, in that they share a common stake in a society that is religiously diverse as well as diverse in the other identities to which people lay claim. That word "citizen" speaks of responsibility and commitment in a way utterly beyond the reach of a certain noun beloved of politicians these days. They call us "taxpayers," as if that were the sum and substance of our social existence, as if all that mattered to living in a great nation were the financial transactions made between individuals and a distant entity called government for services rendered. That's an atomized vision of society, in which rights and personal expectations count for everything, and common life for nothing.

One of the most eloquent expressions of this comes from a distinctly nonreligious figure in his essay that is a profound call for civic engagement in the name of humanity's future. In "Neither Victims nor Executioners," the French existentialist Albert Camus urged people not to be overwhelmed by history's seemingly inexorable forces. Camus's essay contains a clear-eyed recognition that the world is full of violence, that the various forces of destruction will always wage campaigns of fear and horror. But he calls on individuals not to submit to the hopelessness and social atomization that this terror intends. "Yes, what we must fight is fear and silence and the spiritual isolation they involve," he declared. "What we must defend is dialogue and the universal communication of men." Camus wrote his short essay in eight parts in late November 1946. He served as editor of the French Resistance newspaper *Combat*, where the articles appeared. The first part is titled "The Century of Fear," the concluding one "Toward Dialogue." What a time to mount such an argument: Camus surveyed a continent devastated by a fascism that had been broken only eighteen months earlier. At the core of Europe's disaster lay the *Shoah*, the Nazi attempt to exterminate the continent's Jews. It killed six million, grinding on among a population that overwhelmingly considered itself Christian but that, with the exception of certain heroic individuals and groups, declined to intervene to protect its neighbors. What makes Camus's essay memorable is that he calls for people who care about humanity to care enough to foster "universal communication" among us all. A tall order, it means more than merely according one another an unmolested place in society.

But why *not* set the bar higher, especially now, in an era in which religious differences are so starkly involved in the current fear gripping the world? The Jewish philosopher Rabbi Abraham Joshua Heschel once declared that no religion is an island, which he said meant that in no single religion could believers consider themselves self-sufficient, removed from spiritual contact with other humans. To act on that realization is really to move beyond the sphere of coexistence. But how? In 1999, United Methodists at an annual meeting in northern California raised more than six thousand dollars to help rebuild three synagogues in Sacramento that had just been torched by arsonists. The Methodists delivered their check before a multireligious audience gathered in a public building to support the local congregations in their first Sabbath services after the fire. Recalling the moment, one Jewish participant remarked, "Those in my parents' generation were dumbfounded. Whoever heard of gentiles caring about Jews?" Of course, six thousand dollars didn't buy anyone a new synagogue. But who could ignore the symbolism? Through the donation, a group of Christian ministers said, we want you to be Jews, so much so that we're willing to help you rebuild. The act is remarkable but not unique. Something similar happened three years later—this time right in the midst of the war on terror. It was a gift that crossed not only religious boundaries, but international ones too, from Americans to Afghans, a people living in a nation identified with the enemy.

The project began after the Episcopal bishop of New York, Mark S. Sisk, learned that a mosque had been damaged during

American bombing in Afghanistan during the fall of 2001. The
bishop had supported the intervention by American and allied
troops in Afghanistan after September 11, when that country's ruling Taliban government refused to surrender Osama bin Laden.
Sisk heard the news about the damage to the mosque on a radio
broadcast and thought it might be a good idea to respond to it—as
a religious matter, not a political one. When he discussed the issue
with me, months later, he spoke from a position of spiritual empa-
thy. "These are other human beings who innocently had one of the
most sacred places in their life destroyed," he said later. "I'm not
blaming anybody. These things happen. However, that doesn't ex-
onerate you from responsibility for what happens. As a Christian
person, I am responsible for that." If he sounded slightly defensive,
it was because when he had appealed for funds to help rebuild the
mosque, he heard from Episcopalians who thought the idea a very
bad one. Some accused him of wanting to aid an enemy; others said
he risked undermining Christian truth by offering to help Muslims.

Sisk's diocese incorporates a widely diverse set of demographics,
embracing a broad swathe of lower New York from Staten Island
north to Hyde Park, Franklin Roosevelt's old home, and west into
the Catskills. It includes more than two hundred parishes in which
the liturgy is read in fourteen different languages, from Chinese and
Creole to Spanish and Tagalog. In Manhattan and Westchester
County, it includes some of the wealthiest parishes in the Episcopal
Church. Nonetheless, donations came slowly, some from congregations, some from individuals. But publicity about his plea and the
controversy it aroused helped—in a way that crossed religious lines.
Sisk received contributions from Catholics in California, as well as
from at least one Jewish donor, a New Yorker who gave five thousand dollars. It was the latter gift that gave Sisk considerable satisfaction: Jews had helped rebuild a mosque in a Muslim majority
nation. In the end, the diocese raised thirty-five thousand dollars, of
which a bit more than one fifth came from Afghan immigrants in

New York, who contributed during an appeal in their mosque in the city.

I asked Sisk why he lent his efforts to this particular cause. It didn't stem from any great knowledge of or sympathy with the Islamic world. He had "read some books" about Islam, so he felt better informed than he had once been. But his motivation, he said, was that this was an issue that concerned "general humanity," and he made it clear that his education had come from his interactions with people—his parents, for starters, and also the friendship he developed as a priest with a neighboring rabbi. Sisk was the product of a mixed Christian marriage, his father a Catholic, his mother a Protestant. A cousin had married a Jewish man. He remembered being taught that people were of equal worth and value, and that it would be wrong to denigrate anyone based on class, racial, ethnic, or religious identity. Much later, appointed to serve an Episcopal parish in Kingston, New York, he found the church to be located next door to a synagogue. Over time, he and the rabbi became friends; together, they founded a local interfaith council. "He was really my closest clerical friend in the city," Sisk said. As for the fund-raising on behalf of the mosque, the bishop offered an essentially theological argument that Episcopalians in New York and Muslims in northern Afghanistan shared the most profound of similarities: "We're all children of the same God." As such, it made sense for one to help the other. "I would like to think that we are in some way playing a role in softening the edges of the human condition," he said. It was a theological statement: God takes the side of all humanity, an understanding that ought to impel believers toward charity. To reach that point didn't make Sisk less of an Episcopalian, and certainly not less of a Christian.

The day I visited Falmouth, I did not really know what motivated the Congregationalists when they gave the Jewish congregation their building a quarter century earlier. At one point, I called the Reverend Douglas Showalter, a local minister who maintains a

keen interest in the area's Congregationalist history. He had moved
to Falmouth after the gift had been made, but he recalled conversations he had had with a now-deceased member of the East Falmouth community who said they had been using the building as a
seasonal parish, opening it for summer services. "And then they decided they couldn't keep up the building anymore," he said. He was
unsure how the Congregationalists made the connection with their
Jewish neighbors. But he regarded the result as impressive. "Maybe
'tolerance' isn't the best word," he said, reflecting on the town's official statement when I raised that with him. "It's a show of mutual
respect one for another."

That day at the synagogue, Rabbi Lieberman took out a key to
let us in the side door. The pews sat in stiff rows, in an interior that
struck me as very much old-fashioned Protestant. But the pew
racks held copies of the Reform Jewish prayer book and anyone
who took a seat there would face the ark above the *bima,* the platform at the front of the sanctuary. The ark itself held an old Torah
scroll from the Czech Republic, which had somehow survived the
Nazis. When I mentioned the local selectmen's proclamation and
asked Lieberman if he thought what happened in Falmouth could
be described as "tolerance," he said he too would have preferred
another term. "For me, tolerance almost has a grudging quality
about it," he said. In Falmouth, he said, Jews had experienced
"warm acceptance." That went some way toward clearing up the
mystery I had wrestled with, the question of what words might be
appropriate to describe what had happened. The gift of the building amounted to an act of respect, a mindfulness of society. It did
not diminish vital differences between the groups, but it suggested
that they, and all of us, are not simply competitors.

THREE

An Idea Revived for the Battlefield

Why should Americans and Europeans be concerned about the thoughts of a former Egyptian bureaucrat, a man who wrote exclusively for Muslims and specifically about Islam? What's more, the Egyptian in question, Sayyid Qutb, who worked for his nation's education ministry, has been dead for decades. He wrote mainly in jail; his most important book was banned by the Egyptian government. But ideas can be enormously potent tools, assuming a durability and intellectual force out of proportion to the circumstances in which they were first articulated. Ideas can persist despite all the legal and extralegal obstacles that can be thrown in their way—police, courts, censorship, military action. And so it has been with Qutb (whose name is pronounced KOOT-ub). Potentially dangerous ideas demand a bold and attractive counterargument, one that can motivate people looking for something in which to believe, something around which to declare their identity.

About Qutb: Two months after 9/11, the British newspaper *The Guardian* declared his importance with an ominous headline, "Is this the man who inspired bin Laden?" The essay described him as "the most influential advocate in modern times of jihad, or Islamic holy war," and the leading proponent of the idea that Muslims might violently oppose governments "that claim to be Muslim, but whose implementation of Islamic precepts is judged to be imperfect." Since Qutb's execution in 1966, an alleged traitor to the secular, socialist government of Egypt's president, Gamal Abdel Nasser, his books have been published throughout the Muslim world. His most im-portant—its title translated as *Milestones*—contains prose with a chilling resonance in light of recent terrorism: "Humanity today stands on the brink of the abyss. . . . To establish the reign of God on earth and eliminate the reign of man, to take power out of those of his worshipers who have usurped it and return it to God alone . . . this will not be done through sermons and discourse." Beyond words lies the sword. Gilles Kepel, a leading scholar of extremist militants in Egypt, wrote in his book *The Roots of Radical Islam* that Qutb's thought had great impact on Ayman al-Zawahiri, the Egyptian eye surgeon who helped found a militant organization that in the 1990s closely allied itself with Bin Laden's al-Qaeda. Zawahiri had been active in Egypt's Islamist movement since his adolescence in the mid-1960s. These days, he is considered al-Qaeda's second in com-mand, perhaps its chief strategist. When we hear from our more prescient commentators that the contest with terrorists is not just fought with munitions, but with ideas, we ought to think of Qutb.

"The religious extremist's vision—the core idea—is 'My inter-pretation of my religion is the only legitimate way of being, and everyone else needs to be coerced into that way believing and be-longing on Earth,' " Eboo Patel, a young American Muslim, told me one day. He regarded the world as contested ground between what he called the "religious totalitarians"—high-profile fundamentalists of all stripes, some murderous, some simply outspokenly intoler-ant—and the "religious pluralists," of whom he counted himself one. At the time of our conversation, we were sitting in the lounge of a small hotel in London one autumn afternoon, both of us having come from a meeting of Christians, Jews, and Muslims interested in promoting a better, more trusting dialogue among community leaders within the three faiths. Patel had spoken at the conference, but he had a much larger end in mind than simply talking with the people there. He wanted to compete with the religious totalitarians, particularly for the hearts and minds of young people whom he said are typically targeted by extremists who appeal to a younger person's sense that he or she can make a difference in the world. Patel had spent years thinking about this, between graduating from the University of Illinois at Champaign-Urbana in the 1990s and returning from Oxford University in 2002, where he had been a Rhodes Scholar. Later that year, he began to develop an organization called the Interfaith Youth Core. Its central mission was enlisting students from different faith groups to collaborate in socially beneficial projects, something like raising a house for Habitat for Humanity or collecting food for America's Second Harvest or working with a local parks department to clean up urban playgrounds. The main idea was to get young people to identify the source within their own religion for the values—like hospitality and compassion—that overlapped with those of other religions. They would talk with each other about where those values came from within their own faiths, and then they would work together during an "interfaith day of service." Patel's organization had printed a training manual and produced an accompanying DVD, which it could take to college chaplaincies to explain the idea and the process. Patel wasn't entirely focused on college campuses; the Core was open to young people beyond that particular group. But, he said to me, "When you're trying to start a movement, you're trying to find a way to pick it up. The best place to start is college campuses, because diversity exists there, the chaplain may be interested, plus there's an office of volunteer services. You've got the social capital on campus to run this." By 2006, Patel's organization had launched programs at nearly three dozen locations. I'd once encountered it at Princeton, where a young woman from the office in Chicago had come to speak at a gathering of some seventy students, from colleges around the nation, about getting involved in collaborative service work. Still, by Patel's own admission, the organization had only begun its work. There were twenty-six hundred colleges in the United States, he said. "Why shouldn't fifteen hundred of them have a day of interfaith youth service? Why shouldn't there be a network of those things?"

"Our ultimate goal," he said, "is launching an idea into the culture." Based on Patel's background, he might not have seemed a natural choice to run an organization so deeply concerned with religious identities. By his own account, he had not been particularly mindful of his religious identity until after college. These days, he would be what the news media would call "a moderate Muslim," a label bestowed on nonextremists—the vast majority of humanity, the people we needn't fear on religious grounds. But to call Patel a "moderate" seemed hardly to do justice to his energy and creative passion. He adamantly rejected the idea that the world had entered into a religiously based "clash of civilizations," a phrase made famous by the Harvard political scientist Samuel Huntington in a highly influential article he wrote in *Foreign Affairs* magazine in 1993. "What we have to understand," Patel said, during a subsequent interview we had, "is, religious identities have to be in various interactions with each other. Conflict is not inevitable. It's not about Muslims versus Christians, but people who want to build diverse societies where people thrive, versus people who want to build societies where people suffocate."

Patel, a tall, slim man, wears small gold earrings and has a stud in his tongue—an ornament I heard remarked upon by older people who had met him. He was born in India in 1975, but his family moved to the United States while he was still an infant, after his father had been accepted into the master's degree program in business administration at the University of Notre Dame. Patel recalled that religion formed a basic part of his family's life, but in a quiet way. "We said *bismillah* at dinner, but we didn't always make it to Friday prayers," he said. Similarly, in high school, he hung out with adolescents who also came from religious backgrounds—a spiritually eclectic crowd, they included a Jew, a Catholic, a Lutheran, a Mormon, among others. But no one talked much about faith or how it might be linked to one's life or actions (outside, perhaps, of why one kept certain dietary practices, like not eating pork). When he went on to college, at the University of Illinois at Champagne-Urbana, Patel encountered a similar silence regarding spiritual identity. Students talked often of diversity, but they meant race, ethnicity, social class, gender, sexual orientation. It seemed to him that something important was going unspoken among students—even as it became increasingly obvious as a subject shaping the world around them. "I would flip on the TV and it was religious wars raging all the time," Patel said. "What was happening in the Balkans at that time? What was happening in Northern Ireland?" Often enough, the stories about violence indicated that many of those involved—as aggressors and victims—were young people. If one wanted somehow to try to stop that, or at least to make some difference, then one had to talk about religion and what it might mean to individuals.

Movements can grow out of ideas, when the conditions are right—often during times of painful social and economic change. Marx's theories found a following amid European industrialization and worker ghettos. And Qutb's critique of secular Muslim regimes gained an audience during demographic change in the Middle East, as people quit tradition-bound villages to seek work in overburdened cities like Cairo. But there are equally powerful, influential examples of people who articulated ideas of peace and social service—Dorothy Day, during the Depression; the Reverend Dr. Martin Luther King, Jr., amid a movement of African Americans to claim their civil rights; and the fourteenth Dalai Lama, after the Chinese invasion of his homeland, Tibet. Patel admired all three. He had closely looked into Day's legacy while at the university. Day, a journalist and Roman Catholic convert, launched first a newspaper, *The Catholic Worker,* then a national network of shelters called Catholic Worker Houses, on the strength of a passionate conviction that Christian belief demanded advocacy for and attention to the poor. The Dalai Lama, an unshakable advocate of peace and reconciliation even while exiled, had captured Patel's imagination, too. In the late 1990s, Patel received an introduction to the Tibetan leader. He traveled to India with a friend; the two of them made the trek to Tibet's exile capital in the Indian city of Dharamsala. "You are a Muslim," the Dalai Lama told Patel, speaking to him for the first time, this when Patel was only just beginning to come to grips with his religious identity. "Islam is a very good religion," the Dalai Lama continued. "Buddhists and Muslims lived in peace in Tibet for many centuries." He told Patel that "religions must dialogue, but even more, they must come together to serve others."

In our conversation, Patel told me he didn't believe his path toward reclaiming his religious identity was so peculiar. "I actually think that my story, it's a lot of people's stories—minus the Dalai Lama part—a lot of people look at their religion with a lukewarm sense until they meet someone else of another faith who deeply inspires them and that causes them to look with more interest at their own tradition."

That basic idea the Dalai Lama articulated, about dialogue and service together, can be found in teachings of Gandhi, King, Pope John Paul II, and others who have waged campaigns for peace in recent decades. They have left deep imprints on millions of people. King drew Protestants, Catholics, Jews, Unitarians, Buddhists, agnostics, and atheists to the cause of civil rights. In 1965, a religiously mixed group marched together in Selma, Alabama, right into the truncheons of Alabama law enforcement authorities. Bloody Sunday, as the event came to be called, proved crucial to bringing about the political momentum to pass the federal Voting Rights Act. Within two years, King had taken on broader work, becoming an outspoken critic of American involvement in the Vietnam War. He had befriended Thich Nhat Hanh, who had worked to forge a peace movement in Vietnam. In 1967, King nominated Nhat Hanh for the Nobel Peace Prize. He also wrote an essay called "The World House" in which he identified the "great new problem of mankind," the divisions that separated people from recognizing that they lived together and had a responsibility to one another. "We have inherited a large house, a great 'world house,' " King wrote, "in which we have to live together—black and white, Easterner and Westerner, Gentile and Jew, Catholic and Protestant, Moslem and Hindu—a family unduly separated in ideas, culture and interest, who, because we can never again live apart, must learn somehow to live with each other in peace."

King's collaborative vision, expounded with a grace and power that makes so much of his writing memorable, stands in contrast to the narrow theorizing of Qutb, and especially the ways in which Qutb's ideas have been realized by his most radical disciples. And yet the essence of King's vision, the religious cooperation he expressed in 1967, predates him by nearly a century. Its introduction to the United States—on an earlier September 11, in 1893—came by way of India, where it emerged from within the meeting of two religious Hindus, one a teacher, the other a man who would become his disciple. On that earlier September 11, it was the younger of the two—the disciple—who rose to speak to an American audience. He came from an urbane, middle-class background, and in fluent, appealingly accented English, he addressed a largely Protestant audience at an unprecedented religious gathering in Chicago. Known by his monastic name, Swami Vivekananda, he denounced sectarian violence in terms that brought him a standing ovation and, soon enough, national fame.

His presence at the opening session of the World's Parliament of Religions was the result of a decision he had made years earlier after seeking out one of the modern era's greatest mystics, Ramakrishna. Vivekananda had been born Narendranath Datta in Calcutta in 1863. At eighteen, he went to see Ramakrishna, the priest at a temple on the Ganges River near Calcutta at a place called Dakshineswar. Ramakrishna was forty-five and had gained a reputation as an extraordinary sage whose visions had given him a deep understanding not only of various aspects of Hinduism, but also of Islam and Christianity as well. Have you seen God? Datta asked Ramakrishna upon meeting him. Yes, the mystic replied, the same as I see you here but with a greater intensity. Ramakrishna stands as one of the great theological universalists of the modern world, a man at the opposite end of the spectrum from religious fundamentalism. He had a deep impact on Vivekananda, who became his student during the five years remaining in Ramakrishna's life. "It is not good to say what we ourselves think of God is the only truth and what others think is false," Ramakrishna said, "that because we think God is formless, therefore He is formless and cannot have any form; that because we think of God as having form, therefore He has form and cannot be formless. Can a man really fathom God's nature?" Basic to Ramakrishna's teachings was his conviction that religions can exist in harmony because they all ultimately lead to God. It is in some ways ironic that this idea, which Vivekananda would take to the West, came to him from a priest who officially served the Hindu goddess Kali, whose portraits typically represent her as a ferocious figure whose image has repelled and (sometimes) fascinated westerners for generations. Kali is depicted as dark-skinned, her blood-red tongue protruding from between her lips, her hair wild. She holds a demon's head in one of her four hands, a bloody sword in another; her neck is hung with a garland of human heads and her waist with a skirt made of human arms. She stands with one foot atop the chest of her unconscious consort, the god Shiva. But her appearance symbolizes her positive power; Ramakrishna worshiped her as the Divine Mother. Few photographs of him exist, but those that do show him as a small man, bearded, barefoot, simply dressed in a white robe drawn about his waist. In one photograph, we see him with his right arm raised, his left bent at the elbow. The fingers of both hands are splayed. His eyes are closed and a deep smile crosses his face. It is a look of a man caught in a spiritual experience of beatific intensity. Four or five men sit at his feet; another stands behind him, lightly supporting him, with a hand under that elbow. His disciple and biographer, Mahendranath Gupta, would remember their first meeting in Ramakrishna's room in the temple. During the visit, the guru "seemed to become absent-minded," Gupta wrote. Later, he learned that Ramakrishna was known for slipping into and out of states of spiritual ecstasy. "It is like the way an angler acts when sitting with his rod: the fish comes and swallows the bait and the float begins to tremble; the angler is on the alert; he grips the rod and watches the float steadily and eagerly; he will not speak to anyone."

Seven years after Ramakrishna's death and after emerging as the mystic's most important disciple, Vivekananda would travel at the urging of his friends and students to the United States to try to gain entrance to that first-ever gathering of representatives of different faith traditions, the World's Parliament of Religions. The event had been organized as a feature of a great fair in Chicago that year, the World's Columbian Exposition. The parliament—a nonvoting event despite its political name—had been organized specifically to allow representatives of different faiths to meet and talk about what they believed, without overtly trying to convert one another.

These days there are about one thousand organizations in the United States that try to involve people across faith lines in their work, according to the Reverend Bud Heckman, a United Methodist minister who formerly headed one such group and did a sort of census of this movement in 2004. He found most had been around only since the mid–1990s and were small, local, or regional operations. A few were more ambitious. The Interfaith Alliance, for example, had been founded in 1994 with headquarters in Washington, D.C., and a stated purpose of bringing Americans together across faith lines to promote shared civic values. Its origins lay at least in part in a movement among different religious believers to provide a counterweight to Pat Robertson's Christian Coalition, which promoted an ideologically and theologically conserative approach to political activism. Another organization, the World Conference on Religions for Peace, had been working with the United Nations' agencies to bring religious believers into cooperative efforts against civil wars and on behalf of child welfare. The conference dates to 1970, the result of collaborative efforts by prominent Jews, Protestants, Catholics, and Unitarian-Universalists. In the 1990s, it sought to try to bring together religious leaders in the Balkans and West Africa to defuse armed conflicts. It also joined hands with several large charities like CARE to try to help African children orphaned by the HIV virus. There were other groups as well, including Bishop Swing's United Religions Initiative and Eboo Patel's Interfaith Youth Core.

But before 1893 there had been nothing like the event toward which Vivekananda traveled. It hardly seems an era in which human diversity, religious or otherwise, would be valued. Vivekananda's India was firmly under British rule. In the United States, Native Americans had been largely and forcibly confined to reservations. The nation itself, thirty years after the Emancipation Proclamation, was becoming a society of legalized racial segregation. But at the same time the American religious landscape was undergoing a tectonic shift, as a flood tide of immigration, largely from Europe, built up communities of ethnic and national groups. Since the Civil War, the nation's Roman Catholic population had tripled, to 9 million, 1 in 7 Americans. Jews, far fewer to begin with, were undergoing an even more rapid increase. From a population of 250,000 in 1885, they would grow exponentially to 3 million Americans by 1914.

Against this backdrop, a largely Protestant committee in Chicago decided to convene a forum for people of different faiths—in effect, a temporary school of comparative religions, in which representatives of various faith groups would be invited to talk about what made them distinctive. The event, the World's Parliament of Religions, took place on Chicago's South Side. The parliament was never intended to function as a law-making body. Instead, its organizing committee made it plain that the event was primarily about valuing religion, in a broad sense, as a singular human asset. The committee wanted to clear a space in which people "of all faiths may speak for themselves without hindrance, without criticism and without compromise, and tell what they believe and why they believe it."

The parliament should not be considered an oddity of its time. It is, in some ways, representative of an era revolutionary in technological and intellectual changes. By the 1890s, new modes of transportation and telecommunication were knitting people worldwide into an unprecedented contact with one another. By 1893, a network of transatlantic telegraphic cables linked North America and Europe; the telephone and electric light were more than a decade old and the first four-wheel automobile had been built. Colonialism, with its economic and political exploitation, made the world a smaller place too; European powers had extended their control over Africa and southern Asia. Although their global imperialism worked primarily for the economic benefit of people in the Northern Hemisphere, it had the unintended consequence of exposing the colonialists to the religions and cultures of the people whose lands they occupied. Gradually, in a process that continues, this meant a transmission of knowledge—about Buddhism, Hinduism, and Islam—to the West, laying the ground for the academic study of comparative religions in the United States and Europe.

By the time of the parliament, too, some Christian missionaries—having had close experience of the adherents of eastern religions—had begun to reevaluate their traditional stereotypes of non-Christian faiths as empty and unworthy of study for the ethics and values they contained. A very gradual (and halting) reassessment of Christianity's relationship to other faiths had begun. Finally, the parliament coincided with the beginning of a civil rights movement—vitally important for the successful anticolonialist movement of the next century—in South Africa. In that British colony, a young Indian lawyer named Mohandas Gandhi founded an organization to fight legislation designed to deny South Africa's Indian minority the right to vote.

The idea for the parliament came from a New York–born lawyer named Charles Bonney, a man with a broad forehead, a pair of widely set eyes, and a passion—not unusual among spiritual seekers of his era—for the writings of Emmanuel Swedenborg, a Swedish mining engineer who had lived a century earlier and recorded his vivid and distinctly unorthodox spiritual experiences in numerous books. Swedenborg described an otherwise invisible divine order surrounding the earth; he claimed to have visited heaven and hell. In 1889, Bonney became concerned that the leading Chicagoans bidding to host a world's fair in their city were too focused on showing off humanity's material accomplishments, at the expense of its intellectual, artistic, and spiritual achievements. "Something higher and nobler is demanded by the enlightened and progressive spirit of the present age," he wrote, optimistically but persuasively. The fair's planners took heed of his appeal. In matters of faith, Bonney was inclined to discern more common ground than differences among various believers whom he met. He spoke often in different churches on issues related to his specialty, the law, and in so doing formed friendships that left him convinced that his understanding of human spirituality had been enhanced. "Thus I came to know the distinguishing characteristics of various religious organizations," he wrote, "to respect their sincerity and zeal; to understand the reasons for their peculiar views; to learn that all creeds have meaning which only those who profess them can explain." He also came to "feel kindly," he said, not only toward various Christian churches, but to other faiths as well. That feeling was shared by other parliament organizers, to the extent that they decided to extend invitations to people from major religious traditions worldwide. Many who received them accepted, ensuring that there would be Buddhists, Hindus, and practitioners of Japanese Shinto, among others, at the parliament, where they would be provided with an unprecedented public platform from which to speak to Americans. But a number of prominent religious figures did not approve of the parliamentary idea at all. The Archbishop of Canterbury, spiritual leader of the Church of England, strongly objected that Christianity could not be presented alongside other religions, as it alone contained truth. The Sultan of the Ottoman Empire, who also held status as Islam's caliph, flatly refused to send anyone to speak for Muslims, a decision that undercut the possibility of an early recognition of Islam among Americans. When the parliament convened, it had but a single Muslim as a speaker—a recent convert, American born.

Vivekananda arrived in the United States uninvited to the parliament and unknown to its organizers. The event was still months off, but its speakers' roster had already been closed. It was only through a series of remarkably fortuitous encounters with people who knew the parliament's organizers that Vivekananda received an invitation to speak Visually, he cut a unique figure. On the opening day he dazzled the audience as he advanced to the podium clad in an orange robe over his trousers, a saffron turban fixed above his handsome, smiling face. He started by acknowledging his "brothers and sisters of America" and received a two-minute standing ovation. His speech was short. He denounced religious intolerance and violence. His audience, thousands of people packed into the meeting hall, gave him an ovation. "Sectarianism, bigotry and its horrible descendant, fanaticism, have long possessed this beautiful earth," Vivekananda declared that day. "They have filled the earth with violence, drenched it often . . . with human blood, destroyed civilization and sent whole nations to despair. Had it not been for these horrible demons, human society would be far more advanced than it is now. But their time is come; and I fervently hope that the bell that tolled this morning in honor of this convention may be the death-knell of all fanaticism. . . ."

These days, a statue of Vivekananda—larger than life-sized—stands on an artificial hill in Chicago's suburbs, within the grounds of a major Hindu temple. But his real legacy is the vision he articulated, which saved the parliament from being lost to history, a curious footnote from Victorian America. Instead, it became the founding text of the idea of conversation and cooperation among adherents of different faiths. When I asked Eboo Patel if it held any significance for him, he almost seemed startled. "It's a huge reference point for me," he said. "Part of it is that it happened in Chicago." Another source of inspiration was that the event's heroic figure was a thirty-year-old Indian.

Even if the the 1890s seem terribly distant from the vantage point of the early twenty-first century, calling to mind black-and-white images of men in handlebar mustaches and women in hoop-skirts, the parliament's era has parallels to our own. Richard Hughes Seager, a professor at Hamilton College who has closely studied the parliament, says it ought to be viewed more generously, as occurring within a world's fair that emphasized American inventiveness and material progress. Symbolically, the fair heralded the arrival of the United States as a world power. Electric lights illuminated the six-hundred-acre grounds; telephones connected the event to the world. Speakers at various public "congresses" (the parliament among them) took up a vast array of subjects, including whether English had become an international language, the requisite tongue of anyone who wanted to do business in the world. The fair unveiled the world's first Ferris wheel, more than three hundred feet high. It impressed Vivekananda, who discerned a theological message in its rotations. "Nature is like the chain of the Ferris Wheel, endless and infinite," he said, "and these little carriages are the bodies or forms in which fresh batches of souls are riding, going up higher and higher until they become perfect and come out of the wheel. But the wheel goes on." The fair, Seager said, marked "the take-off point of what we call globalization."

But the fair's era also coincided with the beginning of a great rift among the nation's dominant Protestants. The challenge of new, scientific knowledge, especially Darwinian evolution, and increasing interest among scholars of Christianity in a critical, historical approach to the Bible began to drive Protestants apart. Mutually antagonistic camps arose, one leaning toward accommodating the new ways of thinking, the other rejecting them. Tensions were keenly felt among Presbyterians, who comprised one of the country's most significant religious groups, socially and politically. Grover Cleveland, president at the time of the Chicago fair, was a Presbyterian, as had been his immediate predecessor, Benjamin Harrison. In the same year the parliament took place, Presbyterians in New York City suspended a well-known scholar, Charles A. Briggs, from preaching, in part for declaring that Moses had not written the first five books of the Bible, as Jews and Christians traditionally believed. To combat thinking that struck conservatives as heretical, a new movement would shortly arise that emphasized the idea that Christianity contained fundamental, unquestionable truths. The movement began among Presbyterians with the publication of a series of pamphlets called *The Fundamentals*, a title that would eventually lend the movement a name, fundamentalism.

But it was also a Presbyterian whose leadership of the parliament and enthusiastic endorsement of allowing non-Christians to speak there helped make the event as memorable as it would become. The Reverend John Henry Barrows, a prominent Chicago minister, served as chairman of the committee that organized the parliament. He was no fundamentalist, but he cannot be categorized as a theological liberal either. These days, he would be described as a man of orthodox Christian views, albeit with an adventurous streak. On the parliament's opening day, September 11, he delivered a speech posing a central, rhetorical question for Christians like himself in a religiously diverse world: "Why should not Christians be glad to learn what God has wrought through Buddha and Zoroaster— through the sage of China, and the prophets of India and the prophet of Islam?" From the way in which he framed the question, we can assume we know what Barrows thought—that God is active in other people's religious lives, such that they cannot be dismissed as simply spiritually misguided. It's an idea that lays the basis for dialogue, even while it stops well short of a far more radical claim—that people may achieve salvation outside Christianity. If Barrows avoided going in that direction, it was because of his bedrock commitment to Protestant Christianity. At the parliament, he said repeatedly he believed faith in Jesus to be intended for all humanity. He promised the last words he would speak from the platform would be Jesus' name. He kept his word. What makes him interesting is he showed himself capable of holding two ideas at once: a certainty about his own faith, along with a willingness to listen respectfully to others.

And that mattered, because it provided an opening for individuals whose religions had been subject to stridently negative stereotypes to speak for themselves. Foremost among these was Vivekananda. If Americans and Britons could claim to know anything about Hinduism, then what they knew largely derived from the reports of Christian missionaries and those reports could be terrifying. Hindus were typically portrayed as idol worshipers, practitioners of a faith that degraded women and allowed chaos to envelop major festivals. One missionary, upon visiting a temple, reported shivering with the conviction that he had come close to hell itself; he described a statue of the temple's resident deity as "a little ugly black image." Vivekananda, good-looking and gracious, could not have presented a starker contrast. He refuted the attacks with his personal dignity as well as what he said. The effect could be measured in the public's response to him. "He is undoubtedly the greatest figure in the Parliament of Religions," a New York newspaper declared. "After hearing him we feel how foolish it is to send missionaries to this learned nation." Vivekananda offered a living counterpoint to an ugly stereotype. For a time, he became a national celebrity, embarking on a lengthy lecture tour in the United States.

The parliament shut its doors without a plan for a successor. Barrows went on to publish two immense volumes recording the speeches made. But outside of a few individuals, its message became marginal. The twentieth century was a time of ideology, of uprisings against colonialism, of fascination with technology, of nationalism, of belief in race and blood, of global warfare. Not that there weren't efforts by individuals to create permanent networks of different faith groups dedicated to the cause of peace, among them the World Congress of Faiths and the Religious League of Mankind, the latter an idea of German philosopher of religion Rudolph Otto. It is not a well-known landscape, although it has been carefully chronicled by an Anglican priest, the Reverend Marcus Braybrooke, a veteran observer and participant in interreligious organizing. At the least, the postparliament period was enlivened by one especially colorful individual, British explorer Sir Francis Younghusband. A near-contemporary of Vivekananda, swashbuckling and introspective at once, Younghusband specialized in journeying through Asia's remotest reaches, the Gobi Desert and the Himalayas. In 1904, the British government ordered him to lead an armed invasion of Tibet, to counter alleged reports of Russian influence. Younghusband crushed Tibetan militia who tried to resist, and briefly drove the thirteenth Dalai Lama into exile. But while in Lhasa, Tibet's capital city, he had an overpowering religious vision, which he would later describe as being "in touch with the flaming heart of the world." He spent years promoting the idea that an essential unity underlay all faiths.

But it was really Vivekananda who kept the idea of multireligious meetings alive. He outlived the parliament by less than a decade, dying at age thirty-nine on July 4, 1902, not long after completing a second tour through America. But beforehand, he had created an organization that would directly contribute—much later—to reviving the idea of the parliament. Intent on spreading Ramakrishna's teachings to the West, Vivekananda founded a small religious order in 1895 that would operate outside India. Called the Vedanta Society, it holds that God is a single entity, even if the divine is worshiped differently within various faiths. Life's goal, the society teaches, is for men and women to understand their divine nature. It remains a small movement. In the late 1980s, some of its members raised the idea of commemorating the parliament on its centennial. Initially, talk centered on arranging a scholarly meeting, with academic papers. But as word spread and local religious groups became involved, the plans evolved to create an event for a much broader constituency, a public forum for adherents of different faiths, a bit like the original parliament itself. Organizers eventually raised nearly two million dollars and hired staff, including the Reverend Dirk Ficca, a Presbyterian minister who became executive director of the event's planning council. Like its predecessor, the new parliament was held in Chicago. But it was a far more decentralized proceeding. In place of a series of lectures from a single platform, the 1993 parliament featured numerous workshops, panel discussions, and demonstrations of religious rituals alongside its plenary gatherings. Eight thousand people showed up, including the Dalai Lama, who may come as close as anyone today to holding a status—sage and celebrity—similar to that accorded Vivekananda. After the 1993 parliament, the Tibetan leader would write about his vision of interreligious cooperation: "If we are each to contribute to religious harmony and a more peaceful world, followers of different religions must be true to what they believe. When you discover the deeper value of your own tradition through actual practice, you will come to recognize the value of other traditions as well."

Dirk Ficca, in an interview I had with him years afterward, added his perspective: "The point of interreligious dialogue is not commonality, it's not consensus, it's not compromise. It's understanding. And we can understand each other and have profound differences." He went on to offer a rather homey analogy: "Often, I say to people, 'What relationship do you have with anybody where you agree on everything, or even substantially agree?' If that were the basis of relationships, many of us would have no relationships at all." Since 1993, an organizing committee has held two more parliamentary events in two different locations—Cape Town, South Africa, in 1999 (with Nelson Mandela as its main guest) and Barcelona, Spain, in 2004. The parliament could claim to be a flagship for a global interreligious dialogue. I attended the 1993 meeting in Chicago as a journalist and remember being impressed with the sheer variety of people there—a response that echoed the impressions held by Americans a century earlier who had encountered Vivekananda and others from outside Christianity and Judaism. I missed the event in South Africa, but did travel to Barcelona, where the gathering took place in a neighborhood directly on the Mediterranean seacoast. An auditorium, a hotel, and a multitiered meeting hall held down the corners of an undulating plaza, beyond which lay the Mediterranean's luminous blue waters. The week-long schedule was extremely eclectic, with a few central events, including a concert at Antoni Gaudí's Sagrada Familia Cathedral. But the program, printed in a volume with the heft of a phone-book, defied easy description. What did the Vatican say about interreligious dialogue? A panel would tackle that one. What might African indigenous religions contribute to peace? A workshop would address that one too. What did different traditions say about the environment? A session dealt with that. What did Zoroastrian worship look like? Well, there would be a service that morning, observers welcome.

Yet nothing could obscure the fact that the parliament—quite coincidentally—took place in the shadow of recent, intense religious violence. Only four months earlier, on March 11, terrorists linked to al-Qaeda detonated ten bombs at commuter rail stations in Madrid at the morning rush hour's peak. Nearly two hundred people died and eighteen hundred were injured. The next day, an estimated eleven million Spaniards—more than a quarter of the nation's population—took to the streets to demonstrate their peaceful outrage. In such circumstances, it may be impossible to match the rhetoric of peace against the fact of sheer terror. But some tried. "Under no circumstances, theological or nationalistic, is this massacre justified," said one Catholic bishop, presiding at burial services. Shortly before preaching at a state funeral attended by King Juan Carlos I, the church's highest authority in that nation, Madrid archbishop Cardinal Antonio Maria Rouco Varela declared that "to kill your own kind, to kill a brother, is to attack God himself."

Given the proximity of this mass murder to the parliament, it seemed fortuitous that the gathering had provided a platform for other Muslims to speak at length and to take questions, in a clear effort to distinguish their faith from that of the terrorists. "What is Islam?" the title of a panel discussion that included a pair of American women and a British imam, promised to explain essentials by which religious Muslims live. The principles are easily grasped. Islam has Five Pillars, starting with the *shahada*, the declaration that there is only one God and that Muhammad, a seventh-century Arabian trader, was his final prophet. Muslims are also to pray five times a day, give an annual percentage of their worth to charity, observe a dawn-to-dusk fast during the lunar month of Ramadan, and if they are physically and financially able, make a pilgrimage to Mecca, the Saudi Arabian city where the faith's holiest sites stand. More than one hundred people squeezed into a too-small room for the presentation. The panelists seemed to make the closest connection with their audience when they spoke about themselves in relation to their faith, as did one woman who described Islam as affording her "a personal relationship" with God, unmediated by any clergy. I went up to speak with her afterward, but before I could, a young man stepped between us and thanked her, saying her remarks gave him an idea about how to respond to coworkers who disliked Muslims and were unafraid to say so. He had felt uncomfortable listening to them, the man said, but he had never heard from a Muslim and so lacked a means to challenge them—until now.

Later, a lively Muslim woman who wore her dark hair in a long braid down her back told me sessions like that one made a mass meeting like the parliament useful. "People are at different levels of being informed," said Rabia Ali, a Pakistani woman I met there, in interviews I had with her. She had just graduated from Princeton and come to Barcelona with a group of fellow students. "It's absolutely essential that we have these '101' sessions." The students with whom she traveled belonged to a multifaith group affiliated with Princeton's chapel. She had an interesting personal story to tell. Before Princeton, she had grown up in Lahore, Pakistan, as a Muslim not familiar with anyone outside the faith. As a child and adolescent, she heard many news reports directed against Hindus, the dominant group in neighboring India. The two nations had gone to war against each other several times since they had become independent in 1947. And the news bulletins she had often heard while growing up suggested that open conflict might break out again at any time, with fighting over the Himalayan province of Kashmir. She recalled the tenor of the reports, with the religious element woven into the political. "You see yourself in opposition to this religious philosophy which you don't understand."

In her senior year, Ali had applied to join the interfaith group that operated from the university's chapel. She became a member and went on a trip with the group to Washington, D.C., where they met with people from different religious traditions and visited their houses of worship. What was most useful, she said, was the opportunity simply to talk with her fellow students, who included Protestants, Roman Catholics, Jews, Buddhists, Unitarian-Universalists, neo-pagans, and, yes, Hindus. "It was a mind-blowing experience," she said. Each night, the students stayed up late, talking about the differences between them. "We were functioning on maybe three or four hours of sleep a night. We were having the most amazing conversations. This was the first time I felt I could talk about the things that mattered without being judged." Within the group, she had befriended a Hindu student from Bombay, India, named Ritu Kamal. At Princeton, the two marched side by side in a student parade, Ali carrying a flag of Pakistan, Kamal a flag of India. The young women told me their friendship worked in part because each took her faith seriously. They had that in common.

Ali's experience points toward a larger trend. While the news media have paid a great deal of attention to the worrisome work of South Asian Islamic *madrassas,* schools that incubate a militant religion in their young charges, little notice is paid to an opposite trend. Universities like Princeton possess an international influence; the students they draw become social, cultural, and political leaders. In such places, living arrangements and many activities are designed specifically to foster interaction among students of different backgrounds. As one hopeful chaplain told me, "I think universities are the perfect place for this to happen. I do think it's an antidote to fundamentalism."

That's a high bar to clear. But it is increasingly possible to find on college campuses creative responses to a growing religious diversity among students—the field that Eboo Patel wanted to tap for his vision of cooperative work. "I deeply, deeply believe that young people are the best architects of pluralism," he told me. Any space created for a peaceful meeting of people of different faiths he called one of pluralism's cathedrals. "The cathedrals of pluralism are spaces where people of different backgrounds are coming together in mutual trust and loyalty," he said. They needed to be created in such numbers "that there aren't enough terrorist bombs in the world to destroy them."

If one wants to think about what such a place—in concrete form—might look like, there is one in Baltimore. In 1999, a new building opened across the street from Johns Hopkins University to bring students together across religious lines. By then, the number of student religious organizations officially recognized by the university had grown to twenty, nearly twice what it had been a decade earlier. I visited the Bunting-Meyerhoff Interfaith and Community Service Center one rainy spring morning. The chaplain, Sharon M. K. Kugler, a Roman Catholic laywoman, showed me around. The building had once been a United Methodist church, but had since been renovated to serve as home to a truly varied constituency—Buddhists, Hindus, Jews, and Muslims as well as Catholics and Protestants. The renovation had been sensitively done, so the building did not appear as an anodyne space, reflecting an imagined "melting pot" of faiths where differences are supposed to be blurred. Instead, the center's designers had left the old church sanctuary largely intact, with the stained glass windows depicting stories from the Christian Bible remaining in place. Frosted glass shutters had been installed beside each of them, which could be swung into position to cover the images, if a non-Christian group were using the space for worship. In a smaller room just off the sanctuary, Buddhist students had arranged cushions on the floor for seated meditation. In a room off the former church basement, Hindu students had set up statues of their deities. A large meeting room dominated the space downstairs, where representatives of all the different groups met for the center's student interfaith council. At one point, Kugler held up a T-shirt designed by members of the council. It identified the group as having been started in 1991. It also carried a slogan: "Listening to each other ever since."

Listening is a discipline, one that takes patience as well, of course, as a desire to do it in the first place. You can't force it. But anyone who does listen to another carefully is acknowledging that words matter, that they are central to knowledge, and that the people participating may be changed as a result. Ultimately, words may be the chief resource that peacemakers have to muster against religious extremism and violence. To say so may suggest how slight a reed it is we cling to in the face of all manner of bombs—unless, that is, one thinks about the durability of language and the capacity of well-articulated thought to inspire people to acts of humanity. To doubt the power of words is to doubt a great deal, including the enduring examples set by all those extraordinary figures—Dorothy Day, King, Gandhi, Malcolm X—whom Patel told me had influenced him. They were all long dead by the time he got around to studying their work. When I raised the subject of the 1893 parliament, he responded with a quote—another example of how words can live on and inspire. These words came from one of the Protestants involved—either Barrows or Bonney, he wasn't sure which: "From this point forth, let the great religions of the world make war not on each other but on the giant ills of our time." Patel himself made a similar declaration—not perhaps as elegant, but eloquent nonetheless—when he hired his first staff member for the Interfaith Youth Core. As he told it she was a recent college graduate, an evangelical Protestant from Minnesota, who had been pushed out as president of her college Christian group after members rejected her suggestion that they volunteer to help a local Muslim congregation rebuild its mosque, which had been torched by an arsonist. In recounting the story in a memoir he wrote, Patel said the young woman worried she had not appeared "Christian enough" for her college group, but might be "too Christian" for Patel's organization because she believed Christianity to be uniquely true and Jesus to be Lord. "I sure hope you think it's true, because otherwise there would be no reason to stay committed to it," Patel told her, referring to her faith. "I think my religion is true, too. So let's make a deal. We can both believe our religions are true, we can even privately hope the other converts, and we can work together in this organization to serve others." Barrows and Vivekananda might have had a similar conversation.

Patel and I could have left things there, closing on hopeful notes, rather as the first parliament had for many of its participants. But Patel offered a stark counterpoint to his earlier quotation about the religions of the world cooperating—and by implication challeng- ing Vivekananda's hopefulness that religious violence would even- tually meet its match. "The idea of religious extremism is enormously powerful in the world," he said. "And the reason for that is that reli- gious extremists have built enormously powerful institutions." He mentioned Hezbollah, the Shi'ite Islamic political and military force whose name—"God's Army"—seems appropriate to an era so marked by fierce religious certainties. "My organization closed its books with $750,000," he said. "What do you think Hezbollah closed its books with?" And there was not just the financial dimen- sion, but also the question of what about the people who didn't fall anywhere near the extremist camps, but still opted not to get in- volved in opposing them.

Good people, well-intentioned people often do nothing in the face of religious harassment or worse. One of his friends in high school had been Hindu, Patel said. "And I remember other kids in high school going to throw rocks against the small Hindu *mandir* around the corner," he said, referring to a temple with a statue or print of a god or goddess. "I never participated in it, but I never did anything about it. That stuff happens all the time," he said. "Plural- ism can go up in the flames of a suicide bombing. But it also dies in the face of a thousand silent betrayals."

FOUR

Hospitality

On a summer weekday evening, I got caught in rush-hour traffic heading east on the Northern Parkway through Queens, New York. I had naïvely believed that in driving toward the city late in the day, I would be going against the traffic's flow, westbound from Manhattan. I hit the brakes, stopping opposite the oldest standing house of worship in New York City, the Flushing Quaker Meeting House. It's a wooden building, with hand-hewn beams, dark shingles, and nine rather unevenly spaced windows facing the street. Local farmers put it up in 1694, but the building has a richer history than its age alone would suggest. Once built, it followed a period of intense religious persecution in which Quakers—a new sect in the New World—suffered the indignities of corporal punishment, imprisonment, and exile from New York. Later, after that period passed, William Penn visited the meeting house. So too did George Washington. At some point early in the twentieth century, a very young Thomas Merton once attended with his father, during the time that his mother lay hospitalized with a terminal illness. While healthy, she had sought spiritual refuge within its ancient walls during the short period the Merton family lived in the neighborhood. In his autobiography, *The Seven Story Mountain,* Merton recalls his father telling him "that the people came and sat there, silent, doing nothing, saying nothing, until the Holy Spirit moved someone to speak."

As early immigrants to America, Quakers were terribly unpopular in many places. The Dutch, who controlled Manhattan and adjacent territory, whipped them and sent them packing; in Massachusetts, the Puritans were determined to keep out the Quakers, whom they viewed as heretics. They punished some by branding them, others by cropping their ears, and, finally, the Puritan establishment's patience at an end, they hanged four on Boston Common—the ones who simply refused to be scared off by threats, jailing, or exile. For decades, that monstrous moment of judgment has found its silent rebuke in the form of a statue of one of the four, Mary Dyer, which sits on the grounds of the Boston State House, facing toward the common. In Flushing, the meetinghouse can be seen as a symbol of triumph over persecution—and also as an embodiment of the principle of religious hospitality. The latter idea seemed especially meaningful that afternoon, as I had come from a synagogue whose rabbi and lay leaders had devoted themselves to a yearslong project of hosting and in turn being hosted by members of a Long Island mosque. The previous October, the synagogue had celebrated Sukkot—the seven-day Jewish harvest festival—by building a thatched shelter hung with fruits and vegetables outside the mosque itself, whose members were then beginning their dawn-to-dusk fast during the lunar month of Ramadan.

Hospitality is a virtue, an ancient one, to be sure, but still exceptionally meaningful to those so welcomed. Injunctions to hospitality run deep in the Hebrew Bible. In the Christian tradition, the one with which I am most familiar, they are laid out explicitly in Matthew's Gospel, in chapter 25, in which Jesus tells his followers what he requires of them. "Then shall the righteous answer him," declare verses 37 through 40, "saying, Lord, when saw we thee an hungered, and fed thee? or thirsty, and gave thee drink? When saw we thee a stranger, and took thee in? or naked, and clothed thee? Or when saw we thee sick, or in prison, and came unto thee?' And the King shall answer and say unto them, Verily I say unto you,

Inasmuch as ye have done it unto one of the least of these my brethren, ye have done it unto me."

Those who are shown hospitality across religious lines may be no less different for it in their religious beliefs and practices, but they will cease to be strangers. Instead, they become people among us. And in such instances is society—contemporary society, diverse society—constructed, which is the subject of this chapter.

Tony Blair, on his last visit to Washington as British prime minister, in May 2007, articulated a first step in this direction during a radio interview. Two years earlier, he had joined the growing fraternity of heads of government whose nations had been ravaged by terrorism, a list that included not only the United States and Spain, but also Indonesia, India, Jordan, Morocco, Pakistan, and others. In the interview, Blair's remarks followed a trajectory that moved from commentary on mass violence to something quite different, and more universal—what a single concerned person might do to promote peace among people of different faiths. Unsurprisingly, his conversation with the reporter began with his continuing, outspoken support for the war in Iraq, a conflict by then even more unpopular in Britain than in the United States. From that point, he turned to the violence that sprang from young Muslims' indiscriminate rage. In London, on July 7, 2005, four suicide bombers—all British nationals, three native to England—had blown themselves up on commuter trains and a bus during morning rush hour. In addition to themselves, they killed fifty-two people, a group vastly varied by age, ethnicity, and religion. Among the dead was Atique Sharifi, a twenty-four-year-old Afghan refugee, whose parents had died in his country's long internal war. He had supported himself by delivering pizzas and had managed to send money back to a younger sister still in Afghanistan. His English teacher remembered him as a "high achiever" who was able to put others at ease. He died on the same commuter train as Helen Jones, a twenty-eight-year-old Scottish accountant who had taken a first-class honors degree in divinity at her university. A minister would recall how she helped him once prepare himself emotionally to conduct a child's funeral, telling him, "In tragedy, it is never God's will." A younger person, Shahara Islam, died in the explosion that tore the roof off a bus in Tavistock Square. At twenty, she had been a bank cashier who dressed neatly and stylishly. Her family remembered her as "a Londoner and British, but above all a true Muslim and proud to be so."

Blair, twenty-two months later, took a long view of the religious violence: "This terrorism has been a generation growing. It'll take a generation to knock it out." Yes, he knew people believed the American and British intervention in Iraq had ultimately fueled radical Islamist hatred of the West. But he wouldn't leave it at that. "The criticism that I think is more telling is that the only way you are going to knock out this terrorism eventually is not just through the force of arms, but through the force of ideas." To American ears—used to hearing government officials speak mainly of security measures and military means as our defense—Blair was offering something more, and not just about the need to promote western ideas of "freedom," but global efforts on behalf of social justice and economic opportunity. Action needed to be taken against African poverty, on climate change, and in the Middle East. Not only that, he said, but the Islamist critique of western society had to be confronted intellectually. "I think this question to do with religious faith and how the faiths come together and understand each other better is an important part of this," Blair said. "I mean, one of the things that's very difficult sometimes in the twentieth century was a century dominated by political ideology. . . . And then at the end of the twentieth century, really, those fundamental divides of political ideology have largely disappeared. You know no one, apart from a very few people, argue for the old communist position—I mean it's all a form of market economy. And what's strange is that suddenly in the early twenty-first century it's almost as if a religious

ideology has become more prominent. And I think what is important is that we try to get a better understanding and better dialogue
between people of different faiths, because of it's—you know, a lot
of it's just based on misunderstanding. And I think this is why it's
interesting for Christians to read the Qur'an, to get an understanding of the fact that, for example, Muslims revere Jesus as a prophet.
And it's important for Muslims to understand that Christianity is
not about, you know, the Crusades of the centuries ago."

As prime minister, Blair had been publicly known as a religious
man, a churchgoing Anglican married to a Roman Catholic. How
he would promote his conviction that there ought to be better
communication between members of different faiths he left an
open question. He acknowledged the possibility of setting up a
foundation, as former president Bill Clinton had done for other
causes. But one really did not need the stature of a former head of
government to do such a thing, nor did one need the fund-raising
ability of an Eboo Patel, who had put together $750,000 in one
year for his Interfaith Youth Core. The possibilities of which Blair
spoke can be found at the local level, both in the United States and
Britain. And they have become more numerous since 9/11. But
what is it that ordinary people are doing—and have been doing?

Back in 2000, the Hartford Institute for Religion Research, a
scholarly organization that specializes in analyzing Americans' spiritual practices, undertook a sweeping study of the life of 14,000
congregations of all denominations nationwide. Among its findings, the report, "Faith Communities Today," stated that within the
preceding year, 7 percent of American congregations had gotten
together with another group of religious believers, across faith lines,
and held a joint worship service; during the same period, a slightly
higher number, 8 percent, said they had collaborated in a community service project with another such congregation. Proportion-
ately, the figures may seem small—at least until one considers there

are an estimated 335,000 churches in the United States, in which case the institute's findings pointed to between 20,000 and 25,000 involved in interreligious activities. But the original survey provided a baseline for a second, more intriguing one five years later. This time around, the institute reported that the number of houses of worship participating in interreligious worship had tripled to more than 22 percent, while the number that joined in community service had risen more than fourfold to 38 percent. (The increase was not evenly spread across the religious map; far more mainline Protestants and Roman Catholics reported participating in these events than did evangelical Protestants, while the greatest participation of all came from among non-Christian congregations, nearly two thirds of whom said they had joined with Christians in social service projects.)

A cultural shift had taken place. David Roozen, who directs the institute (based within Hartford Seminary in Connecticut), said he believed at least two factors were at work. On one hand, old ecumenical networks—local organizations that brought Protestants and Catholics (and sometimes Jews) together—were reaching out to include Muslims. But even more so, he said, a mutual curiosity was bearing fruit: In a time of war, people had become more curious about one another, more determined to reach out. "A high percentage of the United States is college educated," Roozen said, adding that among those there were a good many people who were asking questions about what other people believed, and were finding that those others were often—not always, but often—willing to respond and might be able to meet their Christian or Jewish neighbors at a socially equally level. "New immigrants of almost any of the faith traditions tend to be at least somewhat educated, if not very educated, partly as a result of the way immigration laws are written these days," he said. "And so they really are part of the mainstream of American economic life, which is where most of us spend most of our time. They are not marginal, not—to use an old term—'ghettoized,' as the old immigrants were. There's a wanting to be accepted." Given estimates like those made by Hartford, it's tempting to call these interreligious activities a movement—and some people do. But what happens tends to occur at the local level, which makes it no less important, but does leave people in one town unaware of what may be going on only a few miles down the road.

For example, I had spent some time talking to a nascent interreligious group that began forming in Queens in 2001 and 2002. It is possible I simply missed the discussion, but I never heard anyone mention the unusual work going on a few miles east in Great Neck and Westbury, across the borough line in Nassau County. Their story began a decade earlier, in 1991, when Rabbi Jerome K. Davidson, spiritual leader of Temple Beth-El, asked one of his lay leaders to see if there might be a mosque not too far from the Great Neck synagogue. Founded in 1928, Beth-El held a unique status in its community, a commuter town on Long Island Sound, as the oldest local synagogue. Spiritual home to twelve hundred families, it was affiliated with Judaism's Reform movement, the faith's largest liberal branch. Among his fellow rabbis locally and nationally, Davidson was well known, enough so that by 1994, he would be named "rabbi of the year" by the New York Board of Rabbis, the first time the honor had ever been bestowed on someone within the Reform movement. For some years, Davidson had been in charge of inviting prominent non-Jews to speak to the biannual national meetings of the Reform rabbis, bringing in Protestant ministers, a Catholic bishop, even American Muslims who served as officers of national mosque organizations. But it nagged at him that such events occurred so rarely and only among the movement's clergy. "Nothing really had been done at the local level," he said. "And I felt it was important to try that."

At the time, Davidson knew the United States had a growing Muslim population, but he didn't know how many people that meant or where they might actually live. He did feel that Americans lacked much sympathy for Muslims, even at a time when news reports told of a large Muslim population in Europe—in newly independent Bosnia-Herzegovina—that had come under brutal siege from its Serbian Christian neighbors. In 1991, the Persian Gulf War had only recently ended and many Americans, if they thought about Islam at all, associated the faith with Saddam Hussein, a Muslim in name if not in practice whose secular dictatorship survived his army's defeat and retained a tenacious hold on power in Iraq. It might take a while for another image of Muslims—as victims of a massive crime—to begin to sink in. But in the summer of 1992, Long Island's main newspaper, *Newsday,* published reports describing how Bosnian Serbs had established a concentration camp—the first in Europe since World War II—to intern thousands of the Muslims with whom they had once coexisted. The stories came with photographs, showing emaciated, shirtless men standing behind barbed wire. A journalist working for *The Guardian,* a British newspaper, visited Omarska, as the camp was called, and reported it as "a monstrosity: an inferno of murder, torture and rape." By then, however, Davidson's quest had paid off. For weeks, the synagogue had come up against dead ends; the mosques they contacted in western Long Island either didn't seem interested or lacked anyone willing to take on such a project. Some of those who answered the phone said they had no idea where other Muslims lived and worshiped. But Davidson said, "Somehow, we got wind of a mosque maybe ten miles away in the town of Westbury. We called them and they responded very quickly that they were interested."

The mosque was the Islamic Center of Long Island, a rectangular building with a high archway over its front door, the structure set back behind a neatly tended lawn and flower garden in a largely residential neighborhood. Its clientele comprised an ethnic mixture fairly representative of the diverse American Muslim population, with immigrants from India, Pakistan, Afghanistan, Iran, Egypt, and

Eritrea, as well as converts born in the United States. Back in the 1970s, its earliest members had met in members' homes and rented spaces in local churches. But their numbers growing, they had broken ground for a mosque of their own in the 1980s, replacing the flat roof with a green dome. By the time Beth-El got in touch, one of the mosque's principal figures was Dr. Faroque A. Khan, a cardiologist who taught medicine at the State University of New York at Stony Brook. "It started in January 1992—their initiative," Khan said. "The rabbi made some inquiries: 'Are there any Muslims living on Long Island?' They somehow connected with us."

Davidson recalled that at first people on both sides seemed a bit tentative about embarking on the project. "But we picked a good bunch from the temple and they picked a good bunch from the mosque," he said. All together, about two dozen participated, a small enough group to gather in someone's living room, on couches and chairs around a coffee table. They made it a point of steering clear of obviously controversial topics—after all, they didn't know each other, so where would it get them to jump into a debate over who had historic rights to Jerusalem? "We sat together," Khan said, describing the two groups' initial meeting (perhaps an achievement in its own right), "and planned what we are going to do, and said, 'Look, we're not going to solve the Middle East problem—you have your views, we have our views.'" Instead, they talked about issues they were sure to share: family rituals, the milestones in a person's life. What do you do in your religion to celebrate a baby's birth? What are the procedures you follow at a wedding? What happens with a funeral and mourning? The questions naturally led to a discussion of their respective scriptures, the Torah and the Qur'an, which in turn raised theological issues. What does yours have to say about God? What is expected of humans in relation to God? As time went on, people got to know one another; the group grew and topics became a bit more daring—discussion of women's roles in mosque and synagogue, and what religious minorities need to know about protecting their civil liberties in the United States. One of the most-talked-about sessions occurred when Beth-El members went over to the mosque to speak specifically about the American Jewish social and economic success story. Davidson recruited some of his older members, people who had grown up on Manhattan's Lower East Side, had worked all hours, and had pushed hard for their children to take advantage of enough educational opportunities so they would become professionals, firmly ensconced in the upper middle class. The Muslims found the presentation riveting.

"Then we got into the sophisticated stuff," Davidson said. They began a series of conversations about conflicting claims to the city of Jerusalem; they argued about the grounds for the Palestinians' second intifada, or uprising, which began in 2000; and after 9/11, they talked about why a group of Muslims had directly attacked the United States. At times, the conversations grew heated. At one event, Davidson said, an Israeli Arab, with a reputation as a moderate, spoke about how he and other Israeli Arabs felt discriminated against in Israel. "Some of our people got very angry," he said, and argued that the allegations could not possibly be true, as Israel is a democracy and all are equal. A similar response followed a mosque member's criticism of American foreign policy as too weighted toward Israel in the Middle East. But Davidson took it in stride. "Some people got uptight about that, but that's just part of the dialogue." And even so, he said, most of those who took part in that discussion managed to stick around for coffee and dessert afterward. "I teach a course in the Hebrew Union College on social action and issues of community responsibility for people who are studying to be rabbis. Every year, I have Faroque Khan come." Khan talks about Islam's basics and how Muslim-Jewish dialogue might work. "One thing that strikes me is how adventuresome in some people's minds this has seemed, like, 'Who would have dreamed of such a thing?'" One year, too, he invited a prominent woman scholar to come to the college and speak about the meaning of the Qur'an to

Muslims like herself. She talked about how the book needed to be read and understood in the context of Islamic tradition and scholarly interpretation. It struck Davidson as similar to the approach Jews—at least non-Orthodox Jews—took to reading the Hebrew Bible. "It was the first time anyone, including me, had heard this very moderate, scholarly approach to Islamic scripture," he said.

Davidson, who grew up in Kansas City, said he had been interested in interreligious relations since his childhood. He had strongly admired his family's rabbi for working to rally Christian and Jewish clergy against the corrupt political machine run by Tom Pendergast, an urban boss who benefited from bootlegging and gambling operations until federal prosecutors jailed him on income tax fraud. "My rabbi would speak at dozens of churches," Davidson said, recalling that the ministers would reciprocate by visiting to speak at the synagogue. "And as a kid, it always struck me how good that was."

By the fall of 2006, Davidson had built a strong enough relationship with the Long Island mosque that he felt comfortable stepping into a particularly high-profile controversy that pitted the mosque against the local, seven-term congressman. In the midst of his reelection campaign, Peter T. King, whose Third District includes the Islamic Center in Westbury, referred to the center as a place run by extremists. King, a Republican who then chaired the House Homeland Security Committee, was known for his outspokenness. He also wrote novels, including one titled *Vale of Tears,* whose plot focuses on a terrorist attack by a Muslim group. In August 2006, King called for people of "Middle Eastern and South Asian" ancestry to undergo more background checks at airports than would be applied to other travelers. King had said that all Muslims were not terrorists, but all recent acts of terror had been carried out by Muslims. When he criticized the Long Island mosque, Khan asked for help and Davidson, among others, responded. The rabbi wrote letters to the editor at *Newsday,* protesting the allegations against the mosque and calling King's statement "plain demagoguery." King soundly won reelection and not long afterward publicly said that Davidson ought to have "a guilty conscience" for defending the mosque. In December, the mosque presented the rabbi with an award for his interfaith work. Davidson showed it to me in his office one afternoon. A six-inch-high piece of Plexiglas, it was cut to resemble a mosque's dome and inscribed with a label identifying it as the Islamic Center's Chairman's Award. Engraved beneath was a personal message, saying Davidson embodied a Qur'anic verse, 7:159: "Of the people of Moses, there is a section who guide and do justice in the light of truth." At the dinner where he received the award, Davidson told Khan and others from the mosque that he was ready to speak out against people who attacked Islam and American Muslims, but he also expected them to speak out against attacks on Jews and Israel.

By that time, the public profile of Muslims in America had risen higher—thanks to local politics—but not those on Long Island. On November 7, 2006, voters in Minnesota's Fifth District, which comprises Minneapolis and its near suburbs, had done the unprecedented in American history by electing a Muslim to Congress. Keith Ellison, a forty-three-year-old Democratic state representative, criminal defense attorney, and married father of four, had converted to Islam two decades earlier, as a college student. Four weeks later, one of his soon-to-be colleagues, Virgil H. Goode, Jr., a Republican whose Virginia district includes Thomas Jefferson's Charlottesville estate, sent a letter to his constituents warning about an increase in Muslims—in the nation and in Congress too. By then word was out that Ellison planned to be sworn into office in a private ceremony, in addition to the public swearing-in all members go through. Other congressmen have similar ceremonies. But Ellison let it be known that he would do so with his right hand on the Qur'an, not the Bible. And in the letter that Goode wrote to the people in his district, he made it clear that this troubled him. Americans ought to rouse themselves, he said, or face the prospect of "many more Muslims elected to office and demanding" similar accommodations. "I fear that in the next century we will have many more Muslims in the United States if we do not adopt the strict immigration policies that I believe are necessary to preserve the values and beliefs traditional to the United States of America and to prevent our resources from being swamped," Goode wrote. That would not have blocked Ellison's election; he wasn't an immigrant, but instead traced his roots as an African American back many generations in the United States. When asked for comment on the letter, he replied with restraint, saying he looked forward to getting to know Goode and reassuring him that the Virginian had "nothing to fear." Ellison told a reporter: "The fact that there are many different faiths, many different colors and many different cultures in America is a great strength." And when it came time for the private ceremony on January 4, 2007, Ellison used a particularly historic—and unequivocally American—copy of the Qur'an, one that had been owned by Thomas Jefferson, a part of the third president's personal library that was now housed in the Library of Congress's rare book collection. (Ellison endured other negative reactions to his election, including at least one national broadcast: In November, a CNN host, Glenn Beck, invited the congressman-elect on his show, then led off by asking him, essentially, to prove his patriotism: "I have been nervous about this interview with you, because I feel like asking, 'Sir, prove to me that you are not working with our enemies.'" Ellison, in response, said the people in his district knew he had "a deep love and affection" for the United States, adding, "There's no one more patriotic than I am." Beck did couch his question in some words of reassurance to Ellison, declaring that he knew and liked Muslims, had visited mosques, and didn't really "believe that Islam is a religion of evil."

Although Goode wrote his letter early in December, it did not surface as news until later in the month. In an ironic piece of timing, the letter hit the news cycle on the very day that another Virginian, an immigrant Muslim from Sudan, was leading an Islamic delegation to meet with Holocaust survivors at the U.S. Holocaust Memorial Museum on the Washington Mall. The group shared in a candle-lighting ceremony on behalf of Jewish victims of Nazi genocide. Why then? Mohamed Magid, imam of a major mosque in Washington's Virginia suburbs, explained that the idea occurred to him as a way to respond to an internationally notorious conference of Holocaust deniers, held in Tehran, Iran, earlier in the month. Magid told *The Washington Post* that he had put out calls, telling other local Muslims they should "show solidarity with our fellow Jewish Americans." Stories like these are worth telling, if only because they are likely to strike many non-Muslims in the United States as counterintuitive. Individuals like Ellison and Magid tend to be vastly overshadowed by their far more sensationally dangerous coreligionists. In June 2006, the FBI arrested seven men in south Florida whom they charged with plotting to blow up the Sears Tower in Chicago, although the accused appeared not to possess bomb-making materials. Nearly a year later, the bureau carried out arrests against six men in New Jersey whom they charged with threatening to attack Fort Dix, an action shortly followed by the arrest of four others whom federal authorities said were intending to blow up John F. Kennedy International Airport. In the absence of all the evidence, we cannot know how carefully developed the alleged plots were. But the heavy coverage such incidents receive— supplemented by daily news of violence in Iraq against American soldiers and Iraqi civilians—conveys an image of Muslims as a group as dangerous, angry conspirators, fixed on creating mayhem. Of course, there are those who fit the image, especially in regions of very heavy conflict, and they often do not seem to mind talking to reporters about their beliefs. Thus, within days after the alleged plot against JFK was broken up, *The New York Times* ran an extensive story quoting several very radical Muslims in the Middle East whose definitions of what might be acceptable in waging jihad against various perceived oppressors included the killing of civilians and innocent bystanders, including children. The obvious question is, whom do these people speak for?

On this side of the Atlantic, the number is very small—although not so as to be utterly nonexistent. In May 2007, the Pew Research Center released a one-hundred-page paper, built around analysis of an extensive survey it had done on the economic status and political attitudes of American Muslims. The title summed up its findings: "American Muslims: Middle Class and Mostly Mainstream," and the papers identified the overall population as two-thirds immigrant, the remainder native born, with half of the total population having attended college and, on average, making an average annual salary comparable to other Americans. Based on random telephone interviews with 1,050 Muslims, conducted between the preceding January through April, the report found that more than 7 in 10 Muslims affirmed the idea that people who want to get ahead in the United States can do so if they are willing to work hard—about as solidly an American conviction as any. An equal number described themselves as satisfied with the communities in which they lived and more than three in every five regarded the United States as a place where life was better for women than in Muslim-majority nations. In addition, 61 percent said they worried about terrorism carried out in the name of their faith. (Several of the findings showed American Muslims to be more at ease in their nation than were their European counterparts, whose opinions Pew also cited. But, then, European Muslims in general have a lower standard of living when compared to the surrounding population.) And yet the Pew report contained responses from American Muslims that indicated their own unease as a religious minority. Just over 50 percent said they believed that being Muslim had become "more difficult" in the United States since 9/11 and that the federal government was singling out Muslims for "extra surveillance." But those perceptions may be stronger than individual realities. Only 25 percent told the Pew interviewers that they had ever been discriminated against as a Muslim in the United States; 15 percent said they had been called "an offensive name." By contrast, one third said that within the past year someone—presumably, non-Muslim—had "expressed support" for them.

In its study, Pew also uncovered a flicker of evidence of possible support for extremist actions: 1 percent of those surveyed said suicide bombings were often justified in defense of Islam, while another 7 percent left the door to such actions ajar, saying they could "sometimes" be justified. Such proportions are far lower than what Pew discovered in asking a similar question in 2006 in such Muslim-majority nations as Egypt (28 percent, combined response) and Pakistan (14 percent) and even among Muslim populations in Britain (15 percent). Nevertheless, in the suggestion that even this very limited level of alienation exists among American Muslims lies the basis for suspicious questions, like the one Glenn Beck, the CNN commentator, put to congressman-elect Keith Ellison. But might there be other ways to deal with a minority's alienation, not only to check its potential spread but also to tamp it down?

In a brief but impassioned essay published on Hartford Seminary's Web site after Pew released its results, Ingrid Mattson called on preachers and politicians to envision and proclaim the need for "a new heroism" that eschews violence and values life for its own sake. Mattson, a Canadian convert to Islam who teaches at the seminary, holds a unique status among Muslims in the United States: She is president of the Islamic Society of North America, perhaps the best-known network of mosques in the United States and Canada, and one whose mission specifically calls for fostering good relationships with people of other faiths. Until her election to the position in August 2006, the organization had never had a female president. (In the same meeting, Mohamed Magid, the Virginia imam who would visit the Holocaust Museum, was elected vice

president.) In her essay, Mattson said she was disturbed by that particular statistic on support for a murderous tactic used against civilians. "How could those who claim to follow Muhammad reject his
explicit teachings on this topic?" She also cited another Pew study,
published in 2005, that found that a majority of American Catholics and white Protestants believed that the use of torture against
suspected terrorists could be justified in efforts "to gain important
information." "How could those who claim to worship Jesus, who
was tortured by political authorities, accept the torture of human
beings?" Popular culture, playing on the fear of those who feel
powerless, creates a false idea of heroism, often in the form of cine-
matically glorious explosions, she said. "Rather, nails and screws
pierce the eyes, hands, abdomens of children and elderly women
whose flesh burns and lungs gasp for a last breath." By contrast,
Mattson said, "Authentic religion teaches one to imagine the
other—to consider another's vulnerability and humanity. The beginning of ethics is this transcendent imagination." The message,
she said, to be expounded by preacher and politician alike is that all
human beings possess a God-given dignity.

There are certainly politicians who speak to this issue, the world
over. But efforts to overcome people's alienation, their suspicions of
one another, may lie much more with individuals and groups far
down the political ladder—that is, among people working in their
own communities, among neighbors they can meet face-to-face. In
one instance, a public official did offer some encouragement in this
direction. Shortly after July 4, 2003, Phil Bredensen, the governor
of Tennessee, acting at the behest of a constituent, issued a proclamation urging fellow Tennesseans to make an effort to get to know
one another across religious lines, specifically by visiting one an-
others' sacred spaces. The underlying idea was that the knowledge
derived from meeting people face-to-face and learning about
their religious values can work to foster peace, even in an era of

alienation and religious violence. That violence was "consuming the world and holding it in fear," declared the document in which Bredensen proclaimed "Different Religions Week" in his state.

If you are not familiar with Tennessee, the idea of its being a multifaith haven may come as a surprise. Nashville, the capital and largest city, serves as headquarters for the Southern Baptist Convention, one of the most theologically conservative Christian organizations in the United States—as well as one of the largest, with 16 million members. In the late 1990s, the denomination's missionary agencies printed tracts urging Baptists to pray for the conversion of Jews, Hindus, and others. But even with such a powerhouse on the block, an economically booming metropolitan area of 1.5 million people is unlikely to reflect a uniformly evangelical Protestant culture. Yes, Nashville sits squarely in a region still called the Bible Belt, but it is as much a focus of contemporary immigration as anywhere else in America. Religious multiculturalism has taken root there, enough so that a visitor can find congregations of Buddhists, Bahais, Hindus, Muslims, Sikhs, and Jains, the latter affiliated with a twenty-six-hundred-year-old tradition in western India. Two months after Bredensen's proclamation, the city's main newspaper, *The Tennessean,* reported that the Sri Ganesha Temple, a Hindu house of worship southwest of downtown, staged a public festival that drew about two thousand visitors. "The reason we have this is to let the community become more aware of our temple and to experience Indian culture," the president of the local Indian Association told the reporter. It wasn't the first time that particular temple had opened its doors to visitors. Shortly after 9/11, worshipers there staged a festival to raise money for the families of the people killed at the World Trade Center and Pentagon. Far more people showed up than the temple officers had expected—upward of fifteen hundred, such was the curiosity about the place. The festival has become an annual event. In 2003, *The Tennessean* reporter interviewed a couple, who had brought their children along, and

remarked that it was the second time they had come to the festival. Built in 1985 on Old Hickory Boulevard (the name a tribute
to Tennessee's most famous son, President Andrew Jackson), the
Ganesha temple forms part of the bricks and mortar that make religious diversity so increasingly visible in the United States. But
even in Nashville, it wasn't unique. In 2006, one academic survey
counted three other Hindu organizations, seven Buddhist temples,
six mosques, a Muslim school, and a Sikh gurdwara, all within the
city or its suburbs. There may well have been more. Given that nascent religious organizations often start up in a low-key manner, in
rented space, and without full-time staff or even a telephone, the
survey may well have undercounted the pluralistic reality.

In opening up to the public, post-9/11, Nashville's Ganesha
temple was not at all unique. The Islamic Center of Long Island,
which had built up the relationship with Temple Beth-El, did so
too, as did many other mosques around the nation. The idea was to
welcome the curious, allow them to take a measure of the building,
its prayer room, and children's classrooms, and then meet and talk
with people who regularly prayed there. Refreshments were served.
"You break through the barrier," Faroque Khan, the mosque's president said to me once. "You go to a house of worship and it's fairly
straightforward—no factories for bomb-making." By 2005, Muslims from twenty-five different communities in and around Los
Angeles were holding an annual "Open Mosque Day." Reporters in
suburban Orange County counted two hundred visitors at one
such mosque, greeted by an imam who said, "We are your neighbors. Please know your neighbors." Stepping into someone else's
sacred space can lead to that sort of interaction—hands shaken,
names exchanged, questions posed, explanations offered. In the
process, the blanks may be filled in or at least the stereotypes replaced—a religion's adherents become something more than a
headline, a darting and possibly frightening image on television, or
simply occupants of an unknown building one glimpses while

speeding by on the highway. "When you encounter another person who's different from yourself—and you drop the labels and assumptions about who they are—there's a kind of integrity of the spirituality and wholeness of that person that emerges," Judith Simmer-Brown, a professor of religious studies at Naropa University, once told me. Naropa, in Boulder, Colorado, was founded in 1974 by an exiled Tibetan teacher, Chögyam Trungpa, a creative and controversial leader within America's Buddhist community. Simmer-Brown, a Protestant minister's daughter, became a Buddhist in the 1970s, and since then has not only participated in many dialogues between Christians and Buddhists, and Buddhists and Muslims, but has also taught a class showing how such events might best be undertaken. "In my dialogue with Muslims," she told me, "when I encounter them and the whole-heartedness and discipline of their practice, it has a very positive experience for me as a Buddhist."

A Christian might admire it too. Pope John Paul II once told an Italian interviewer he felt moved by the devotion of Muslims he had seen at prayer. To be sure, the pope made it clear he found Islamic theology lacking when compared with Christianity. "Nevertheless, the religiosity of Muslims deserves respect," he said. "It is impossible not to admire their fidelity to prayer. The image of believers in Allah who, without caring about time or place, fall to their knees and immerse themselves in prayer remains a model for all those who invoke the true God." Taking the role of a scold, the pope added that the Muslim example might be particularly relevant to Europe's large population of nominal Christians, who, he said, "having deserted their magnificent cathedrals, pray only a little or not at all." Enter another person's sacred space and you stand not only to learn about a tradition, but even come to see the believers as individuals—the underlying message in the Bredensen proclamation. As the twentieth-century Jewish philosopher Martin Buber wrote, "All real living is meeting." An encounter may be much more than a passing thing: experiential, rather than purely intellectual. In his book *I And Thou*, Buber writes that in intimate interactions with a stranger, not only does that person become less strange, but one may actually glimpse the divine. To be invited into someone's home for the first time is to cross a threshold. To be invited into another's house of worship is to take part in an act of spiritual intimacy. Speaking before a multifaith audience, the Dalai Lama, who had visited Jerusalem, suggested his listeners go on pilgrimage with another person to that person's holy site. "The pilgrims should pray together if possible; if not, they can practice silent meditation. This is a very effective way to understand the value and power of other religious traditions," he said.

Nevertheless, to walk into someone else's house of worship unannounced tends to be a mission for the spiritually self-confident. Whether they be churches, temples, mosques, or gurdwaras, many places are not set up to accommodate visitors who want simply to observe, unless it's a special occasion, an "Open Mosque Day." There are neat little roadside signs all over America informing their readers that the Episcopal Church "welcomes you." No doubt it does, but as an evangelistic tool: They want you with them as a fellow worshiper. It is different when the intention is to bring congregations together and when that goal is stated at the outset, as it was between Temple Beth-El and the Long Island Islamic Center. Nonetheless, at least two trends have made the process of visiting more easily done. One change directly affects younger people—college students, mainly, but also some high schoolers and seminarians—in that the expansion of religious diversity within the United States has coincided with a growth in academic programs in religious studies. Religion as a scholarly endeavor, distinct from theology, has taken its place alongside literature and philosophy in university humanities departments and, occasionally, within high school social science curricula. More recently, courses in comparative religions have been included as options for students studying for the ministry or priesthood in seminaries and divinity schools. Typically, these courses come with field trips to supplement textbook readings as only such visual and aural experiences can. As someone who teaches in a religion department, I have been part of the trend, having taken scores of students to local religious institutions, where we have sat in as observers during Eastern Orthodox divine liturgy, Zen Buddhist meditation, Islamic prayers, and Hindu *puja,* the latter while watching as a temple priest recited prayers and offered food and flowers to life-sized statues of the resident deities. To say the obvious, these excursions are intended to inform, not to lay the basis for conversion (which is an entirely personal matter). They supplement what students get in the classroom. The visits are qualitatively different from textbook reading. Students see people in what are essentially private moments, participating in rites many have practiced since they could walk, speaking in phrases they have heard since infancy. Students may have occasion to speak with those they've observed, to learn more about how they practice their faith and what it is they value.

The local mosque—a ten-minute walk from my campus—has always seemed to make a strong impression on students. It is not the architecture, as it is a modest place. But being within its walls allows students to check the impressions of Islam they have absorbed from any number of other sources, not least television news reports. At least they see a wide-ranging ethnic diversity—African American, Bosnian, Nigerian, Pakistani, Palestinian, and more—that is typical of mosques in the United States. The Qur'an enjoins Muslims to pray five times daily, starting with one before dawn and closing with another after dusk. It is a fundamental spiritual discipline—one of the faith's Five Pillars—that helps define a Muslim's submission to God. I have taken forty or more students at a time to the mosque, where they have watched the resident prayer leader guide a group of men and boys through the prescribed positions of physically offering God reverence, through standing with eyes downcast, bowing at the waist, kneeling, touching forehead to the floor. My students tend to be urban, culturally sophisticated, often well traveled. But few have ever previously set foot in a mosque.

"There are a great many stereotypes about Islam and Muslims, and it is only through dialogue that these will, slowly, be dismantled," writes Amir Hussein, a professor of religious studies in Loyola Marymount University in Los Angeles, in a recent essay. The scholar, a Canadian born in Pakistan, acknowledges that this is a two-way street, that Muslims need dialogue as much as anyone else. "It is easy to be taught to hate Christians or Jews (as for example tragically occurs in Saudi Arabia) if there are few actual Christians or Jews in one's country. In the pluralistic context of North America it is a very different matter. The stereotypes that one may have learned, for example that Christians worship three gods and are therefore polytheistic, fall away when one is invited to a Christian worship service and realizes that it is the same One God who is being praised and worshiped."

The vital word in his statement is *invited,* that is, made a guest and welcomed. Hospitality is a theme that runs through all the world's major religions. Among Jews and Christians, one of the most resonant examples is beautifully narrated in Genesis, its eighteenth chapter, when Abraham sees three strangers approach the tent he and his wife Sarah have pitched at the Oaks of Mamre. He rushes to greet them and, bowing, offers bread and water. The three turn out to be divine messengers, who tell the aged Abraham and Sarah to expect a child. In a commentary written many centuries later, the author of the New Testament's Letter to the Hebrews cautions: "Do not neglect to show hospitality to strangers, for by doing that some have entertained angels without knowing it." I heard something of the same point made by a South Asian immigrant at a Hindu temple: "The guest," she said, "is God."

Such invitations are extended, implicitly or quite plainly, by some of the larger mosques and temples in the United States and

Britain. Tour books describing Washington, D.C., suggest tourists check out the block-long Islamic Center on Massachusetts Avenue, above which towers a 160-foot minaret. President Eisenhower attended its dedication in 1957; days after 9/11, President Bush held a news conference inside it to urge Americans not to confuse the words "Muslim" and "terrorist." "The face of terror is not the true faith of Islam," he said. The Islamic Center of America, the Shi'ite Muslim mosque in Dearborn, Michigan, described earlier, has a place on its Web site inviting browsers to "book a tour," as it says "church groups, schools, colleges and individuals" have all done. Similarly, the Regents Park Mosque in London hosts thousands of visitors annually, a spokesman there told me.

A similar possibility exists among the larger Hindu temples. "This is almost universal at temples in the United States," Dr. Siva Subramanian said, in a conversation we had. A professor of pediatrics at Georgetown University Medical Center, he helped found the Sri Siva Vishnu Temple in Lanham, Maryland, outside Washington, D.C., and has also served as president of the Council of Hindu Temples of North America. "At the Lanham temple, we have two or three people who are available on weekdays and weekends to welcome people from schools and colleges and take them on a tour and answer all the questions about theology and practices," he said. "It usually ends with a lunch, a vegetarian lunch." Schoolchildren come by with their teachers, and so do college students, seminarians, and clergy. Subramanian, who moved to the United States in 1970, said he had seen Hindu immigrants pass through three stages in adjusting to living in America. It began with individuals working to establish themselves professionally; once they had begun having children and put some money in the bank, they began building temples and schools, to teach their faith and culture to a second generation. The third stage was outreach, trying to forge friendly relations with the religious neighbors, churches, and synagogues. What helped drive that third stage, too, Subramanian said, was that some Hindus felt a rising level of abuse—some of it physical—from individuals and gangs hostile to immigrants. Temples were scrawled with spray paint; Hindu men and women were singled out for insult and worse. "So the whole idea and concept was, 'Hey, we need to have some relationships with the broader religious community,'" Subramanian said.

Such concerns didn't strike me as at all overblown. In November 1992, during a period of substantial Indian immigration into New Jersey, a colleague at *The Washington Post,* where I then worked, wrote a story reporting on incidents of verbal harassment and beatings directed against Hindus in the state's northern suburbs. One immigrant died in the backlash. A xenophobic gang wrote to a local newspaper, menacingly calling themselves "the dot-busters"—a crude reference to the *bindi,* the small circle that Hindu women often paint between their eyebrows. Around the same time that the Lanham temple was reaching out to its neighbors, Subramanian helped launch a course at Georgetown to train medical students and nurses in how they might better understand basic religious differences among their patients. Again, the idea was a direct response to a growing religious pluralism becoming evident on the treatment wards. Medical staff could no longer assume everyone shared a more or less common cultural background; doctors and nurses would have to take basic religious beliefs and understandings into consideration when discussing medicine and treatment. All this is to say that hospitals, especially in urban areas, have become multireligious crossroads—not only because of their patients, but because the religious and ethnic composition of their medical staffs has diversified. Since the liberalization of immigration laws in 1965, the United States has added thousands of Hindu, Muslim, Sikh, and Buddhist doctors and nurses. For example, the 1980 U.S. Census found that more than 10 percent of the Indians immigrating to the United States were physicians, while even larger proportions listed their training as engineers, architects, or surveyors. It has been those

individuals—upwardly mobile and well educated in their fields—
who are often the most likely members of their faith groups that
Christians and Jews encounter.

That would include Dr. Uma Mysorekar, an Indian-born gyne-
cologist who moved to the United States about the same time as
Subramanian, in the early wave of professionally trained South
Asians who arrived on the heels of the sweeping change in federal
immigration law. By the time I met her, in Queens, New York, Mysorekar served as president of one of the largest and oldest Hindu
temples in the United States, whose prosaic name was the Hindu
Temple Society of North America. It stands on Bowne Street, a
north-south thoroughfare in Flushing, one of the most religiously
diverse neighborhoods in America and also one with a history of
religious hospitality at the local level that dates back to the first arrival of the Quakers in the 1650s. To enter a Hindu temple can be
a richly sensory experience, or it might be disorienting—especially
if one comes from a far more visually and aurally austere background. I recall one day at the Flushing temple: people sat in clusters
on the floor, eyes fixed on the statues of individual deities—
among them the great gods Shiva, associated with destruction and
creation, and Vishnu, known as the preserver, and the goddess of
good fortune—Lakshmi—while priests, robed in white from waist
down, moved among them, chanting prayers and preparing offerings of fruit, vegetables, and flowers they set before the gods. There
might have been a hundred people in the room, but it was easy to
spot Mysorekar, standing attired in a resplendent green sari. She
stood prayerfully gazing at the temple's central deity, Ganesha, embodied in a statue carved from a formidable block of black granite
housed in a three-sided shrine in the middle of the room. Ganesha,
whose elephant head sits atop a portly human body typically shown
cross-legged, is the deity to whom a Hindu might pray first. Not
only is he the god of wisdom, but he is also believed to remove obstacles from one's path, including the spiritual obstacles that might

prevent a devotee from approaching another god. "A child is first introduced to learning with a prayer to Ganesha, the fountain-head of wisdom," reports my lavishly illustrated Indian book on the god. "When laying the foundation of a building, Ganesha is invoked before placing the first stone. No new business or industry is started without a prayer to him. Travellers on lonely roads stop and pray at roadside Ganesha shrines. . . ." From the Flushing temple, Hindus have been publicly celebrating Ganesha's birthday for years, placing a likeness of the deity in a chariot and pulling it through the streets in a parade that begins and ends at the temple. Basic to the Hindu experience of temple-going is a concept called *darshan*. The divine spirit is understood to inhabit the statues of the deities there, such that being in their presence, gazing upon them, means being blessed by a holy vision. A fundamental spiritual transaction takes place: You see the deity, the deity sees you. That day, I had come upon Mysorekar during that experience.

Mysorekar had not always been associated with the Flushing temple, which had been built by other families. After studying medicine in Bombay, she moved first to Columbia, South Carolina. In 1970, even a Roman Catholic might have been considered exotic in a city so overwhelmingly Baptist, Methodist, and Presbyterian. As a Hindu, she struck people as exotic and made them curious, enough so that some asked her to talk to them about Hinduism, often inviting her to speak to them in their churches, the central institution of southern society. She did so. Unsurprisingly, she met women who earnestly wanted to persuade her to convert to Christianity for the sake of her soul—or at least to acknowledge Christianity's superiority. But she did neither, instead taking a diplomatic tack to avoid comparisons. "I'm just telling you what I practice—that is it," she recalled saying to her hosts. Her presentations, then, were about sharing knowledge, the idea being that each would gain from the other, from talking and listening. "Because," she said, "I'd like to learn from you what you practice." These conversations were not restricted to adult Sunday schools, but took place in the intimate circumstances of the hospital, often on the wards. Religion came up between her and some colleagues and patients. She told me that after she moved north to work in New York, she struck up a friendship with a Jewish doctor who specialized in anesthesiology. The two women often spoke during the quiet times they waited for patients in surgery; they spoke of their respective religious faiths in their practices. Mysorekar remembered her friend confiding that she prayed for her patients every time she put them under anesthesia. Some of Mysorekar's patients wanted to talk about matters of faith, especially if they were facing surgery. Hospitals then were home to relatively few female gynecologists, so she attracted clients who preferred a woman as a doctor. Many were practicing Christians, and some felt sufficiently at ease with her to share their religious thoughts. "They would tell me, especially in certain serious illnesses, 'Doctor, I'd like to pray before surgery.'" Mysorekar respected that. Afterward, some of them would share their feelings, narrating their inner experiences. "They would tell me, 'I'm sure Jesus was with me and he was helping you go along.'" What they interpreted as Jesus' presence Mysorekar understood to be something divine but universal. "There is some supreme power, in whatever form we see, we feel. I respected that. It really was appropriate. They really have educated me. And they made me open up my mind."

Twice I saw what she described as her openness put to the test. Violence between Hindus and Muslims in India has been an occasional but often devastating phenomenon in recent years, especially since a Hindu nationalist mob attacked and destroyed the four-century-old Babri Mosque in the Indian city of Ayodhya in December 1992. The nationalists alleged that the mosque stood on the birth site of a god. In one instance, I visited the Flushing temple around the time of a violent encounter between Muslim guerrillas and the Indian Army at a Hindu shrine. The assailants had tried to force their way into a crowded temple belonging to the Swaminarayan movement, a two-hundred-year-old sect based in northwestern India oriented around the worship of Vishnu, one of Hinduism's principal gods. The attackers ended up exchanging extensive fire with elite security forces. The shooting went on for hours, eventually leaving thirty dead; a letter found on the corpse of one of the gunmen declared the attack in revenge for the killings of Muslims by Hindu mobs in an earlier round of violence. In our conversation, Mysorekar was firm in saying such outbreaks involving Muslims could not be blamed on Islam or the Qur'an, its holy book. "Essentially, the Qur'an doesn't teach like that—it's a misinterpretation of the Qur'an," she said. The book, she said, is about "the well-being of humanity." It was a view, of course, totally removed from that of Hindu nationalism. Around the same time, I saw her preside in the temple's capacious new auditorium at an event intended to emphasize peaceful religious coexistence in Flushing. People representing different faith traditions had been invited to speak, a Muslim among them. But one man arrived late and, taking the stage, faulted Muslims as a cause of South Asian violence. The Muslim speaker stood nearby but said nothing. The man then left, and Mysorekar hurried to the podium and apologized, saying he did not represent the temple. Such an example cannot be taken for granted, not given the depth of the hostility that ranges across religious, ethnic, and racial boundaries. Substantial wisdom lies within the simple Hebrew proverb: A gentle answer turns away wrath, but a harsh word stirs up anger.

Anyone who thinks this might be easy needs to think again. The past two decades have seen the spread of a radical sense of Hindu identity—*hindutva,* or "Hinduness." It exists mainly in India, where adherents have often focused their wrath on the nation's Islamic minority, as they did in tearing down the mosque in Ayodhya. Ten years later, mobs in the state of Gujarat killed hundreds of local Muslims in a riot that followed a tragic encounter between militant Hindus returning from Ayodhya aboard a train and Muslims on a

railway platform. A train car caught fire—Hindus at the scene
blamed Muslims for causing it—leaving nearly sixty people dead.
However, there are people with the power to act against such hatred. For example, after the attack on the Swaminarayan shrine, the
head of that religious organization called on his followers to bear
the attack's pain with "prayer, unity, and peace." People listened to
him; there was no retributive violence.

Mysorekar's words about the Qur'an seemed to me something
many Americans would do well to hear from Muslims themselves.
The literature is certainly available. But getting it to a popular audience is another matter. If one somehow happened to pick up a collection of essays titled *The New Voices of Islam,* published in 2006 by
the University of California Press, then one could read words written by Mohamed Talbi, a Tunisian historian and an authority on
Islamic thought. Talbi argues that a reader of the Qur'an must be
very careful not to confuse what the book says about apostasy from
Islam (which it severely denounces) with the possibility of religious
liberty (which it does not reject). "We can never stress too much
that religious liberty is not an act of charity or a tolerant concession
toward misled persons," writes Talbi, sounding a bit like Jefferson or
Madison. "It is, rather, a fundamental right of everyone. To claim it
for myself implies *ipso facto* that I am disposed to claim it for my
neighbor, too. But religious liberty is not reduced to the equivalent
of atheism. My right and my duty, also, are to bear witness, by fair
means to my own faith and to convey God's call. Ultimately, however, it is up to each person to respond to this call or not, freely and
in all full consciousness." There are many ways one can quote from
the Qur'an, but I have often heard American Muslims point to a
verse that has a particular resonance in a pluralistic society: surah (or
chapter) 2, verse 256:"Let there be no compulsion in religion: truth
stands out clear from error. ..." (That's from a popular English-
language version, by Abdullah Yusuf Ali, which includes the foot-

note that "religion depends upon faith and will and these would be meaningless if induced by force.")

Not everyone at the temple shared Mysorekar's views. Indeed, on one visit, a worshiper there approached me and, in reference to Muslims and 9/11, flatly stated, "Now you Americans see what we've been dealing with all these years." And that was it—point made, he walked away. And yet I wondered if there might actually be something in the temple's surroundings that might encourage cooperation among people of different faiths. Mysorekar regarded that possibility quite literally. The neighborhood resonated with multiculturalism, the flourishing of different spiritualities. "That's one of the reasons why they say, at least in Hinduism, the soil is very fertile from the worshiper's point of view," she said. "Nothing can beat the authenticity and vibrations that one feels." She tried to interest children at the temple in the local heritage. "In every class of our kids, I tell them, 'Do you know why this is called Bowne Street?' " If they didn't (usually the case), she told them to go visit the Bowne House, about a mile to the temple's north.

The house, remarkably, is a relic of what New York was back in its first colonial era, Dutch New Amsterdam. Now well into its fourth century, the house belonged to a farmer named John Bowne who happened to live in Flushing when the neighborhood emerged as a testing ground for religious liberty—nearly a century and a half before the writing of the First Amendment. Here's how the story goes: In the mid-1650s, religious dissenters from England began arriving in small numbers on the American shore. They had been influenced by George Fox and like-minded religious radicals who believed that God's truth was available as an "inner light" to all individuals. In Christianity, therefore, there was no need for paid clergy or state-sanctioned churches when anyone could be a minister and any gathering a service. These dissenters, popularly known as Quakers, refused to swear legal oaths and were not deferential to civil authority. They could be spiritually aggressive, too, entering churches to challenge the minister's sermon. They made enemies very quickly, especially among Dutch authorities, after several Quakers landed in the colony in 1657. "The raving Quakers have not settled down, but continue to disturb the people of this province," Dutch ministers wrote to church authorities in Amsterdam. "Although our government has issued orders against these fanatics, nevertheless they do not fail to pour forth their venom." The ministers became particularly worried about the effect these unwanted visitors were having in Flushing, where "many persons have become imbued with diverse opinions." Bowne emerged out of this crisis. Determined to check Quakerism before it could take root, the colony's governor, Peter Stuyvesant, established a law severely fining anyone who sheltered a Quaker overnight. The first conviction came against a Flushing resident, prompting his neighbors to draw up a statement of protest, in which they said that Stuyvesant infringed on guarantees of liberty originally granted to them as settlers. In December 1657, thirty-one Flushing men—including the local sheriff—signed the statement, declaring they felt bound by their religious faith not to abide by the law. They could not "lay violent hands," they said, on those with whom they differed religiously. The document came to be called the Flushing Remonstrance, a seven-hundred-word argument drawn from a close reading of Christian Scriptures. Its central point is that their understanding of Christian duty meant respecting people who lived and moved among them. Yes, the Remonstrance's authors acknowledged, that was a theologically diverse bunch, some with radical ways of understanding the Bible. But they felt bound nonetheless to look on these people as part of God's creation. "And because our Saviour sayeth it is impossible but that offences will come, but woe unto him by whom they cometh, our desire is not to offend one of his little ones, in whatsoever form, name or title he appears in, whether Presbyterian, Independent, Baptist or Quaker, but shall be glad to see anything of God in any of them, desiring to doe unto all men as we desire all men should doe unto us, which is the true law both of Church and State, for our Saviour sayeth this is the law and the prophets."

In inevitable hindsight, the Remonstrance has been viewed as a forerunner of the First Amendment. But it is also one of those key points in American history where political openness intersects with theological generosity. After its publication, Stuyvesant broke up the group that signed it, sending the ringleaders to prison and banning local residents from holding town meetings. But that didn't end resistance; Quakers continued to meet in Flushing, albeit in secret. And in 1661, the authorities came to arrest John Bowne on charges he allowed such meetings in his own home. Convicted, he faced a choice—pay a fine or go into exile. He chose the latter, but used the time to make his way to Holland, where he took his case directly to the colony's masters, the Dutch West India Company's directors. In 1663, he won a ruling from that board; they sent Stuyvesant a warning that his policies would drive away immigrants, leaving the colony weak and militarily vulnerable. Among other things, the directors stated: "Let everyone remain free as long as he is modest, moderate and his political conduct irreproachable."

These days, it seems as if Bowne's old neighborhood took the Dutch directors' decision very much to heart. R. Scott Hanson, a scholar of religions who lived in the neighborhood and studied it closely, calls Flushing a microcosm of the world's religions. A walk along Bowne Street amounts to a tour of the global destination Flushing has become, with store signs in Chinese, Korean, Hindi, Spanish, Urdu, and English, too. The varied spiritual landscape makes it even more distinctive. If you head a bit north from Bowne's house, you will find the Quaker Meeting House that he helped build in 1694. Long before I pulled abreast of it in traffic on the summer morning I came from Temple Beth-El, I had visited the meetinghouse on the day a multireligious council was gathered there. Around a circular table inside, a dozen people had gathered, representing local Protestants, Jews, Muslims, and Buddhists. The discussion was unremarkable, centering on plans to meet with a borough councilman to talk about neighborhood issues. Afterward, one of the Quakers showed me around, pointing out hand-hewn beams that supported the second floor, stark wooden benches where people gathered for largely silent worship. To walk south from Bowne's house is to be immersed in an even more palpable spiritual variety—an imposing brick church affiliated with the United Church of Christ, a synagogue, churches of Korean Presbyterians and Chinese evangelicals, a Sikh gurdwara, and a Hindu temple. A mosque stands a few blocks to the east, and not far beyond that a Buddhist temple. After a mile on Bowne, you reach the gates of the Hindu Temple Society of North America, a building that stands on the site of a former Russian Orthodox church. On July 4, 1977, Hindu families gathered to dedicate the temple. "I think it's one of the reasons there are so many faiths along here," Mysorekar said, referring to the local history. "There are plenty of religious places on this street, which I think has tremendous meaning for John Bowne, who fought for this very idea of religious freedom."

One day when I visited the Hindu temple, I met a group affiliated with a Protestant seminary in Manhattan, taking a tour of the grounds. As a volunteer guide took them around, priests placed carnations at Ganesha's feet and ears, and laid a meal of bananas and coconuts before him. They rang small bells. Incense smoke rose in threadlike streams toward the temple ceiling. At one point, I walked over to a rack of brochures to pick up a pamphlet about the temple. "We also welcome those who belong to other faiths," it stated. "We do invite them to be united with us in prayer." On another occasion, a busload of Methodist ministers from Pennsylvania pulled up to the curb. Their guide for the day, a retired schoolteacher who worshiped at the temple, began their tour. It included a stop outside, where they gazed on a large circular symbol, a mandala four feet wide, decorating the temple's western wall. It is a stylized lotus, open and drawn to appear as if one were looking down at it from above. On each petal is displayed the symbol of a major religious faith: a Christian cross, a Star of David, an Islamic crescent moon, Buddhism's wheel of the dharma, and, at the topmost point, the Hindu symbol for *om,* the universe's essence. In script form, *om* resembles the number 3, with a hooking curve emerging from the back of its upper half, the design surmounted by a small square above a curved shape like a cow's horn. Years ago, someone affiliated with the temple had spotted a similar arrangement of sacred symbols at the headquarters of a popular guru in India. But Mysorekar regarded its presence in Flushing as a sign of openness. "It shows clearly, right at the door, you're made welcome," she said. One of the tour guides told me the number of groups visiting had been gradually increasing. The temple got about thirty groups each year in 2003 and 2004, mainly high school or college students, along with Christian seminarians. The size of the groups varied, sometimes only a dozen, sometimes fifty or more. But by 2005, the number of groups visiting had risen to fifty.

I asked Mysorekar if she found within Hinduism an explicit theological basis for hospitality. She said it existed in the Bhagavad Gita, an essential Hindu scripture that recounts a conversation between the warrior Arjuna and the god Krishna on the eve of a great battle. The book's central message is of selfless human duty and divine love. She quoted one of its concluding verses, containing both invitation and promise: "Abandoning all Dharmas, come unto Me alone for shelter; sorrow not, I will liberate you from all your sins." She explained: "He doesn't say, 'Hindus come to me,' he says, 'Anybody come to me, I will give you that grace and I will shelter you.' So if the Lord is telling us this, who are we to question and challenge the Lord?"

Her speaking about God in the singular should not seem odd. It is often said that Hinduism has 330 million gods. That's nothing like an exact count, but rather a figure of speech, an illustration of a spiritual decentralization. But many Hindus will speak of a single God; the various deities are merely manifestations of one divine essence. Some years ago, Horst Pohlmann, a German theology professor, undertook a personal survey, visiting more than one hundred temples in India and quizzing their priests on the question. Eighty-five told him they believed in one God. That might seem conclusive, but it wasn't quite so simple. Several others said the God had many names, or many forms, or many varieties.

Later on, I mentioned Mysorekar's remarks about the Qur'an to Faroque Khan, chairman of the mosque in Westbury. By then, I had been to the mosque during some multireligious events, including once when the area's new Catholic bishop visited. Already, Khan had gained a reputation for upbraiding politicians whom he regarded as playing on anti-Islamic feelings. Although a registered Republican, he had been particularly outspoken during the 2000 election against remarks made by his party's U.S. Senate candidate, Representative Rick Lazio, a fellow Long Islander. Lazio had faulted his opponent, Hillary Clinton, for taking what he called "blood money" from Muslim donors in Massachusetts. Lazio alleged the donations came from people who tacitly supported terrorism. Khan called it guilt by association. As the mosque had focused much of its outreach in building relations with Christians and Jews, he said he did not really know Mysorekar but had encountered her at an occasional gathering. Nonetheless, he made it clear he appreciated her remarks. "Bless her," he said, adding that Gandhi had also defended the holiness of the Qur'an. "There are some good people out there who can think through the fog."

Gandhi is the gold standard when it comes to talking about interreligious respect. On the night that India became independent from Britain, the goal for which he had worked so hard, Gandhi avoided the ceremonies in Delhi and stayed in Calcutta with members of India's Muslim minority. He had wrestled much of his life with the question of how to relate to a plurality of faiths. In his autobiography, *The Story of My Experiments with Truth,* he told of growing up with almost daily experience of encounters that defied caste and faith boundaries, as a result of his father's openness to speaking with people across Hinduism's internal lines as well as with those of other religions. The senior Gandhi served as a minister to one of India's princes. Jain monks visited the family, accepted gifts of food, and had friendly discussions with Gandhi's father. The elder Gandhi also had Muslim and Zoroastrian friends who, the son reported, would talk to him about their religions, to which he listened with respect. Gandhi at first felt, he said, tolerant of other faiths. But later in life, he found that insufficient as a basis for dealing with non-Hindus. Instead, he adopted a position he described as respecting all religions as equals. He described the world's major religions as being like branches of a tree, in which the trunk contained a dedication to truth and nonviolence. "Tolerance may imply a gratuitous assumption of the inferiority of other faiths to one's own," he wrote, "and respect suggests a sense of patronizing whereas *ahimsa*"—that is, nonviolence—"teaches us to entertain the same respect for the religious faiths of others as we accord to our own, thus admitting the imperfection of the latter."

Khan told me he was born in Kashmir during the final years of British rule. "I would see growing up, when somebody comes to our house, we would offer them food and, if they wanted to stay overnight, 'You are welcome to stay overnight.' It didn't really matter where they were from, whether they were close or distant. That was a kind of a part of Islamic tradition growing up, welcoming your guests." Several non-Muslims came to the home. "They were almost part of our family. Holidays, the Hindu holidays, they would send us gifts, we would send them gifts." I asked him if his parents ever actually discussed this. No, he said, it was part of the family tradition. His early education, in a school run by Roman Catholic nuns from Ireland, added another dimension to this early interfaith encounter. "So I've grown up in an environment of tolerance, acceptance, respecting others' viewpoints," Khan said. "That has helped me immensely in dealing with the issues here."

I had met Khan that day at an Afghan restaurant in Westbury. I walked up from the train station, passing the Islamic Center, whose extensive plantings had been singled out by the local garden club for honor as "lawn of the month." We talked about the dialogue with Beth-El, how they had started slowly, avoiding controversial issues, and eventually built up to being able to talk—and disagree—on such subjects as the future of Jerusalem. I asked Khan what he had gained. "Does it make a difference?" he asked, rephrasing my question. "In the larger global picture, it's a blip. From my personal, grassroots level, if I can help two communities understand each other better, that to me is an accomplishment. It makes life a little easier for my kids, their kids growing up. And breaking down the stereotypes and helping understanding. We're realistic about the end product." Then, speaking as a physician, he added, "In medicine, we need outcome studies—you've done something, what have you accomplished? All I can say is, I have a much better impression of the Jewish community and they have a much better impression of the Muslim community." But ultimately, that was as much as he would venture. He suspected there were similar efforts under way in other communities, but he didn't know what they might be. "I don't know what the other guy's doing, and they don't know what I'm doing. Decentralized—each one doing their own thing. Hopefully, it will have a cumulative effect, and hopefully we will live to see it."

FIVE

An Era of Conversation

A five-minute walk north from Baltimore's Inner Harbor, a block-wide plaza honors the memory of the Jews murdered by the Nazis. The Baltimore Holocaust Memorial is mostly open space but for an eighty-foot-long barrier stretching across its northern boundary. A massive pair of concrete blocks nineteen feet high stand linked together, with railway tracks at each end. The sculpture represents the boxcars that carried European Jews to the death camps. The concrete is undecorated, save for a descriptive statement taken from the autobiography of Primo Levi, an Italian Jew, a chemist and writer, who described his imprisonment in Auschwitz in a 1958 memoir. "On both sides of the track rows of red and white lights appeared as far as the eye could see. . . . With the rhythm of the wheels, with every human sound now silenced, we waited to see what was to happen. . . . In an instant, our women, our parents, our children disappeared. We saw them as an obscure mass at the other end of the platform. Then we saw them no more."

Although the monument doesn't mention it, the passage comes from the book's first chapter, in which Levi describes his arrest in 1944 and subsequent transport with hundreds of other Italian Jews north to Poland. To read the chapter is to be struck by the total collapse of dialogue that Levi experienced after his arrest. His captors barely speak to him or his fellow prisoners—about them, yes, as when one German officer asks another, "How many pieces?" He means Jews. But in general, there is no speech other than the unanswerable questions that the prisoners ask each other about their fates, and the brief, shouted commands that come to them in German, a language few understand. When the train stopped outside the camp, Levi writes, "The door opened with a crash, and the dark echoed with outlandish orders in that curt, barbaric barking of Germans in command which seems to give vent to a millennial anger." Once inside the camp, Levi and the other prisoners have their clothes and shoes taken away and their heads shaved. They are utterly isolated: "If we want to speak, they will not listen to us, and if they listen, they will not understand. They will even take away our name. . . ." He describes the end result as "the demolition of a man."

That part of the memorial—the sculpture resembling train cars—was completed in 1997. Coincidentally, it occurred within a historically remarkable decade in which major Christian organizations in the United States and Europe began publishing critical reflections on the role that their faith's historic theological attitudes toward Judaism likely played in making the Holocaust more possible. In sharp contrast to Levi's experience, the frightening lack of communication that had so isolated him and others taken to the death camps, now words poured forth, in an effort to reconstruct a new relationship between two historically related religious traditions. "The fact that the *Shoah* took place in Europe, that is, in countries of long-standing Christian civilization, raises the question of the relation between the Nazi persecution and the attitudes down the centuries of Christians toward Jews. The history of relations between Christians and Jews is a tormented one." The two sentences, delicate in their tone, come from a document released by the Vatican's Commission for Religious Relations with the Jews, signed by Pope John Paul II, on March 16, 1998. "We Remember: A Reflection on the Shoah" had been in the works for a decade and, perhaps as a result, it read as if it had been written by committee, some of whose members seemed grudging in acknowledging that Christians could have played any role, anytime, in persecuting Jews. As such, the document's reception was tepid, especially among Jews familiar with the bold actions John Paul himself had undertaken to foster positive Christian-Jewish relations. The pope, who as a Polish seminarian had witnessed Nazi cruelty in his native land, had been the first of Saint Peter's successors since antiquity to visit a synagogue. The photograph taken of him outside the building, smiling as he prepared to embrace Rome's chief rabbi, Elio Toaff, showed his intentions better than any formal statement might have. John Paul never lacked for words on this subject: Two years later, in 1988, he pledged to Jews in Strasbourg, France, that he felt "the strongest condemnation of anti-Semitism and racism."

For the most part, Nazism drew its inspiration from crude and inherently violent theories of bloodlines and ancestral purity—in other words, tribal ideas deeply at odds with the Christian understanding of all of humanity as created in God's image. But by 1998, the Vatican was at least ready to pose a question Christians might ponder about how in the heart of Christian Europe the Nazi movement could arise and then act with such focused viciousness. It "may be asked whether the Nazi persecution of the Jews was not made easier by the anti-Jewish prejudices imbedded in some Christian minds and hearts. Did anti-Jewish sentiment among Christians make them less sensitive, or even indifferent, to the persecutions against the Jews by National Socialism when it reached power?" The document might also have asked, did prejudice against Jews make Christians in Germany and elsewhere in the Nazi realm willing to collaborate in genocide? It asked no such question. Instead, "We Remember" demands a future built on a "shared mutual respect" between Christians and Jews. The great question is, how does one get there?

In wanting to discover an answer, I had chosen to come to Baltimore. I had no plans to visit the Holocaust memorial—I would come across that only later, and by chance. Instead, my goal was to visit the Institute for Christian & Jewish Studies, a single, relatively small component within what has become a much larger project, one that spans the Atlantic, involving the Vatican, major Jewish organizations, and Protestant churches, ecclesiastical councils, and academic study centers, as well as thousands of individual priests, rabbis, ministers, and lay people. Because it goes back to the immediate aftermath of the Second World War in Europe and the United States (and even predates the war in some places), this particular conversation has a much longer history than efforts to foster dialogue between Christians and Muslims or Christians and Buddhists. But, then, Christians and Jews have a vastly more contentious ground with which to deal, a "tormented" past, as the Vatican said. In no other relationship of one faith to another is there so much deeply fraught history, in which signal events always seem to begin with a capital letter—the Crusades, the Inquisition. In no other relationship, too, do two faiths stand in such close spiritual proximity. Christianity emerged from Judaism; its original figures, starting with Jesus, were Jews. As Rosann Catalano, a Roman Catholic theologian at the institute, said, "It's that we share and don't share the same text." She meant the Bible—what Jews call the Tanakh, Christians the Old Testament. It can be read (and is read) as a text complete in itself, the history of a God-chosen people and their ultimate expectations. Or it may be read (and is read) as a precursor to another Testament entirely, for another people, lately chosen by God. Churchill once famously described the British and the Americans as two people divided by a common language. Christians and Jews, said Catalano, stand "divided by a common text."

The pressing need to reconstruct and then nurture this relationship has engaged people almost since the day Allied armies reached the gates of Buchenwald, Bergen-Belsen, and other camps in 1945. Work began gradually. But among Christians it has spread through ever-higher ecclesiastical levels as a theological movement, widespread though by no means universal. It did not entirely come after the war—serious and dedicated individuals in both faiths labored hard to create a more equal and respectful relationship before 1939. But in the postwar period, this work received a critical boost from a Holocaust survivor, a distinguished French Jewish scholar already an old man by the time the Germans surrendered. Named Jules Isaac, he holds an obscure but important status in these efforts. Within two years of the Nazis' surrender, he met in Switzerland with dozens of Protestants and Catholics who drew on his wartime research to create a list of ten points for Christians worldwide. They began with a single, declarative statement: "Remember, one God speaks to us all through the Old and New Testaments." That simple statement was and remains an enormous challenge in the face of the last twenty centuries. God speaks to us *all*? If that's the case, then it must mean that somehow people in two separate faith groups not only have to read a text true to what they believe, but also be aware—respectfully aware—that the other group reads the same words differently, yet also hears God speaking authentically to them.

This is not an academic issue, because people's lives depend on it—certainly from the Jewish experience. For the better part of two thousand years, an essential Christian assumption is that God sent Jesus Christ—who lived and taught among men and women, died on the cross, and was then resurrected—as God's new covenant, a replacement for the older one with the Jews, forged at Mount Sinai during their Exodus from Egypt. That understanding of the Christian message meant Judaism no longer existed as a valid faith, which left Jews devoid of a living relationship with God. Or as John Chrysostom, an eloquent and creative fourth-century theologian, once described it: The Jews were branches grown from a "holy root," but they were severed, cut off—and gentiles grafted on in their place. Chrysostom was anything but a marginal preacher. He was one of the great minds of the early church and his outstanding speaking abilities earned him the Greek name by which he came to be called: "golden mouth." His work demonstrates a part of the problem that Jews and Christians face: Vitally important figures within Christianity have among their work texts that attack Judaism.

One need not roam the writings of the church fathers to discover the idea to which Chrysostom gave voice. In medieval Europe, it could be carved right into the fronts of cathedrals and painted on church walls for an illiterate population. There it remains, post-Holocaust. Sister Audrey Doetzel, a Roman Catholic nun with a doctoral degree from the University of Toronto, has seen such depictions on her travels in western Europe. On the front of such Christian landmarks as the cathedral in Strasbourg, she has seen a pair of female statues, designed to represent opposites of each other theologically. One represents Christianity, standing tall; the other Judaism, collapsing. "The theology is inscribed in stone," she said to me over lunch one day. Doetzel, who has long taught Catholic groups about the Holocaust, described an elaborate wall painting she had seen in a church in Alsace-Lorraine in eastern France. Once again, Christianity stood triumphant, while the figure representing Judaism sat astride a donkey, a medieval symbol of ignorance. At the donkey's feet lay an open grave, a skeleton inside. The symbolism seemed obvious, she said: "Dead Judaism." For centuries, these messages stood largely unchallenged. But revelation of the Nazis' genocide against the Jews, fully exposed to light from 1945 onward, gradually provoked among leading Christians a sweeping reassessment of what their churches ought to teach about Jews and Judaism. "Conversion is what happened to the church with the Holocaust," said Doetzel, administrative and programming director at the Center for Christian-Jewish Learning at Boston College. Still, it's important to state plainly here that within the vast and varied landscape of global Christianity, this idea is not universally shared. A lot of people have not converted, to borrow Doetzel's word. There is no shortage of churches that are silent on the subject of Jewish-Christian relations, and many millions of Christians know little, if anything at all, about the half century of meetings, discussions, and books that have focused on this topic. Unsurprisingly, too, there are Christians who continue to emphasize efforts to convert Jews—a work that they often describe as being done out of "love" for God's once-chosen people. In the millennial year 2000, I came upon a large church in Manhattan sponsoring a conference focusing on Jews being in need of evangelization. Nevertheless, the official change in Christian attitudes toward Jews and Judaism is sufficiently widespread that it registers as a major shift within contemporary Christianity. It has not lacked for symbols, as when John Paul hosted a memorial concert within the Vatican in 1994 for victims of the Holocaust.

Among Jews, the fact of the Holocaust lent great momentum to the creation of a modern state of Israel, as well as to its ongoing support. Among many Christians, the Nazi genocide prompted a new approach to what they ought to teach about the faith's origins within Judaism and its relationship to the Jewish people. The two trends have key symbolic dates within a year of each other. In Israel's case, it is the state's independence in May 1948. For Christians, the vital event occurred ten months earlier on July 30, 1947. On that day, seventy men and women gathered in Seelisberg, a village in Switzerland, with Jules Isaac, the Holocaust survivor. In the days that followed, the group drafted a ten-point declaration, the central element of which warned Christians never again to describe Jews as rejected by God.

In building on this message more than a half century later, the Institute for Christian & Jewish Studies played a creative role, one that deliberately tried to involve the public. Catalano, as a Roman Catholic theologian, and her two colleagues—one Protestant, the other Jewish—took the message into churches and synagogues, colleges and high schools. They got people to look together at biblical passages and talk to one another about what they might mean from two different perspectives, Jewish and Christian. It sounded straightforward enough. But it was dauntingly ambitious precisely because it was meant to be a conversation, a respectful and educational exchange of views—not a debate with a winner and a loser. In that sense, the work was highly unusual, cutting radically against cultural norms. "What we are most fundamentally about," Catalano said to me, "is the work of peace. Because what we are trying to say is, can one admit differences without being adversarial? Now, that's a radical thing in the world—that you're not me, and I'm not you, but that doesn't mean a threat. That means difference."

It also means an invitation to a deep, ongoing exchange that can be returned to again and again and on which a new relationship might be founded. Implicit in the conversation is the question, what does it mean to be different *together*? The United States enshrines freedom of conscience as a basic, individual liberty. That individuals have taken advantage of that provision, and continue to do so, has made it a collective fact. To explore that—to "admit differences without being adversarial," in Catalano's words—is to be open to the idea of democratic collaboration. And that in itself represents a high degree of civic engagement. But it is an entirely appropriate—I would say necessary—level of commitment to sustain self-government among people for whom pluralism (religious, ethnic, racial) is an inescapable element of life. It is a subject on which the philosopher Charles Taylor has written eloquently and that he has defined as an activity that transcends the enlightened self-interest of any one individual or group. Instead, it is a foundation for civil society. Taylor likens his idea of mutual participation to a conversation. People are not jockeying for advantage, but creating a social good in which everyone shares. "A conversation," he writes, "is not the coordination of actions of different individuals, but a common action in this strong, irreducible sense; it is *our* action. It is of a kind with—to take a more obvious example—the dance of a group or a couple, or the action of two men sawing a log. Opening a conversation is inaugurating a common action." What's more, conversation creates a bond that exceeds in quality the contractual state of people agreeing to work together in a free society. "On a deeper level, those I talk to about the things that matter to me are my intimates. Intimacy is an essentially dialogical phenomenon: It is a matter of what we share, of what's for us. We could never describe what it is to be on an intimate footing with someone in terms of monological states."

The idea that there might be something vital for Jews and for Christians alike in cooperation and dialogue is by no means unique—or original—to the institute in Baltimore. Long before the institute's founding in 1987, major Jewish organizations like the Anti-Defamation League and the American Jewish Committee brought vital work to the task, asking Christian churches to scrub anti-Jewish material from their religious education curricula—requests that met with positive results. In addition, the Vatican, the U.S. bishops, and major Protestant organizations hired staff and established departments to foster meaningful communication with Jews. In Washington, D.C., for example, the American bishops established a director for Catholic-Jewish relations. I had come to know of the Baltimore institute in 1995, when as a reporter I was invited to participate in a panel it arranged, with funding from a small state humanities grant, that focused on the news media and interreligious relations. But I had lost touch with the organization for several years, until it sponsored four Jewish scholars who published a document assessing how Jews might regard Christians and Christianity in light of the ongoing work to improve relations between the two faiths.

I had another reason for coming to Baltimore, one tied to Maryland's distinctive past. Nearly two centuries ago, a legal battle erupted among the state's politicians that, in some of the debates, foreshadowed the discussions among Christians that would follow the Holocaust. In Maryland then, the issue was whether to grant Jews political rights. Very few Jews lived in the state, but those who did found that for half a century after the signing of the Declaration of Independence, they were denied the right to hold either civil or military office. Only Marylanders who swore to a belief in Jesus Christ could have that privilege. An immigrant, a Scottish Presbyterian named Thomas Kennedy, found that idea outlandish— un-American as he understood the principles of his new country. Elected to the legislature, he fought the ban for eight years, just long enough to win. Kennedy, from his portrait, wasn't much to look at, a man with unkempt hair and a receding chin. But he could be eloquent. After winning his first election to the legislature, he introduced what came to be derisively known as "Kennedy's Jew Bill," by declaring, "We all know and fear the force of our *political* prejudices, but our *religious* prejudices are still more strong, still more dear; they cling to us through life, and scarcely leave us on the bed of death; and it is not the prejudice of a generation, of an age or of a century, that we have to encounter—No, it is the prejudice which has passed from father to son, for almost 1,800 years." He would go on to make a theological argument for his claims as well.

The institute took shape long afterward, founded by a group of local Christians and Jews. The primary purpose then lay in trying to "de-fang Christian anti-Semitism," said the Reverend Christopher M. Leighton, its executive director. That meant directly challenging what for many would be ingrained, even unconsciously held beliefs about Judaism, such as the enduring idea of Jews as bound to a legalistic tradition governed by a wrathful God. Leighton, as I came to know him, had a knack for appearing to speak informally while he was actually laying out complicated ideas. A member of the Presbyterian Church (USA), he held a master's of divinity degree from his denomination's best-known seminary, at

Princeton, and a doctorate from Columbia University Teachers College. But his résumé was more interesting than that (and certainly relevant to his position); he'd gone on to study at Baltimore Hebrew College, Jewish Theological Seminary in New York, and at Yad Vashem, the Holocaust memorial in Jerusalem. He had also helped edit a book-length study guide to the journalist Bill Moyers's public television series on the Book of Genesis. I heard him use the "de-fanging" expression in a study session the institute held one spring weekend before a group of forty priests, ministers, and rabbis who had been invited to participate. But if this were its only purpose, the institute could almost have done without Jews participating, except perhaps as observers. Its bedrock goal was to encourage conversation so that individuals in both faiths could discover each other's religious thinking. Thus, it made sense that weekend that half those present were Jewish and that the institute had a Jewish staff member—at the time I visited, Rabbi Charles Arian.

Affiliated with Judaism's Conservative movement, Arian served a pulpit in York, Pennsylvania, before coming to Baltimore in 2001. While in Pennsylvania, he and members of his congregation had linked up with a local Presbyterian church to spend several weeks discussing the biblical Book of Genesis. In so doing, they used Leighton's text (this happened long before Arian thought about joining the institute). That particular encounter, congregation to congregation, ended up fostering a counterintuitive result. "The Jewish participants had their Jewish identity strengthened," Arian said. You don't know, he said, that that's going to happen until you sit down to read a familiar text with someone who reads the same passages differently. I heard him elaborate on this to a mixed group of clergy. "People tend to think this is diplomacy, that one has to convince the other, or we'll meet in the middle, or the Christians have to give up one person of the Trinity," he said. No, he wouldn't walk away unchanged from such an encounter, he said. "But that doesn't mean I'm going to give up who I am." I thought that a neat way to summarize what I heard many people say about interreligious dialogue. For perhaps the first time, you have to think about what it is you yourself believe, because you've got to explain it to someone who knows little or nothing about it; at the same time, you listen to that person, asking basic questions. You get in touch with your spiritual heritage, your religious foundation. In the process, two identities take form, each gaining insights from the other.

Arian grew up in a household more culturally Jewish than religiously observant, as the son of a father who devoutly believed that religion itself was trouble. Didn't it always lead to violence and war? He found Christianity inscrutable, baffled that serious people could believe what it taught about Jesus as the Messiah. That didn't stop Charles Arian from applying to Georgetown University, a Jesuit-run institution, for his undergraduate study. He emerged with an abiding love of Big East basketball and a commitment to study Judaism in seminary. Georgetown's Jesuits had been very respectful of Arian's Jewish identity. "I went to Georgetown to become a lawyer or a journalist and I came out headed to rabbinical school." After ordination, he took an unusual sabbatical, spending several months as a guest of Trappist monks in northern California. He taught them an introductory course in Jewish studies, in return for which the monks allowed him a cabin, a telephone, and a personal computer. They did not pray for his conversion, but he experienced some uncomfortable moments. When he attended their Good Friday and Easter services, he became aware that the way in which they were reading the biblical text—it was John's Gospel—the Jews appeared to be clearly removed from God's favor. Arian wasn't alone in getting that message. With a rabbi in their midst, the monks suddenly saw something new in the text, freighted with a resonance they had not noticed previously. "Later," Arian recalled, "a number of the Trappists said to me, 'You know, as I was listening to those texts, I was thinking to myself, how must Rabbi Charles be hearing this?' "

When I reminded him of this experience much later, Arian wanted to clarify a lesson he had drawn from it. He had no objection to Christians reading the Old Testament—the Hebrew Bible—as foretelling the coming of Jesus. That, after all, was the Christian tradition. But he added, "Don't at the same time write me out of the texts altogether." In other words, he wanted Christians to understand that the stories they read foreshadowing Jesus also composed the complete, living Bible to Jews. What's more, Jesus himself was Jewish, as was Paul; those New Testament texts that speak negatively about "the Jews" were actually written by Jews as the larger community was slowly, bitterly dividing over its understanding of Jesus. Arian recalled that it was a Trappist, the monk Thomas Merton—the single most famous American in the order—who recognized and wrote about the Christian tendency to read the Bible as if Judaism was a thing of the past. "Merton has written some really good stuff on this. He said, what Christians have historically done is empty the scriptures of their Jewish context."

"That's what supercessionism is," Arian said. "It writes the Jews out of their own story." The word is inescapably awkward. But it gets to the heart of what half a century of work in Christian-Jewish relations has been directed against. If Christians and Jews read the same text, as Arian said, it "can have multiple meanings at the same time—it's not one or the other." What the word *supercessionism* itself lacks in felicity, it possesses in precision. To supersede means to replace someone or something in power, to strip away its authority and render it ineffective. When a consumer product is superseded, it becomes obsolete, at best a museum piece. When the same process happens to political systems—say, in the fall of monarchies or dictatorships—it is often amid violence. But if the object being superseded is bigger than a government, and perhaps instead is an entire religious faith whose adherents cross national boundaries, what then? What happens once their identity is pronounced dead by another group that lays claim to it?

To Catalano, doing battle with supercessionism meant persuading Christians to approach their texts anew—certainly not by challenging Jesus' divinity or his place as Christian messiah, but by placing him and his teachings in historical context, as a man born and raised a Jew, living and teaching among Jews. "Getting the Gospel right," she called it. To describe this as an ambitious goal would be an understatement. It seemed even more so in light of the institute's size and appearance. In a gradually gentrifying neighborhood of brick row houses several streets north of Inner Harbor, the institute kept a low profile. Anyone looking for corporate-style offices or an ivy-covered townhouse with a shiny brass nameplate—appearances that would suggest the self-conscious power of a Washington think tank or an outlying center of a university campus—would be disappointed. The institute, when I visited, occupied the topmost floor of a former parson's home adjacent to a Presbyterian church. A railroad magnate's widow had paid for building the three-story, gray stone building a few years after the Civil War. Inside the aging suite of offices the institute occupied, a visitor had the overwhelming sense of being in a place where words matter. It had the feel of a well-used library, what one might find within a seminary. It contained thousands of books—on history, theology, biblical commentary—shelved in room-length rows, piled in precarious stacks on the floor, even shoved into bookcases lining the narrow corridor to the bathroom.

In its mission, the institute stands within a growing trend. Over the past two decades, two dozen or so organizations have been founded with a broadly similar purpose, focusing on study and learning through thoughtful interaction between Christians and Jews. At St. Leo University, north of Tampa, one can find the Center for Catholic-Jewish Studies. Muhlenberg College in Allentown, Pennsylvania, is home to the Institute for Jewish-Christian Understanding. Seton Hall University, in Orange, New Jersey, has its Graduate Department of Jewish-Christian Studies. By 2002, there were enough such places to form an association, affiliated with the Center for Christian-Jewish Learning at Boston College. Even so, they exist within a larger framework. From the 1970s onward, major Christian churches had been drafting and publishing detailed statements calling their members to a more respectful relationship with Jews and Judaism. "Episcopal conferences and diocesan agencies, general assemblies and conferences, synods and councils—have produced reams of documents, many now available on the internet," writes the theologian Mary C. Boys. Written in plain terms for laypeople, not professional theologians, these statements often express the anguish of Christian leaders recognizing that a historic anti-Judaism contributed to creating the grounds for lethal anti-Semitism. In 1994, the five-million-member Evangelical Lutheran Church in America adopted a statement that includes this sentence:"Grieving the complicity of our own tradition within this history of hatred ... we express our urgent desire to live out our faith in Jesus Christ with love and respect for the Jewish people." Episcopalians, Methodists, Presbyterians, Congregationalists, and at least one Baptist group have written their own statements. The Alliance of Baptists, a small organization some of whose members broke away from the larger and much more conservative Southern Baptist Convention, drafted their statement in March 1995, with a reference to the Nazi extermination camps liberated by Allied soldiers fifty years previously. "The madness, the hatred, the dehumanizing attitudes that led to the events collectively known as the Holocaust did not occur overnight or within the span of a few years, but were the culmination of centuries of Christian teaching and church-sanctioned action directed against the Jews simply because they were Jews."

As eloquent as some of these declarations are, few have achieved the impact of those written by Roman Catholic authorities, a function of their church's size—hundreds of millions of people worldwide—and its hierarchical nature, which lends immense weight to any official statement. The Catholic bishops in Germany in 1995 and their French counterparts two years later issued documents lamenting that the church in their nations did very little to help Jews during the Holocaust. The French prelates titled their statement "A Declaration of Repentance." Both documents fit within a larger pattern, an official response to Jews and Judaism unimaginable four decades earlier. In 1994, the Vatican recognized the state of Israel, a decision with immense significance for Jews worldwide. Several years later, a group of Catholic scholars acting as delegates for a bishops' committee issued another document stating that Catholics did not target Jews for conversion. Titled "Reflections on Covenant and Mission," it essentially acknowledges Judaism as a living faith, in which Jews, like Christians, "are called by God to prepare the world for God's Kingdom." Although it says that "individual converts," Jews and others, will always be welcomed into the Catholic fold, the church is no longer trying to absorb entirely the Jewish people. For one thing, it says, Judaism is unique among non-Christian faiths, because God's covenant with Israel is contained in Scripture. Not only that, the document states, but that agreement endures: "Both the church and the Jewish people abide in covenant with God." The document is unofficial; the bishops as a body voted neither for nor against it. It does not explicitly say that through their relationship with God Jews actually receive salvation, as Christians understand that concept. Instead, it is ambiguous. But in that ambiguity, some people have found space to raise that possibility. And a number of Catholics have advanced the question, if the divine covenant with the Jews was never abrogated, then aren't Jews assured of God's grace? To be sure, this is a Christian question, one well outside a Jewish theological framework, but the way in which it is answered affects Jews as a minority within a larger Christian population.

Among Catholics, people intimately concerned with Jewish-Christian relations take the upbeat view that the various declarations and statements have laid the foundation for permanent realignment, such that the post-Seelisberg era is one profoundly and lastingly different from what prevailed in the previous nineteen centuries. In this view, the momentum that has built up is such that it is best expressed in an old cliché: You can't put the toothpaste back in the tube. When I went to visit him in Washington, D.C., at the offices of the United States Conference of Catholic Bishops, Eugene Fisher, associate director of the Secretariat for Ecumenical and Interreligious Affairs, described the work as permanent in its impact. "This could be slowed down and stopped for a year," he said. "A new pope, let's go on to other things—but it's too embedded an idea to be turned around." As it happened, Fisher seemed to speak prophetically. In his first trip abroad, to Germany, Benedict XVI repeated what many consider to have been John Paul II's most moving act of showing respect to Jews, when he visited Rome's synagogue in 1986. Benedict, himself a German who had been a (deeply reluctant) member of the Hitler Youth, visited the synagogue in Cologne, which had been rebuilt in the 1950s after the Nazis had destroyed it. He called on Christians and Jews to show each other mutual respect.

The value of such an event is that it calls attention to itself and, by extension, to the positive developments between Christians and Jews. The world's press had joined Benedict on his pilgrimage, just as they regularly covered John Paul. The popes' symbolic gestures provided visual symbols and sound bites that served as signposts to a much deeper trend. Still, as experts who specialize in this field point out, the important documents on Christian-Jewish relations remain pretty much the province of those who move in official circles, even if their spirit can occasionally be discerned at pew level, courtesy of informed priests and ministers. Again, the Catholics have an advantage, in that events associated with their hierarchy frequently attract news coverage. In 2002, *The Boston Globe* reported on "Covenant and Mission," the document that said that the church was not working to convert the Jewish people. The statement received an even higher public profile when it drew criticism by theological conservatives within and outside the church. That in itself was hardly unusual. Efforts by groups of Christians to establish a new relationship with Jews, based on mutual respect and eschewing efforts at conversion, have triggered other backlashes. A year after the Alliance of Baptists spoke out, their statement was rebutted by a resolution from a much larger organization, the sixteen-million-member Southern Baptist Convention, which called for renewed efforts to convert Jews. In the process, the denomination even went so far as to appoint a missionary for the task. Later, one Southern Baptist agency published a booklet encouraging members to pray, on the eve of the High Holidays, for Jews' conversion. Not surprisingly, Jewish organizations, the Anti-Defamation League prominent among them, expressed outrage. What further complicates this situation—Christians divided among themselves on how to relate to Jews—is the problem that some organizations that have sought to promote reconciliation between the two faiths have also espoused a low view of the Judaism out of which Jesus emerged. As the New Testament scholar Amy-Jill Levine has written, Jesus is sometimes portrayed by progressive Christians as a liberator—of the poor, of women, of cultural outcasts—an image sharpened by the idea of first-century Judaism as oppressive, rigidly patriarchal, and uncharitable. This shows the challenge an organization like the Institute for Christian & Jewish Studies faces. In groups ranging from a couple dozen to well over one hundred people, Catalano, Leighton, and Arian brought Christians and Jews together with seeming comfort in churches and synagogues where they directed them into friendly but intellectually challenging discussions of biblical texts.

One spring evening, I met one of these groups at a small synagogue, newly built, on a commercial strip in one of Baltimore's northern neighborhoods. Several round tables, encircled by folding chairs, had been set up in a capacious meeting room. By 7 P.M., about twenty-five people had gathered, an interracial audience about evenly divided between men and women. One of the texts to be discussed that evening describes what for Christians is one of the most famous incidents in Jesus' ministry. As told in John's Gospel, Jesus has gone to the Temple in Jerusalem, where Jewish officials bring him a woman caught in an act of adultery. They note that the penalty laid down in the biblical book of Leviticus calls for stoning adulterers to death. They ask Jesus his opinion in order to entrap him into an explicit rejection of legal tradition. Instead, he turns the tables, saying, "Let he who is without sin cast the first stone." The crowd melts away and Jesus is left with the woman, whom he tells to go "and sin no more."

This evening, people were asked to read the text, printed on sheets handed out and passed around to them, and then come up with words to describe the Jewish authorities and Jesus. Jews and Christians reacted much the same way: The authorities had been "vindictive," they had an "agenda"; by contrast, Jesus showed patience, compassion, forgiveness. Given how the text is written, their responses shouldn't have been surprising. The responses gave Catalano an opening to talk about very early Christian history. When reading how John's Gospel describes Jewish authorities, one must keep the period's history in mind, she said. John's Gospel, which comes fourth in the New Testament sequence, was also the last to be written in the view of most scholars, after Matthew, Mark, and Luke. And in that particular period, the closing decades of the first century, tensions were rapidly escalating among people who followed Jesus but still identified themselves as Jews and other Jews who rejected claims that Jesus was the Messiah. The rift had long since passed civility: Synagogues had lost patience with people who belonged to the Jesus movement. Amidst this breakdown in community, why should it be surprising that John portrays Jewish authorities as unfriendly to Jesus? But Catalano's lesson went further. Jesus' moving act of showing mercy to the accused woman wasn't

itself out of keeping with religious practice of that time. Other rabbis would not have demanded enforcement of Leviticus's code for
stoning an adulteress. "No one in those days would say, 'Stone her!' "
Catalano said. I suspected that few Christians had ever heard the
famous story presented that way in a sermon. But would it have
shaken anyone's faith in Jesus' divinity or even his mercy to hear
that he worked more closely within his own tradition in this instance than John states?

Before the evening began, I had spoken briefly with one of the
people present, Maggi Gaines, who once sat on the institute's board.
Afterward, I asked her if she thought sessions like this made a difference in helping Jews and Christians better understand one another's
religious traditions. There were, after all, more than six hundred
thousand people living in Baltimore. "Why don't we have more of
them here tonight?" she asked. But then she smiled and added that
education across religious lines depended on the quality of the encounter, rather than on the number of people present.

I had been curious about why someone like Rosann Catalano
had decided she needed to focus on this particular work, rather than
teach theology in a seminary, where she had begun her career. She
had, after all, grown up in an environment where similarity was
pretty much the rule. Her parents were of Sicilian background—her
mother an immigrant, her father the son of immigrants—who lived
in a town north of Boston. When they had guests over, they invited
people of similar background. "It wasn't like we had a lot of people
in the house. We had aunts and uncles and cousins and they were all
Sicilians and they were all white." Her father worked as a mechanic,
a quiet man who had never reached third grade. Her mother, a lively,
voluble woman, had gone a bit further in grade school. Despite the
homogeneity around her, her parents had communicated to her that
they held a broader view of the world than what their immediate
surroundings suggested. How did she know it? "Somehow very

early on, I knew something—now I couldn't express it this way—about a basic dignity and equality," Catalano said. It boiled down to this: Differences were not necessarily negative. "And if I play pop psychology with myself, it's because my mother had this incredible love for life. I suppose just this notion—that you would not respect someone, because they weren't like you—was an abhorrent one." That supplied a foundation. How she actually got involved in trying to change Christian attitudes toward Jews and Judaism came much later, the indirect result of an invitation casually extended. By then, she was finishing her dissertation and teaching theology part time at a Catholic seminary in Baltimore. One day in 1984, the seminary's head, its rector, called her into his office to ask if she might be interested in a small fellowship. An anonymous donor had given the seminary a grant that would cover the expenses of a faculty member who might like to attend a national conference on Christian-Jewish relations in St. Louis. The rector had already polled the full-time faculty. None wanted to go, he said. Did she?

Catalano recalled thinking, "My goodness, four days on Jewish-Christian relations? I wonder what that will be about?" Nonetheless, she took up the offer. How often did such opportunities come round to part-time, junior faculty? Years later, she vividly remembered two responses she had to the conference. On one hand, she felt astonished by the crowd she encountered: "I was stunned that there were maybe two thousand people there." The audience ranged from high school teachers to scholars at elite universities and seminaries. But far more crucial was what she learned about Christian anti-Judaism. "I know I'm Sicilian and prone to overstatement and embellishment, but I cannot tell you what it was like to sit in a room and hear about the anti-Semitic teaching that was embedded in church life and got into preaching and hymns and was part of the air that the church in Europe breathed." Even two decades later, she could still recall the sick feeling she got in the pit of her stomach. To be confronted with this information, she said, did not simply alter the course of what her intellectual study would be. It was, she said, "a theological and spiritual turning point."

When it comes to Christian anti-Judaism, you do not have to reach back very far in time to come up with examples that seem startling these days, such are the changes that have happened in only four decades. Even after the Holocaust, a Catholic could still hear the Jews described in severe theological terms in a prayer within the Good Friday liturgy. "Let us pray also for the perfidious Jews," the prayer stated. "That our God and Lord will remove the veil from their hearts so that they, too, may acknowledge our Lord, Jesus Christ. Almighty, Eternal God, who does not withhold thy mercy, even from Jewish perfidy, heed the prayer we offer for the blindness of that people that they may acknowledge the light of thy truth which is Christ, and be delivered from their darkness." In 1949, Pope Pius XII altered the prayer slightly in translation from the Latin in liturgical books by replacing the word "perfidious" with "unbelieving," a change that might still suggest that Jews remained spiritually empty, void. But of course the problem extended well beyond an annual liturgy. Parochial school religion textbooks used "the Jews" as a synonym for Jesus' enemies. Passion plays, public performances that recounted the biblical stories of Christ's death and resurrection, typically cast Jews as God's murderers, a people guilty of deicide, who call down a lasting persecution on themselves when the play's actors repeat the line uttered by the crowd in John's Gospel: "His blood be upon us and our children." Furthermore, the picture of Jews as a people deficient of God's love extended well beyond the Catholic church. After all, the leading figure of the Protestant Reformation, Martin Luther, had followed his break with Rome with a steadily darkening appraisal of the Jews' place in the world. Some of his statements are colored by such a venom that they can hardly be read today without feeling such language helped lower the barriers against the most lethal forms of anti-Semitism. *Concerning the Jews and Their Lies* is the title of a tract he wrote in 1543; he described Jews as rejected by God, no longer his people. It was partly for this that the Evangelical Lutheran Church in America apologized in 1994.

Some of the greatest figures in Christian history have said some terrible things about the Jews. Yet the overall historical picture of Jewish-Christian relations is more complicated than those examples imply. As Mary Boys writes, the past two millennia contain long stretches of tolerance by Christians of Jews, as well as work by individuals in church and civil government to prevent outright persecution of Jews. What's more, she points out that anti-Jewish persecution had other bases than the purely religious—it arose from political issues, broad economic problems, and societal change. Even then, the record of relations between Christians and Jews is highlighted by some instances of fearless generosity, as in those individual cases of gentiles who rescued their Jewish neighbors from the Nazis by hiding them or helping them cross a border. At Yad Vashem, the Israeli monument to the Holocaust, they are honored as "righteous gentiles." Still, the overall record of Christians toward Jews and Judaism is discouraging. The Reverend Rowan Williams, Archbishop of Canterbury, has written that Christians "have conscripted Jews into their version of reality and forced them into a role that has nothing to do with how Jews understand their own past or their current experience."

After that first day in St. Louis, Catalano went back to her hotel room feeling terribly distressed—not only about what she had heard, but also that she felt she was hearing it for the very first time. "How could I not know this?" she wondered. "I have a master's degree and I'm four and a half years into my doctoral thesis and I had no hint of this." Educated as she was, she said, she felt like a deeply naïve adult. "I went to dinner that night and I was like a two-year-old, weeping into my soup." But she wasn't alone at that meal. Her dinner companions included others attending the event from Baltimore. They struck up a conversation about how they ought to organize the next meeting of the conference in their city. A plan was set forth, and Catalano found herself on the organizing committee, which laid the groundwork for the conference two years later. Momentum carried over; the meeting's organizers declared a need to continue their work. Eventually, they decided to launch the institute itself. As its work (and funding) expanded, Catalano joined the staff in 1992. In her work there, she maintained a personal credo, which she mentioned on more than one occasion when we talked about what she did. "If the gospel truly is the word of God, it can withstand the hardest questions I can ask it and the toughest challenges I can throw at it. And if it can't, it's not worth my devotion."

In taking this approach to the issues within Jewish–Christian relations, Catalano stood in a line that historically, at least, is still very short, encompassing as it does barely half a century of work. But her phrase about asking the "hardest questions" is an important one, as it recalls a remarkable project that lies very close to the root of this work—by now a global venture, involving Catholics, Protestants, and Orthodox Christians, as well as Jewish partners in the United States, Europe, and Israel. Coincidentally, that project began at roughly the same time that the German government launched the final phase of its genocide against Europe's Jews, following the Wannsee Conference in January 1942. That same year, an elderly French Jew began a searching examination of the Gospels, intended to persuade Christians to renounce their contempt for Jews and Judaism, and to do so out of gratitude for their own faith. Christianity owed its origins to Judaism, he said. "For what Christians received above all from Jews is faith in God, in God One and Eternal, the God of Abraham, Isaac and Jacob. What more miraculous gift could there be!"

The writer was Jules Isaac, a French historian and well-known educator who would have a substantial impact on improving relations between Christians and Jews. But at the very time that he embarked on the task of attempting to alter nearly twenty centuries of Christian attitudes toward Jews and Judaism, he was living increasingly on the cliff edge of mortal danger. Prior to World War II, Isaac was known as coauthor of a series of textbooks used in French secondary schools; he also held a high government position as supervisor for high school education. But after the German armies defeated France in June 1940, his family's safety became imperiled. The Isaacs moved often, but the Gestapo finally caught up with the family. One day in 1943, they came looking for Isaac, found him momentarily away, and arrested his wife. The distraught husband turned himself in to the local police, saying he would not be separated from her. But it was the end of the day and the local authorities, with a Gallic sense of priorities, told him they were closed for the day, to go home, and come back in the morning. Friends dissuaded him from that course, and instead pointed him toward the French Resistance, which in turn found him a safe house, under the care of two young Catholics, Germaine and Jacques Bouquet.

The Bouquets hid Isaac in a farmhouse in the Berry region of central France. During the days, Isaac and Germaine Bouquet took long treks across the surrounding fields. "When spring came the two of us used to go for long walks in the countryside—he was a tireless walker," Bouquet would remember, her words recounted by scholars Michael Phayer and Eva Fleishner, who have chronicled wartime Catholic rescuers of Jews. As she and Isaac walked, they talked. "Always he would come back to the subject that preoccupied him more than any other: Christian teaching about Judaism." Bouquet, aided by a sympathetic priest, began borrowing books on Christian history and theology from local libraries, surreptitiously passing them on to Isaac, who studied and wrote. His accomplice, as Isaac would discover, was unusual among French Catholics. Her parents were atheists who had raised their daughter in public schools. She had converted in her adolescence as an act of rebellion. Her religious instructor was a disciple of Jacques Maritain, a theologian ardent in his rejection of anti-Semitism. Isaac completed his manuscript in 1946. The book, he said, was addressed to readers' "consciences and heart." It was published the next year under the title *Jesus and Israel*. Its effect lies in the driving force with which it expounds a single idea: A close reading of Christianity's origins do not support the anti-Jewish message embedded for so long in Christian teaching. Thus, Christians should recognize that antipathy toward Jews and Judaism is an insult to God; they should replace it with respect. As a Jew, he called Christians to a renewal and purification of their own faith and to a thorough examination of their conscience. "Such is the major lesson that emerges from meditation on Auschwitz, which I cannot release myself from, which no man of heart could abstain from," he wrote in his conclusion. "The glow of the Auschwitz crematorium is the beacon that lights, that guides all my thoughts."

But Isaac's book is remarkable in another way, too. We can't forget how a project begun by an outcast, living on the knife edge of enormous personal peril, would come to have such influence on people of another faith. At its beginning, everything hung on a conversational relationship between Isaac and Bouquet, two dissimilar people unlikely to have met under other circumstances but those imposed by the Nazi cataclysm. Against this background, it is foolish to discount ongoing efforts at Christian-Jewish reconciliation—or, indeed, at fostering other, positive relations across religious boundaries. Sure, they may draw limited crowds. But who knows what individuals might be there—and what they might then do with what they learn?

I took a copy of Isaac's book with me when I went to Baltimore, because I wanted to hear what Rosann Catalano might say about the author. In so doing, I felt as if I were completing a circle. It had been at a conference organized by the institute that I had heard someone mention the meeting of Christians and Jews in the Swiss village of Seelisberg shortly after World War II. And that was what had led me to Isaac, whose name I had not previously heard. In July 1947, Isaac traveled to Seelisberg to meet with more than five dozen Christians from Europe, the United States, and Australia, under the authority of a new, global organization, the International Council of Christians and Jews. *Jesus and Israel* contained eighteen recommendations that Isaac had formulated to combat Christian anti-Judaism. Over the course of a week, the men and women in Seelisberg drew on these recommendations in composing a declaration addressed to the world's churches, demanding they forge a new relationship with Jews. Their statement contained ten points. Four declared that Christians must remember certain basic facts about Jesus—that, for example, he and his followers, as well as the church's first martyrs, were Jews themselves. Christians must remember, too, that their faith's "fundamental commandment," to love God and one's neighbor binds everyone "without any exception." The other six points dealt with what Christians must henceforth avoid—among them, disparaging Judaism to lift up Christianity, using the word "Jews" as synonymous with Christ's enemies, and presenting Jesus' Passion "in such a way as to bring the odium of the killing of Jesus upon Jews alone."

But the Seelisberg declaration didn't end there. The council that sponsored the meeting added some "practical suggestions" to its report, which boiled down to this: From now on, make sure that nothing in religious instruction, especially directed at children, conflicts with these points. The report's authors closed this section with a brief passage from the New Testament, a quotation from the Apostle Paul's letter to the Romans, chapter 11, verses 28–29, in which he says that Jews "are beloved for the fathers' sake. For the gifts and calling of God are without repentance."

Reading a copy of the report, more than a half century afterward, can impart an eerie feeling. For one, its authors have no name for the Nazi genocide; the term "Holocaust" would not come into general use for several more years. But even more startling, they say that they do not necessarily believe it is over. After all, the report states, the Seelisberg meeting was called not just to work against anti-Jewish bigotry, but also "to study the present extent of the evil of anti-Semitism and the contributory factors to its persistence and growth in post-war Europe." *Persistence and growth?* Only twelve months earlier—on July 4, 1946—residents and soldiers in the Polish village of Kielce had massacred more than forty Jews, many of them survivors of Nazi extermination camps, who had returned and taken up shelter in a building in the village's center. The killing began after two men and a boy had spread rumors related to the old anti-Semitic blood libel, that Kielce's Jews were killing gentile children. Other pogroms broke out, too, in the war's aftermath; hundreds of Jews lost their lives. But the attack in Kielce deeply frightened Europe's Jews. The Seelisberg group saw their work as urgent.

Isaac had at least two more ecclesiastically high-level conversations as a result of his book. The first took place in 1949, with Pope Pius XII, who had been enthroned a decade earlier. For his role as wartime pope, Pius remains an elusive and controversial figure. He condemned violence against peoples, but he did not speak out publicly against the Holocaust. For that omission, in the face of the twentieth century's greatest crime, he has been a subject of mounting criticism, especially since the production in February 1963 of Rolf Hochhuth's accusatory play, *The Deputy*, which portrayed the pope as more interested in Germany's role as an aggressive counterweight to Russian Communism. Nonetheless, Isaac would report his meeting with Pius XII as having been cordial. It did lead to the change in the Good Friday prayer. Still, his conversation a decade later with Pius's successor, Pope John XXIII, helped produce a much more historically significant outcome. By then, the French historian was eighty-four, older still than his elderly host. Pope John, elected in 1958, had served during much of World War II as the Vatican's ambassador to Turkey, during which time he had is-

sued thousands of baptismal certificates to Hungarian Jews, allowing them safe passage out of their nation ahead of Nazi plans to ship
them to the death camps.

"Isaac was absolutely pivotal in the thinking of John XXIII,"
Catalano said. "When they met, John XXIII said, 'What can I do?'"
she continued. "And what does Isaac say to him? 'Stop teaching
contempt.'" Isaac had identified, in a single phrase, the issues that
the Seelisberg conference had worked to address. As long as Christians taught that Judaism was something other than a living faith
and, worse, that Jews were responsible for the death of the Christian
messiah, then the relationship between Christians and Jews would
be so dangerously out of balance as to open Jews to the possibility
of enormous violence. After their conversation, John dispatched
Isaac on a personal errand within the Vatican. The pope sent his
guest to speak to Cardinal Augustin Bea, to tell him that the church's
relationship with Jews must be a subject taken up by the church-
wide council, the planning for which was already in the works, at
the pope's request.

That gathering was the Second Vatican Council, which opened
in 1962 and would include more than twenty-six hundred bishops.
It ran for three years. Just before it closed, the assembled prelates
produced a document describing the ways in which the church
would henceforth regard religious people who did not accept Jesus
as the Messiah. As noted earlier, "The Declaration on the Relationship of the Church to Non-Christian Religions" (nearly always
referred to by its opening phrase in Latin, *Nostra Aetate*), deals in
turn with Hinduism, Buddhism, and Islam. But its central section,
about one third of its twelve hundred words, focuses on Jews and
Judaism, with both of whom the church will chart a new course.
At the time, the document did disappoint some, both Jews and
Christians, not least for wording in its final draft that seemed to fall
short of what it might have been. (The declaration "decries" anti-

Semitism when it might have simply condemned it.) But regard for the declaration has steadily grown since its publication. It is impossible to read *Nostra Aetate* today without thinking back to Seelisberg and to Isaac—for its rejection of the lethally charged accusation of deicide against the world's Jews and for its denial that Jews can be portrayed as "rejected or accursed by God." Instead, the document says that Christians and Jews share a "spiritual patrimony," and it recommends joint theological studies and dialogues. And although the declaration does describe Catholics as "the new people of God," it also includes the very same biblical passage that turns up at the end of the Seelisberg points, Paul's statement that "God holds the Jews most dear for the sake of their Fathers; he does not repent of the gifts he makes or the calls he issues. . . ." In that verse lies the basis, forty years later, for Pope Benedict XVI giving a greeting in his inaugural homily "to my brothers and sisters of the Jewish people, to whom we are joined by a shared spiritual heritage, one rooted in God's irrevocable promises."

By the time the *Nostra Aetate* was published in October 1965, Isaac was dead, as was Pope John. But if one goes back nearly four decades, one can find a remarkable commentary that seems to prophesy the spirit of Isaac's project, if one can see that project in its broadest sense—not just the book, but the long, important discussions with Germaine Bouquet, the people at Seelisberg, and finally, John XXIII. The Jewish philosopher Martin Buber wrote the passage; it can be read as anticipating the era Isaac began. "A time of genuine religious conversations is beginning—not those so-called but fictitious conversations where none regarded and addressed his partner in reality, but genuine dialogues, speech from certainty to certainty, but also from one open-hearted person to another open-hearted person. Only then will genuine common life appear, not that of an identical content of faith, which is alleged to be found in all religions, but that of the situation, of anguish and of expectation."

That many Jews will accept an invitation to come discuss biblical texts these days is remarkable in and of itself, because for many centuries within the past millennium, the idea of such an encounter could only call up some very ugly images. In medieval Europe, civil and ecclesiastical authorities arranged a verbal counterpart to sculptures and paintings that portrayed Christianity as triumphant over Judaism. These staged events were called disputations, and they typically pitted a Jewish convert to Christianity against Jewish scholars who—given their minority status in an overtly Christian society—inevitably stood on the defensive. In Paris, in 1240, the charge against Judaism was that the Talmud—the commentary on Jewish oral tradition—contains negative references to Jesus. The event ended in fire, with the authorities ordering the burning of twenty-four cartloads of Talmuds.

In one way or another, events like this, involving the symbolic desecration of an entire faith, become embedded in the historic memory of people born generations later. Thus, as Isaac developed a friendship with Germaine Bouquet, he felt compelled to ask her why she appeared not to carry a contemptuous attitude toward Judaism and a condescending attitude toward him as a Jew. In response, she told him how she had become a Catholic and that her primary teacher was a follower of French philosopher Jacques Maritain. Maritain became his nation's ambassador to the Vatican after World War II, as well as a chairman of the global council of Christians and Jews several weeks after its meeting in Seelisberg. When that event's declaration was published in the United States, he would write in its foreword: "The struggle against anti-Semitism is a fundamental obligation for conscience, the first duty of moral hygiene for what remains to us of civilization."

The day I brought up Isaac with Catalano, she said something that took me right back to his project to show Christians how they might read their own tradition in such a way as to appreciate its historic relationship with Judaism and so disengage Christian teaching from any tendency to attack that faith. "My passion isn't really for dialogue," Catalano told me, a statement that struck me, initially, as surprising, given the work of the institute.

"My first passion is to contribute to getting the gospel right," she said. "And I don't mean that with any kind of arrogance." Rather, she said, anti-Jewish teaching hindered the church itself from being transformed by Jesus' gospel of love. "I'm committed through the church's relationship with Judaism and the Jewish people to doing everything I can to right that. I want to participate in righting that wrong, not only because of the Jewish people, but because it's detrimental to the gospel of God." Catalano added: "I have said this before, but if there were no Jews in Baltimore, we would still have to do this work."

Later, I thought I heard an echo of her words when I read again Maritain's short introduction to the Seelisberg document. Barely two years after the war, he had written: "The restoration of honor is but a sad and bitter consolation which would end in travesty, if we could not come decisively and realistically to the destruction of the shameful evil against which we are fighting. So long as the world, which boasts a Christian civilization, is not cured of anti-Semitism, it will continue to sin. . . ."

One evening I went to see again how the institute was approaching its mission. This time it had arranged with an Episcopal church to provide space for a four-week seminar on a reading of Paul's Letter to the Romans. The session was called "Rescuing Paul," a title that had everything to do with arguing against a traditional reading of several verses in his letter as denigrating Judaism. The teacher was a lay scholar affiliated with the institute. A slender, short-haired woman with a no-nonsense manner, she started the session on time to the minute, after distributing single-spaced sheets containing background reading. One, I noticed, was a two-page discussion of a single phrase in ancient Greek in the light of new scholarship. In terms of content, then, the evening would be heavy.

But she managed to lighten the mood considerably, calling attention to certain verses by honking a child's toy horn just before she read them aloud. "You have to read between the lines and look in the cracks to find out what he thinks about the Jews," she said. Her message seemed clear: Paul did not believe God was excluding Jews from the covenant, but rather was arguing that God had sent Jesus to include gentiles within it. Her audience had come armed with legal pads and they took notes, occasionally looking up to ask questions. "You know the rabbis have this great saying," Catalano said. "'You redeem the world one soul at a time.' That's who we are. We're not going to remake the world—much to the disappointment of our board! But we provide an environment where people can ask questions and cross lines and go and come back alive."

Some years before I began visiting the institute, four prominent Jewish scholars affiliated with universities in the United States and Canada had written a response, under the institute's sponsorship, to the various efforts by Christians to forge a new relationship with Judaism. The publication of the document, titled "Dabru Emet," clearly signaled that Jews were not mere observers of this process, but would have a hand in shaping it, as Isaac had done. The document offered eight statements to guide Jewish-Christian relations, beginning with the idea that Jews and Christians worship the same God and seek authority from much the same text. Their work also included the statement that "Nazism was not a Christian phenomenon," not inevitable, even if centuries of Christian anti-Judaism had created an atmosphere in which the Holocaust could occur. Later, I spent some time talking with one of the document's authors, Peter Ochs, a professor at the University of Virginia. He began by noting that during the Nazi era, there had been relatively few Christians who saved Jews from extermination. In institutions that memorialize the genocide—the United States Holocaust Memorial Museum in Washington, D.C., and Yad Vashem in Jerusalem—these people are referred to as "righteous gentiles" or as "rescuers." Ochs said he thought the time had come, half a century after Seelisberg, for a new category, the "theological rescuer," the Christian who works among Christians to create a new respect for Judaism as a living faith. "If there were Christians who rescued us bodily in the *Shoah*, there's been a generation and a half of Christians who are rescuing us theologically," he said. "They're doing the very brave work of risking themselves in their own community for the sake of the Jews."

One of "Dabru Emet's" statements anticipates the document put out by the Catholic scholars' committee—the one that rejected the idea of targeting Jews for conversion. But Ochs and his colleagues had taken a broader perspective here. "The humanly irreconcilable difference between Jews and Christians will not be settled until God redeems the entire world as promised in Scripture," it stated, adding that in the meantime, "Neither Jew nor Christian should be pressed into affirming the teaching of the other community."

About the time that the scholars finished their work on "Dabru Emet," the institute published a book of essays, each cowritten by a Christian and Jew, titled *Irreconcilable Differences?* The punctuation in the title seemed to beg some response, so I put the question to Christopher Leighton: Did he believe the differences between the two were in fact irreconcilable—and did he think that was a bad thing? "It's a blessing," he said. "God intended for us to have irreconcilable differences." In that way, neither side could absorb or swallow up the other. If differences could be reconciled, then those differences would be dispensable, he said. "I think what's scary about it is it really entails a commitment." In other words, this particular relationship went well beyond the idea of a single transaction or a series of transactions, leading to an inevitable goal. "I think that's the most daunting thing about it," Leighton said. "If you're going to honor the irreconcilable differences, you're going to have to remain in the relationship over the long haul."

"The endpoint is forging relationships that are resilient enough and deep enough that they will remain intact for all eternity," Leighton continued. He offered an illustration to explain what he meant. Think of a *yeshiva*, a traditional Jewish school in which adolescents and adults discuss and debate the Torah, with a commitment and a zest that expects only learning, not ultimate agreement. "I tend to think that is the heaven for which I'm working," he said, adding that he neither expected nor wanted a "harmonic convergence" between the two faiths.

To make sure this process lost none of its potential, Leighton also said it was important that the Jewish-Christian encounter continue to move forward, so as not to be "frozen" by making the Nazi genocide its central reference point. "While the Holocaust has led to this transformation, in a fundamental way, the work has gone beyond making theological reparations—Christians cleaning up their mess," he said. Instead, he wanted to see Christians and Jews study and talk together about God, about how each tradition demands living in the world. "That's why it's so important to go back to our sacred texts. The way we read our sacred texts is how we read the world."

Before I left Baltimore, I realized I needed to look up Thomas Kennedy—or at least find what I could of his memory. I felt a nagging question: Did we miss an opportunity to launch some of these conversations much earlier, long before the fact of the Holocaust? A little familiarity with Maryland's past reveals that its early shame as a state lies not only in its long history of legalized slavery, which endured until 1865, but also its disenfranchisement of Jews. Only in 1826, the fiftieth anniversary year of the Declaration of Independence, did the state's legislature finally adopt a law allowing Jews to hold elective office. The measure was often called "the Jew Bill," or "Kennedy's Jew Bill," after its author, the legislator who spent nearly his entire political career pushing it.

Kennedy immigrated to the United States around the turn of

the nineteenth century from Scotland. A fervent admirer of Jefferson, he claimed to know nothing of Maryland's restrictive franchise until shortly after he won election as a back-country legislator. Then he fixed on it as an offense to human liberty. Putting his oratorical power behind fighting anti-Semitism, he said he feared a single opponent, which he described as prejudice. "Our prejudices, Mr. Speaker, are dear to us," he said, upon introducing the bill in 1818.

I spent one long afternoon at the Jewish Museum in Baltimore reading his words, which I found in texts in its archives. He appealed to history—why should Christians persecute anyone, having endured persecution under the Roman Empire? He appealed to a sense of fairness, religious and secular in value: "There are few Jews in the United States; in Maryland, there are very few, but if there was only one, to that one we ought to do justice." And he spoke personally, describing the value of American religious pluralism. His Presbyterian father hated Roman Catholics. Kennedy admired the old man, but had come to a different view. "I never expect to be so good a person as my father, but having seen so many more Catholics than him, and having been intimate with many of them, and having found them as amiable in all respects as the professors of other doctrines—my prejudice against them, if I ever had any, is at an end."

Finally, Kennedy appealed to theology, too. He quoted from Paul, that very verse in Romans that the group at Seelisberg and the bishops of the Second Vatican Council would put in their documents: "God has not rejected his people whom he foreknew." Well, if one way to read this particular Christian text is that God didn't reject the Jews, then could it be that their faith is still alive and valid in God's eyes?

It took him eight years, a period during which he twice lost reelection bids, for Kennedy to win the bill's passage. He died six years later, a victim of a cholera epidemic. By then, he had retired from politics and was serving as a postal official in western Maryland, an office to which President John Quincy Adams appointed him. Does anyone remember Kennedy? Every time I visited Baltimore, I found myself wondering. I'd heard that there was some kind of memorial, a very different monument from the one I had found near the Inner Harbor. But people with whom I spoke weren't sure where it was. Finally, I was given the name of a rabbi who told me where I could find it. That would be in Sinai Hospital, a historic Baltimore institution. Sure enough, embedded in a wall on a ground floor is a carved stone, perhaps four feet high. It identifies Kennedy as "a Christian gentleman and an earnest advocate of civil and religious liberty." As a memorial, it seemed to be in a fitting place, surrounded as it is by display cases celebrating the hospital's history and achievements, an institution founded by Jews and dedicated to saving life.

SIX

Gatekeepers

Around the corner from the Cathedral of the Assumption in downtown Louisville, Kentucky, a bolt of what must have seemed to be pure, spiritual lightning erupted out of the blue one spring day in 1958. No one actually saw it, but the incident is known among many thousands because the person to whom it occurred would write so eloquently of it later. His experience—some admirers refer to it as an "epiphany," an elastic word that can mean a sudden insight or a real manifestation of the divine—was about being swept by a feeling of transcendent joy in humanity, as if the barriers between people had been abruptly uprooted, leaving an overpowering sense of oneness. "In Louisville, at the corner of Fourth and Walnut, in the middle of the shopping district, I was suddenly overwhelmed with the realization that I loved all these people, that they were mine and I theirs, that we could not be alien to each other even though we were total strangers." The words are Thomas Merton's, one of the most famous Catholic writers on spirituality in American history, recorded in his journal, *Conjectures of a Guilty Bystander.*

The times I visited Louisville, I almost expected to discover some mark on the ground, a sign of what had occurred that day, perhaps a residual glow on some portion of the sidewalk. I had not come to hunt for ephemeral evidence of one man's experience, but rather to explore a decidedly human project, an annual effort at increasing people's knowledge of—and, ideally, respect for—different religious faiths, a project focused on the Catholic cathedral.

Called the Festival of Faiths, its prime mover was an ebulliently energetic Catholic laywoman named Christy Brown. At the festival's heart lay two linked ideas—to educate people about spiritual differences and to do so with an emphasis on hospitality, with individuals feeling welcome to visit other houses of worship and speak and even break bread with those they met there.

In that sense, it was about the experience of being invited, of passing through gateways, and of crossing thresholds one had never before traversed. And because of that—before I further describe Brown and her vision for a wider movement—it is useful to return briefly to Merton, whose presence can seem almost palpable among some people to whom one speaks in Louisville. His reflections, so deeply searching of himself, so curious in his later years about the great religious world around him, make him a gatekeeper to a broad experience of human spirituality.

By the time Merton experienced his particular moment in downtown Louisville, he held the unique distinction of being internationally famous while also belonging to one of the most rigorously ascetic orders within the Roman Catholic Church—the Cistercians of the Strict Observance, popularly known as the Trappists. They lived simple lives of work and prayer within cloistered communities. For Merton, that place was the Abbey of Gethsemani, an expansive monastery created by French monks who fled a mid-nineteenth-century revolution in their nation and found welcoming shelter amid the rolling hill country south of Louisville. A full decade before his experience at Fourth and Walnut, Merton had published a spiritual autobiography, *The Seven Storey Mountain*, which described his journey from the life of an agnostic intellectual, the son of expatriate artists living in France, through studies in England and at Columbia University in New York, where a spiritual quest eventually led him to become a Catholic in 1938. Three years later, he took monastic vows. Published in 1948, the book sold a remarkable six hundred thousand copies in hardback, becoming a best seller in a nation of fewer than 150 million people. A decade later, but several years before the Second Vatican Council would declare the church to be the whole people of God (not simply its clergy and religious orders), Merton felt a message of radical inclusivity. Cloistered or not, he was no longer set apart, but embraced the life around him on Louisville's streets, filled with Catholics, Protestants, Jews, whites, African Americans. "It was like waking from a dream of separateness, of spurious self-isolation in a special world, the world of renunciation and supposed holiness," he wrote. No, he didn't lose his faith or question his calling, but he was shriven of a vocational pride. "The sense of liberation from an illusory difference was such a relief and joy to me that I almost laughed out loud. . . . It is a glorious destiny to be a member of the human race, though it is a race dedicated to many absurdities and one which makes many terrible mistakes: yet, with all that, God Himself gloried in becoming a member of the human race."

One day in Louisville, I attended a discussion in the city's renovated cathedral, in a capacious conference room in its basement, a space called the undercroft. The subject was Merton's relationship to Jews and Judaism, the occasion the publication of a new book, *Merton & Judaism: Holiness in Words,* by Fons Vitae, a local press that specializes in scholarly work about world religions. Several dozen people had turned up, in a Catholic building to hear of the monk's friendships with prominent Jews and his respect for Judaism. One speaker, Brother Paul Quenon, a monk who had known Merton, described him as a gatekeeper, through whose writings a reader could encounter the lives of other faiths. Quenon had been a new monk at Gethsemani during Merton's last years and had also been in charge of taping some of his lectures to young monks, which included introductions to the spirituality of other faiths. "He opens the doors to things and you go through on your own," he told me later, when I went to see him at the monastery. "It was a lifelong thing," Quenon added. "He was always looking for the fullest, deepest meaning of the sacred. I think his interreligious interests came from his quest for God." Merton, while remaining a monk at Gethsemani, began a serious and scholarly exploration of other religious traditions, entering into long, serious correspondence with scholarly Jews, Muslims, and Buddhists. It continued until his untimely death, at age fifty, in 1968.

One could talk about gateways in Louisville, but one could not also dismiss the city's historic fault lines. Being in Louisville reminded me of my visit, earlier, to the Parliament of the World's Religions, in Barcelona in 2004. That event, organized in the name of interreligious peace, took place in a nation lately shaken by terrorist bombings representative of the most dangerous strand of religious exclusivism. "The brighter the light, the deeper the shade" someone had remarked to me at the time. So in Louisville, one had to take account of the past when examining the present. The late 1990s and the early years of the twenty-first century were marked by a project in cross-faith understanding—but this took place in a city in which Protestants and Catholics, a century and a half earlier, had given up on cooperation and almost literally gone to war against each other, an event remembered as Bloody Monday. Draw a generous circle around the site of Merton's epiphany and you would take in a wide range of collective experiences—cooperation among religious people and active enmity, the local history of slavery and the triumph of the city's best-known African American citizen. The past and present could be read as side-by-side texts, one about collaboration, the other exclusion. Early on, Catholics and Protestants forged some remarkably friendly alliances, but that broke down, spectacularly in 1855. For more than half a century, too, Louisville was a place where slavery was legal and slaves were exported as commercial goods down the Ohio River to the Deep

South. A historic marker identifies the site of mid-nineteenth-century slave pens, the cages in which African American men and women were kept pending their shipment down the river whose opposite bank was free soil, where slavery was illegal. Today, the marker stands virtually in the shadow of a cultural center named for the boxer Muhammad Ali, a native of Louisville. The Ali Center, built both to honor him and promote his ideals, declares that its mission is to foster "respect, hope and understanding" among all people. To be sure, Ali has not always had the image of a humanitarian. By 1965, after he achieved great fame as a boxer, he had joined the Nation of Islam, a black nationalist sect that previously had provided a spiritual home to Malcolm X. In the 1960s, he said some things that reflected the Nation's beliefs—a rejection of integration, a disbelief in positive black-white relations—that look as narrow today as when first uttered. But in 1975, Ali, along with a majority of the Nation's members—acting under the guidance of its new leader, Imam W. Deen Muhammad—embraced orthodox Sunni Islam, abandoning the rhetoric of racial separation. Perhaps it was simply coincidental, but within three years, Louisville's governing council had narrowly voted to rename Walnut Street, upon which Merton stood that day in 1958, as Muhammad Ali Boulevard. The Ali Center opened in 2005. By then, Muslims had begun settling in Louisville, building a mosque on River Road, on the city's eastern edge. There were smaller groups of Buddhists in town, and Hindus and Sikhs as well. But people assured me that Catholics and Baptists remained the biggest players in the city. The two groups had also been moving in opposite directions theologically for some years.

The Festival of Faiths arose out of a Catholic project, a story that goes back three decades. Just after Christmas 1981, Pope John Paul II selected the Reverend Joseph C. Kelly as Louisville's new archbishop. He soon set about planning the restoration of the archdiocese's architectural jewel, the Cathedral of the Assumption—a project that would lead to the establishment of the Festival of Faiths.

Built of brick with a distinctively tall steeple, the cathedral dated to 1852. As it entered its fourteenth decade, it badly needed physical repair, new money for programs aimed at aiding the large population of poor who lived downtown, and new energy to restore a dwindling congregation. In the 1960s and 1970s, Catholic Louisvillians had moved away from the city's center, and attendance at the cathedral's masses had withered. A good Sunday might bring in one hundred people, in a space built for more than one thousand. In his restoration plans, Kelly made two key appointments—Christy Brown, a businesswoman with a keen interest in historic preservation, to a foundation that would raise money for the cathedral's restoration, and the Reverend J. Ronald Knott, a gregarious priest with a doctorate from McCormick Theological Seminary in Chicago, a Presbyterian institution, as the cathedral's new rector. Brown, the wife of Owsley Brown II, chairman of Brown-Forman, a beverage and consumer products concern whose holdings include Jack Daniel's Whiskey and Fetzer wines, was not only well connected with Louisville's business community, but regarded as a civic leader in her own right. "She was known to be a woman of strong Catholic faith who would understand and appreciate the cathedral," Kelly said. "And also she was a woman of enormous energy and deep conviction. You knew when she took something on, she'd do it." Kelly also knew that Brown, who is married to an Episcopalian, would not take a parochial view of the project, but would see it as an opportunity to do something for Louisville itself. "Her life and her marriage—which is extremely successful—went into the mix. All of these qualities made her perfect for the choice."

As for Knott, his appointment coincided with a gradual economic renewal in downtown Louisville, especially with the construction of new hotels. To build up the parish, he set about reaching out geographically, often to the suburbs, where many Catholics had moved, and socially, letting it be known that divorced Catholics would be welcomed to worship where he served. Pews began to fill

back up. Knott had begun his priesthood studies at a time of fundamental change in the Catholic church, during the years of the Second Vatican Council. He remembered the impact that *Nostra Aetate*
had on the church's relations with non-Christians, and on his own
seminary education. The priests who were his teachers began to take
a new attitude toward other faiths; now, if a class were to discuss Judaism, the seminary would invite a rabbi to come speak. That spirit
of openness encouraged him to go on to McCormick for further
study. But when he returned to ministry in Kentucky, he had a different experience of ecumenism. Sent to serve as a missionary priest
in the state's rural, southern tier, Knott signed up to join the local
ministerial association. But when he came to his first meeting at a
Protestant church, its pastor got up and walked out, telling his secretary that the group would not be welcome there again. In this part
of the country, the fires of the Reformation still burned.

Both Brown and Knott discovered that there was no shortage of
businesspeople in Louisville interested in the cathedral's renovation.
But many hesitated to contribute to a strictly Catholic project; instead, they made it clear they wanted the cathedral to serve a broader
purpose as the city's spiritual center, open to the public for cultural
and educational events. In other words, the Cathedral of the Assumption might play an almost medieval role, but within a pluralistic context. Knott recalled coming away from fund-raising meetings
convinced that business leaders, reflecting local sentiment in a
southern city, clearly valued religion itself; they also saw the clergy
as uniquely able to fulfill a peacemaking role in cases of crisis. Two
examples were cited: Once, not long before, the city had been
deeply shaken by a shooting at a local company in which several
people died; in another case, a white supremacist group secured a
permit to march through downtown. After the first incident and
during the second, local clergy across a wide range of traditions had
met at the cathedral to pray together for the city. By the end of its

fund-raising campaign, the Cathedral Heritage Foundation had secured pledges of more than twenty million dollars for the restoration work. Two thirds of the sum, Knott told me, came from people
who were not Catholics, evidence of a generosity that he regarded
as obligating him as the cathedral's pastor to make sure the building
was put to the community's use. "I think it would have been ob-
scene if Catholics had twenty million dollars and spent it on themselves," he said. "In the heart of downtown, this monumental
building—I felt a responsibility that it should be used as much as
possible by as many people as possible."

While this project went on, a historic, national change was under
way among Southern Baptists, setting off tremors felt at another important religious institution in Louisville, Southern Baptist Theological Seminary, which traced its history to the same pre–Civil War
decade as the cathedral. The Southern Baptist Convention, with sixteen million members the nation's largest Protestant denomination,
had become locked in a political struggle for its control between
two factions—one well organized and exceptionally gifted at articulating its theologically conservative beliefs, and another that claimed
to stand for a historic Baptist heritage that valued individual com-
petency when it came to interpreting the Bible. Within a decade of
annual battles for control of the convention's presidency and its
appointive powers, one faction (called fundamentalists by their more
moderate rivals) had triumphed. The victory was strongly felt at
Southern Seminary, the oldest of the denomination's schools for
training ministers, which stands atop a ridge east of downtown
Louisville. Life within the denomination changed quickly: Women
were discouraged from becoming pastors; congregations regarded
as condoning homosexuality were expelled; and convention officials proclaimed the Bible to be "inerrant"—literally true not only
in matters of faith, but in science and history too. Southern Baptist
leaders put the brakes on the small steps the denomination had

made lately toward closer ties with other Christian groups. Southern Baptists have always been evangelical. But with the change in
the denomination's leadership came a much stronger emphasis on
ministers and laypeople alike sharing their faith with those outside
the fold, so that the latter could be brought to a saving knowledge
of Jesus Christ. The seminary felt the changes as acutely as any other
institution within the denomination.

By the time I began visiting Louisville, these changes—within
the archdiocese and at the seminary—were largely complete. The
cathedral had been fully restored, its sanctuary enlivened with fresh
colors, including a vaulted ceiling painted deep blue with golden
stars. The undercroft—the area downstairs where I had gone to the
conference on Merton—had been renovated as a public meeting
space. By 1996, too, the foundation had begun sponsoring an annual
event each November, the Festival of Faiths. Actually, it was struc-
tured as a weeklong series of events, intended as a cultural, educational, and conversational approach to familiarizing local people
with Louisville's emerging religious pluralism. Along with the Catholics, various Protestant and Jewish congregations were participating,
as well as groups of Baha'is, Buddhists, Mormons, Muslims, and others. The first event I attended—inside the cathedral sanctuary—was
a lecture about the Qur'an by a Harvard professor, a Muslim, who
had come to speak about how Islam's sacred book viewed other
faiths. I counted more than two hundred people present. On another
day, an authority on the Dead Sea Scrolls spoke to a packed house in
a nearby hotel's ballroom. There was a film series on Hollywood's
various portrayals of Jesus, a roundtable discussion of Hinduism's sacred texts, and a workshop on African American gospel music. A year
later, I returned to join about five hundred people at a prayer break-
fast the festival organized to hear Mohandas Gandhi's grandson Arun
speak about the practice of nonviolence. On another occasion, I
went to see a group of visiting Tibetan Buddhist monks select from
among forty vials of colored sand to create a mandala, a symbolic

representation of the universe. They would complete the picture, as wide as a kitchen table, then—in a demonstration of Buddhism's conviction of the impermanence of things—sweep up this small masterpiece and pour the sand into the Ohio River. At other times, the festival brought in a group of scholars to discuss what Muslims meant by the word "jihad," hosted a choir of Israeli and Palestinian teenagers, and arranged a roundtable discussion of faith and charitable giving. Local Sikhs discussed the concept of justice within their faith. And a well-known evangelical Protestant writer arrived one evening to speak about the religious responsibility to relieve world hunger. There was a lot from which to choose. To Christy Brown, the variety sprang from her conviction that events like these, especially when hosted by different houses of worship, ought to signal a new era of hospitality and community building. "I think when you invite someone into your house of worship, you're inviting them into the most intimate part of your being, of your family and your culture," she said. If only such events could happen more widely, she said, people who valued religious faith itself might get to know one another better, for the betterment of all. Hearing her speak made me think that Brown might have fit well within the culture that created the first World's Parliament of Religions, in Chicago in 1893. But her vision extended further than that one-time meeting, momentous as it was. Hers amounted to a layperson's plea to religious leaders to open up their churches, synagogues, mosques, and temples to allow spiritually involved people to meet and get to know one another. By its tenth year, a foundation staff member told me, the organization was drawing several thousand people to the festivals. Banks and law firms had signed on as sponsors, as had a hospital and an array of religious groups.

Still, participation could hardly be described as citywide. One noticeably absent organization was the Southern Baptist seminary. In the 1990s, when I worked as a journalist, I had gotten to know the man who would become become its new president under conservative rule. R. Albert Mohler, Jr., a Southern graduate, was younger than most of the denomination's new leadership, but he was also one of their leading intellectuals, whose voice was respected not just among Baptists but conservative evangelicals nationwide. Mohler possessed a gift in his ability to speak clearly and briefly when the occasion demanded, which earned him regular invitations to nationally broadcast talk shows like *Larry King Live*. It also made him a natural source for news reporters seeking someone who could articulate a conservative, evangelical view. Theologically, he could succinctly articulate the conservative critique of interreligious encounters like the one in downtown Louisville. "I have no option," he told me, "but to stand with Christ, who said that he who has rejected the Son has no life in him. And there is no way to know the Father but through the Son, so that to reject the Son is in essence to reject the Father." I drove over to the seminary one radiant autumn afternoon to speak with him in his office, in a neo-Georgian building on the broad and busy campus. At that time, he had just returned from teaching a class and looked like a well-dressed professor, with dark sport coat and tie. It had been clear to me why Southern would not be interested in the Festival of Faiths. From its inception, the festival's organizers had laid down a rule by which they expected all participants to abide—there would be no proselytizing during festival events. It didn't always work— Christy Brown told me that at one early festival, she had been upset when one of the participants had flatly told her that only Christians would ever make it to heaven, to which she replied that she had non-Christian friends whom she expected to see there. The festival's organizers held that people didn't have to like each other and certainly didn't have to agree theologically, but they were not to try to convert one another during that one week.

"That's why we're out," Mohler said, in our interview. But he hastened to add, "We're not 'angry out.' " Still, he said, the seminary would not enter into the sort of conversation that the festival's organizers envisioned. I asked if by that he meant it was not possible to have a theological conversation with non-Christians. No, he responded, that was eminently possible, provided one matter was clear. "It has to begin with, 'I very much want to understand who you are—but not just so that I can celebrate that—but that so I can understand how I can present Christ to you.'" In other words, the primary goal of such an encounter would be his holding out the possibility that the other person involved in their conversation could consciously accept Jesus as savior and thereby receive eternal life. Christianity was by necessity exclusive, he said. "I don't see God at work at all in these other world belief systems. I see God at work within individuals, but not within the systems of thought."

Beyond the principle involved, Mohler made it clear he thought little of the title that the foundation had chosen for its event, the Festival of Faiths. On one hand, there was no basis in Christian theology for referring to "faith" apart from faith in Jesus Christ, he said. In addition, there was about the word "festival" something celebrative of differences concerning ultimate matters. "Buying into that project is to affirm that it's a good thing that there is such diversity," Mohler said. "Now, I'm willing to affirm that such diversity is constitutionally protected, but I can't affirm that such diversity is a theological good." From a legal standpoint, he stood on unshakable ground; there's nothing in the First Amendment that requires one to suppose religious diversity might be God's will. James Madison, the amendment's principal author, regarded religious diversity as a reality, a positive one that kept the pretensions to political power among the Protestant churches he knew handily in check.

Yet as we spoke, Mohler made it clear that his convictions did not mean he found conversations with people of other faiths to lack intellectual value, even in the absence of conversion. He said he was involved in substantive discussions with conservative Catholics and Orthodox Jews about specific issues upon which they found some common interests—theological and ethical matters related to the family and human sexuality. These conversations had a useful by-product: "We actually understand each other more adequately." The conversations had proved useful in clarifying his thoughts on the issues under discussion. "There are aspects where we serve as a catalyst for each other's thinking." (I couldn't help but note that advocates of interreligious dialogue made a similar point about their own theological conversations.) Nevertheless, Mohler said, the conversations in which he engaged could not exclude the possibility of overt evangelism. "When I talk with my Jewish colleagues and conversation partners, I want them to know Jesus as the Messiah," he said. But although that was his wish, he had no desire to hector about it. "I have no power to coerce that, nor will I ever be rude. What I mean by rude is failing to treat them as genuine human beings who deserve respect in this conversation." And so I gathered that a civility prevailed in these conversations that might well be admired by the people at the festival, but then I was privy to information that the two groups themselves had apparently not exchanged.

One day, over lunch, I asked Christy Brown if there had been any single moment in her life in which she had decided she needed to become involved in a multireligious project like the festival. She thought a moment and then recalled that, early in the planning stages for the cathedral's restoration, she and her husband had contributed personally by hiring an expert in historic preservation to review the cathedral site and discuss his findings with others involved in the project. What he found might help the foundation envision what the cathedral's new role could be in the city. And so the foundation came to focus on the local past. "We kept uncovering this history," Brown said. Specifically, that discovery concerned an ecumenical thread that runs through Louisville's early history. Protestants and Catholics—often overt foes elsewhere in the world—had cooperated on *religious* projects in the city, including construction of the cathedral's forerunner, a parish church named for Saint Louis of France. "What became very clear was that the building had non-Catholic money to help build it," Brown said. That struck her with the force of a revelation, as it suggested that there was something about Louisville's past that might be pointed out, to benefit the city's future. "So that, all of a sudden, is an 'ah-hah' moment," she said. In other words, if people in Louisville could cooperate across significant faith lines 150 years earlier, then why not once again?

In American history, Louisville is a distinctly post-Revolutionary city, the creation of the trans-Allegheny migration that followed peace with England. A basic settlement existed by the time Lewis and Clark launched their exploration down the Ohio, from a point on the Indiana side of the river. When it came to erecting sacred architecture in Louisville, Protestants struck first, with a Methodist church going up in 1809. Within two years, Catholics dedicated their own building, the church named for Saint Louis. But remarkably, a large majority of its donors were Protestants and two even sat on its board of trustees. Later, after Catholics had outgrown their space and begun putting up a larger building, they celebrated the laying of the cornerstone with a special service in a Presbyterian church. Two thirds of those who came to celebrate were Protestants. And again, in 1848, when Louisville's bishop consecrated the Reverend Martin John Spaulding as his assistant, local Protestants turned out, sitting respectfully through a service that lasted three hours. Their attentive attitude drew favorable notice from the city's Catholic newspaper. "Ninety percent of the money to build the first Catholic parish in this city came from non-Catholics," Ron Knott told me. "It was before the 1850s, when the nativist movement grew, so that there was an ecumenical climate in early Kentucky. At least my sense is that in early Kentucky, relationships like this occurred out of need. They needed each other on the frontier. Now, they didn't agree theologically, but I think this flat-out need brought them together."

Knott's comment struck me as insightful, not just for its focus on Kentucky's past, but also because it seemed that he identified a particularly American reality. Our vast lands may long since have been settled, but we as a nation have never lost the idea of the frontier, a place where personal dreams could be ventured. The frontier in the American experience was never entirely about individualism; it also required individuals to work together to avoid perishing alone. Think of the collaboration as an exercise in democratic community—neighbors joining hands to raise a barn or pooling resources to shelter a family burned out of its home. (None of this is meant to idealize the reality of the frontier itself—its dark, brutal, and racist sides are well documented.) But the spirit of collaborating for a collective good that was possible within it has not been lost. I believe it was embodied in the will toward the preservation of civil society that immediately followed 9/11, when many people like Frank Hubbard, the New Jersey priest, and Alice Woldt, the church council official in Seattle, reached out to the newcomers in their midst—in those cases, the Muslims whose welfare seemed perilously at stake.

Eventually, the spirit of cooperation in Louisville broke down, quite spectacularly. The nativist movement to which Knott referred—a Protestant backlash against the floodtide of heavily Catholic immigration that began changing American cities in the 1840s—struck Louisville with a resounding blow during Kentucky's 1855 elections. On August 6, voting day, the city collapsed into mayhem as a mob attacked Catholics and their property. Its members wrested a cannon from the courthouse lawn and, at one point, turned up in front of the cathedral, threatening to break down its doors to search for weapons they were sure were stashed inside. The quick-thinking archbishop turned the keys over to the city's mayor, who made a symbolic inspection, then told the would-be attackers to move on. It may seem strange now to reflect on the violence of that era, when Catholics were often viewed as a potentially subversive force. But crude anti-Catholicism, which erupted on Louisville's "Bloody Monday," as it came to be called, had a long history in Protestant portrayals of Rome as the headquarters of a dictatorial plot to undermine American democracy. Lay Catholics would be its pawns, driven by their priests to impose upon America the power of an absolute ruler, the pope. Days before the election, local newspapers did their best to stir citizens to fury, calling for them to support an antiimmigrant slate for the state legislature and warning that the stakes were high, that the future of republican government could be under threat. Ancient history? Not if one considers various claims, easily found on the Internet, that American Muslims may harbor the same designs—that is, they're after our liberties, too.

On my visits to Louisville, I found the festival had emerged as an umbrella of sorts for other multireligious events that had been organized separately. For example, a local mosque, a Presbyterian church, and a Reform synagogue had begun sponsoring an annual meal together, rotating the occasion among the three buildings, while the members of each took turns cooking. They called it the Children of Abraham Dinner and in its deliberate use of a variety of sacred spaces, it reflected the idea I heard Christy Brown promote. Once, when the occasion took place at the synagogue, the one hundred or so diners headed over to the sanctuary after the meal to listen to a quartet of musicians play. The music became sufficiently lively that people actually began dancing in the aisles—Presbyterians, Jews, and Muslims joining hands and snaking around the pews in a long line.

Later, I spoke to the rabbi, Stanley R. Miles, who told me of an experience he had after he had moved to Louisville in the 1970s that indicated the local possibilities for interreligious cooperation. At the time, the synagogue, Temple Shalom, lacked a permanent home and held services in rented space. But the arrangement fell through, pushing the congregation into a hurried search for new quarters. Word got out, enough so for Miles to receive a phone call from the chaplain at Bellarmine University, a Catholic institution astride a hill in Louisville's Highlands neighborhood. The chaplain suggested the synagogue's congregation come use the college chapel as its worship space, holding services Friday evenings and Saturday mornings, while the university's Catholics would make use of it Saturday evenings and Sundays. Miles accepted. For the next twelve months, Temple Shalom met on a Catholic campus. "We built our sukkah in front of St. Robert's Chapel," the rabbi recalled, "and a lot of students came and helped us." But that wasn't quite all. In 1996, long after Temple Shalom had put up its own building, word reached Louisville that the Southern Baptists, in their annual convention, had adopted a resolution calling for new efforts to convert Jews to Christianity. Money was set aside to hire a missionary to direct the work. (Quoted in *The New York Times Magazine*, the missionary would use strong language, saying not only that hellfire lay ahead for nonbelievers, but that the Holocaust itself would "fade into insignificance in comparison with God's future judgment.") In this instance, the resolution produced a direct, albeit quiet, reaction in Louisville. Miles got a call from a Baptist friend, who identified himself as an intermediary for other Southern Baptists, some of them clergy. They wanted to meet with Miles over lunch. The rabbi was curious enough to agree to go. The gathering took place at a house, well out of the public eye. When Miles arrived, he found fifteen men waiting for him. Over the course of the next hour or so, they took turns assuring him that they did not agree with the convention resolution. Indeed, they offered their personal apologies for it. "I tried to be reassuring to them," Miles told me. For one thing, he had known too many Southern Baptists to indulge in the fantasy that they all thought and acted alike. The same, of course, could be said for any other group.

In addition to Southern Seminary, the city is home to the Louisville Presbyterian Theological Seminary. It occupies roughly the same neighborhood as Southern, but the denomination to which it belongs—the Presbyterian Church (USA)—has not undergone a rightward shift in its policies. Indeed, news organizations often identify the church—with more than two million members—as "liberal." But it is difficult to know what this means. The Presbyterians ordain women as ministers, elders, and deacons, but they have adamantly resisted calls from within the denomination to extend that possibility to openly gay men and women. Twice, I found the Presbyterian seminary sponsoring events at the Festival of Faiths—a lecture by religious historian Martin Marty and a speech on poverty in the world by the Reverend Robert Edgar, then general secretary of the National Council of Churches of Christ, whose headquarters are in New York. When Edgar arrived, Archbishop Kelly was on hand to greet him. Once on the campus, I stopped by to visit one of the seminary's Old Testament professors, W. Eugene March, whom I had been told was then at work on a book explaining how Christians might find within the Bible itself a means for acknowledging God's presence among non-Christians. March told me his project had begun long ago, back when he was a graduate student. He had studied under Jewish professors and with Jewish students, in the process coming to respect them as people whose religious lives were every bit as deep as his own. "There is a defensible way of saying we should be open to others and assuming God is working through them," he said. Later, I picked up a copy of March's book, *The Wide, Wide Circle of Divine Love,* a title that prepares a reader for his message, which is that Christians ought to take a generous view of God's favor, understanding it to reach people beyond the bounds of the church. March elaborates on this through his analysis of several major biblical stories—of Noah, Abraham, Ruth, and Naomi. And he also examines John 14:6, a verse typically cited as definitive among those who would close discussion as to whether salvation might be possible for non-Christians. In it, Jesus says, "I am the way, the truth and the life. No one comes to the Fa-

ther except by me." March said the verse, and the Gospel that includes it, ought to be read within the context of the late first
century, when scholars believe John's Gospel was written. In that
way, he echoed the message I had heard from Rosann Catalano in
Baltimore. At the time of which March spoke, tension had developed between Jewish authorities and Jesus' followers, a largely Jewish movement then gradually—and often painfully—separating
itself as a minority from Jewish communities. Read the verse not as
a "policy statement," March would declare in his book, but as encouragement to those who would live a life faithful to God by following Jesus. "These words do not define how Christians should
understand others but how Christians should structure their own
commitments and priorities." I called March to see how his book
had been received. It had been criticized by a conservative Presbyterian organization, he said, but he had also received invitations to
speak in congregations in some places that would not usually be
linked with theological liberalism—New Mexico, Oklahoma, West
Virginia. In writing the book, he said, he meant "to offer words and
ideas to people who have felt some of this, but didn't know it was
defensible."

Several times Christy Brown said she hoped that the Festival of
Faiths could serve as a model for people in other cities, and not just
in the United States. But when I mentioned this to Archbishop
Kelly, he seemed somewhat hesitant. "I think everybody would be
better off if they could do it as we do," he said. "But I know the ecumenical climate is different in other cities." By then, the archbishop had greeted two Nobel Peace Prize winners within the
cathedral on their visits to the city. Elie Wiesel, the Holocaust survivor and writer, had visited before giving a public interview in the
local civic center. And earlier, the fourteenth Dalai Lama had visited during a speaking tour in the United States. Kelly spoke of receiving the Tibetan as a moment of "welcoming inclusivity" for
the cathedral, which he regarded as the building's hallmark. "That

doesn't mean we're shedding one ounce of Catholic identity," he said. "I think we're expressing it to the fullest."

In coming to Kentucky—which he had done at least twice—the Dalai Lama was completing something of a spiritual circle. In 1968, long before he had traveled to the United States, Thomas Merton had gone to see him, in the Tibetan exile capital of Dharamasala, India. Merton, by then deeply interested in the spiritual disciplines of Buddhist monks, had asked for a single meeting with the Dalai Lama. But the two men found they so much enjoyed the intellectual and spiritual encounter they had that Merton stayed on a while longer and met with the Dalai Lama twice more. In his *Asian Journal,* published after his death, Merton wrote that their final meeting, on November 8, was the best they had shared. The two monks discussed the meaning of monastic vows, how individual monks progressed in their spirituality, whether religion could coexist with established Marxism, among other topics. At the end, the Dalai Lama called Merton a "Catholic *geshe,*" an honorific that one of Merton's friends described as a compliment equivalent—coming as it did from the Dalai Lama—to receiving an honorary doctorate. Merton traveled through India and, early in December, went on to Sri Lanka, where he made a point of going to see the four immense stone Buddha statues at a place called Polonnaruwa, a former capital city in the island nation's northeast. The statues had been hewn from the face of a rock hillside; one depicts the Buddha engaged in deep meditation on the eve of his enlightenment. When he came face-to-face with the rock carving, Merton had an experience every bit as unexpected as his Louisville epiphany. "Looking at these figures, I was suddenly, almost forcibly, jerked clean out of the habitual, half-tied vision of things, and an inner clearness, a clarity, as if exploding from the rocks themselves, became evident and obvious," he wrote in his journal. "I don't know when in my life I have ever had such a sense of beauty and spiritual validity running together in one aesthetic illumination." The rapture he described was among the very last things Merton ever wrote; at a conference in Bangkok the next week, an event attended by Buddhist and Catholic monks, he accidentally touched some exposed wiring in his room and died from the electric shock. His body was returned to Gethsemani for burial on the abbey grounds.

Long ago, Merton had written about the importance of not rejecting others' spirituality outright, as what they knew might help one's own spiritual self. "I will be a better Catholic, not if I can refute every shade of Protestantism, but if I can affirm the truth in it and still go further. So, too, with the Muslims, the Hindus, the Buddhists, etc. This does not mean syncretism, indifferentism, the vapid and careless friendliness that accepts everything by thinking of nothing. There is much that one cannot 'affirm' and 'accept,' but first one must say 'yes' where one really can. If I affirm myself as a Catholic merely by denying all that is Muslim, Jewish, Protestant, Hindu, Buddhist, etc., in the end I will find there is not much left for me to affirm as a Catholic: and certainly no breath of the Spirit with which to affirm it." To describe his statement as one of spiritual generosity is only to credit him halfway. Merton declares his identity in a world in which he is fully cognizant of other forms of spirituality. But he recognizes that those religious identities are alive for those who hold them, and those people are as beloved by the divine presence Merton felt so acutely, flowing through him on that otherwise ordinary day in Louisville in 1958.

In July 1996, the Dalai Lama traveled to Gethsemani, Merton's former monastery. The occasion was a major meeting of Christians and Buddhists, an event that drew more than fifty people, about equally divided between the two traditions and composed of monks and academic scholars from Europe, Asia, and the United States. The weeklong meeting became known as the "Gethsemani Encounter," and the formal speeches its participants made were published in a book under that title. Early on, the Dalai Lama called for respect and appreciation to be paid to the world's major religious traditions; he also offered a special tribute to Merton. "As a result of my meeting with him, my attitude toward Christianity was very much improved. It greatly changed. I always considered him a strong bridge between Buddhism and Christianity. So his sudden death was, I think, a great loss. Now while we remember him, I think the important thing is that we must fulfill his wishes." One such wish, the Dalai Lama said, was that "genuine practitioners of different religious traditions" speak seriously with one another.

Much later on, after I had read some of the speeches, I had the opportunity to speak with one of the Gethsemani participants, Judith Simmer-Brown, a professor of religious studies at Naropa University in Boulder, Colorado. She said the gathering at the monastery, although long in the planning, had become complicated by remarks that Pope John Paul II had made about Buddhism in an interview published as part of a book in which the pope reflected on issues within the Catholic church and its relations with other faiths. In the course of the interview, the pope had offered a negative assessment of Buddhism, a tradition that holds that the universe is uncreated, lacking the concepts of god and soul as Christians, Jews, and Muslims understand them. Thus, the pope said, central Buddhist ideas about life and the world were plainly negative, and were in fact radically different from Christian understandings of the earth as God's creation and what human beings should do in it. He implied that he believed Buddhists were disengaged from society, not inclined by their faith to try to improve the world. Unsurprisingly, the remarks were considered insulting by many Buddhists in Asia and the United States. The meeting at Gethsemani provided an opportunity for leading Buddhist figures to reply, discussing concepts within Buddhism (like *maitri* or *metta*, the same word in Sanskrit and Pali, respectively, which translates as loving kindness for one's fellow beings) that directly challenged the pope's assessment. But what also helped break down the gathering's formality and latent tensions, Simmer-Brown said, was when some participants turned to discussing a recent incident that seemed to involve multiple religious dimensions—love, sacrifice, and violence. In Algeria, that past spring, members of a radical Islamic guerrilla group kidnapped seven French Trappist monks—members of Merton's order—and executed them. The monks had known they were endangered; they had been warned to quit Algeria, a nation riven by a gruesome civil war. But they had chosen to stay on in their monastery in the town of Tibhirine as a gesture of love for the local Muslim community whom they served with a medical clinic. Muslims in France had condemned the abductions and offered prayers for the monks' release. The bodies were finally discovered in May, weeks after the kidnapping. Church bells tolled across France. Paris's archbishop, Cardinal Jean-Marie Lustiger, extinguished seven candles that he had lit two months earlier, for the monks, a ceremony attended by French Muslims and Jews. Simmer-Brown said that at Gethsemani, half a world away, the example set by the monks created an emotional intimacy that transcended religious differences.

In 2006, the Cathedral Heritage Foundation adopted a new name, the Center for Interfaith Relations, hired a longtime local community activist, Jan Arnow, as its executive director, and adopted as its motto the phrase "Many faiths, one heart, common action." Arnow told me the organization's mission would be three-pronged: It would stage educational events year-round, create social action projects (such as working against violence among young people) that would draw in congregations across faith lines, and start up a program specifically for middle-school students. She saw the emphasis shifting to shared action—interfaith relations, she said, "as people crossing their faith traditions to work together."

In the meantime, the Festival of Faiths would continue. In 2007, she said, the center raised and spent about $150,000 on it. "For what we do, for a whole week—twenty-three events in seven days—it's reasonable, and most of those events are free to the public." Echoing Christy Brown, she wanted to see the festival idea picked up elsewhere. "I'm hoping cities across the country will do them," she said. "So I'm rewriting the manual."

Before I left Louisville a final time, I caught up with Ron Knott, who had moved on from the cathedral to another position in the archdiocese. "We are simple, down-to-earth people," he said, by way of commenting on why a Festival of Faiths might work there. "We aren't known as sophisticated intellectuals." For that reason, perhaps, you could get a crowd at events like an interfaith prayer gathering or a discussion of the Qur'an by a Harvard professor. But then, you would just as easily have people who would be dead set against coming, seeing in such events a compromise of their deepest-held beliefs. I asked Knott what he said in those cases; people had certainly argued that case with him. "I wish I had a great response," he replied. "I always go back to that fable about the blind men and the elephant, where everybody touches the elephant in a different spot and claims to know the whole elephant. Well, the elephant as far as I'm concerned is Truth. By my understanding and perception of it, there is one Truth. But my understanding of that is limited."

"Yes, God is one and Truth is Truth," he added. "I don't understand everything, but I think I'm to the point in my life where I'm not afraid of different opinions. If I thought Southern Baptists had the answer to everything or that the McCormick Seminary had the whole truth, I probably would have joined them." He offered to say that more bluntly, put his words into what he called the "street version." I told him to go ahead. "I hope to God everybody in heaven is not Catholic. I will be bored out of my mind."

Words over Bullets

Early one morning, an hour or so before sunrise, I pulled into the driveway behind a Craftsman-style bungalow on the crest of a low hill, in an urban neighborhood a mile west of downtown Los Angeles. From the start of my research, I had followed a path that took me from east to west; now I was coming to the end of my travels among interreligious groups. Crunching over pebbles scattered across the driveway as I approached the house's entrance, I passed a porcelain-white figure of the Buddha seated in meditation, a half life-sized statue vaguely luminous in the predawn moonlight. As I knocked on the door, I noticed that of all the houses on the street, only this one appeared to have a light on. I had been invited to observe the meditative chanting that began the day of the half dozen monks who lived there, in a monastery called the Dharma Vijaya Buddhist Vihara. Afterward, I sat with their abbot and founder, a small, bespectacled man with a gentle voice, who tried to explain to me the concept of *metta*. The word comes from Pali, the Latin of Theravadan Buddhists; it can be translated into English as "loving kindness," as my host, the Venerable Walpola Piyananda, did for me. Theravada is the Buddhist tradition most prevalent in Southeast Asia and it is also the oldest (it literally means, "the way of the elders") and so predates Mahayana Buddhism, historically dominant in China, Korea, and Japan, and Vajrayana Buddhism, common among Tibetans.

Piyananda's telling me about *metta* was no idle gesture. Instead, it sprang directly from his religious experience in Los Angeles. For more than fifteen years, he had regularly taken part in a discussion group of Catholics and Buddhists, in which people in each tradition had sought to explain their basic concepts of belief and practice to the other. "We've tried to understand each other," he said to me. "The number-one thing is trust and friendship." It had not been an easy conversation. The distance between the two faiths is vast theologically, and for Southeast Asians like Piyananda it is also fraught with a legacy of conflict, as European colonialists left behind deep memories of their disrespect for Buddhist property and beliefs.

Early on, the dialogue group to which he belonged had issued a short report: "It challenged us to articulate to one another what we took for granted among ourselves." At times, the group—a small one, numbering perhaps a dozen people—had spent an hour or more puzzling over a single word from one of their traditions, trying to explain it to everyone's satisfaction. Sometimes they failed. "At the same time, we also found that we could continue to speak and to hear each other even if we did not have a precise understanding of each other," their report said. In a few words, the authors captured a difficult challenge that lies within interreligious conversation. The discovery of common ground and, beyond that, of the beginnings of mutual understanding may well involve a very long journey. In this case, the participants had persisted and the benefits to those in each group seemed important. Piyananda, for one, had felt moved to write a fifty-page essay—"Love in Buddhism"—discussing *metta* as a concept basic to the faith. To read it as a Christian is to come away thinking that Buddhism possesses a discipline paralleling the Christian ideal of self-giving love, as embodied in Jesus. *Metta* is one of the "sublime states" (another is compassion) within Buddhism. But for many outsiders, it's easy to miss—thus, Buddhism's reputation among some westerners as literally negative. Siddhattha Gottama, the Indian prince who renounced his wealth and privilege, eventually achieved a state of enlightenment. As the Buddha, he preached that human life is characterized by suffering; that suffering is caused by desire or craving; that there is a way beyond suffering and that way means following Buddhism's path of wisdom, meditation, and mindfulness. Some have perceived this as a call to social disengagement. Pope John Paul II once did, in an interview that dismayed Buddhists worldwide.

At the time I met him, Piyananda held an important position in a region with a larger Buddhist population—immigrants and converts—than any other in the United States. He served as president of the Buddhist Sangha Council of Southern California (sangha means "community"), an association of about three hundred temples and religious centers. Like many people I'd met involved in interreligious activities, he had not come from a religiously diverse background. Born in Sri Lanka during World War II, when the island was still under British rule and called Ceylon, he had little knowledge of Christianity as a child. "We were not educated," he said. "We did not know Catholics or any other churches. And they did not trust us either. Before coming to this country, I never touched a Bible." Contact between Sri Lankan Buddhists and European Christians goes back five hundred years and its start was not propitious, including European destruction of Buddhist religious sites and aggressive missionary activity. Piyananda, ordained as a monk at the age of twelve (the monastic name by which he is known translates as "pleasant joy"), studied first in Sri Lanka, then in India, where he learned about Hinduism, and finally in the United States, at Northwestern University and later at the University of California at Los Angeles. While at Northwestern, he had taken housing just off campus at Garrett-Evangelical Theological Seminary, a United Methodist institution. He read the Bible and also the Swiss theologian Karl Barth, whose resistance to Hitler cost him his teaching job in Germany. Piyananda felt respected by the young Methodists studying for the ministry there, with a single exception—a fellow student who warned Piyananda that his Buddhist identity would land him in hell. After being told this publicly before a classroom full of students, Piyananda replied that he fully believed his Christian colleague would go to heaven, but once there would engage in noisy theological disputes with others, creating a racket that would disturb Piyananda's meditation. Therefore, Piyananda said, as a Buddhist he would voluntarily choose hell, where he might compassionately serve suffering souls. That ended the proselytizing.

At the outset, the Buddhist-Catholic dialogue group in Los Angeles presented another challenge. Piyananda told me that when he was invited to join, at least one Buddhist warned him against it, saying the enterprise was intended to convert him and others. At the time, a book claiming the existence of a "Catholic plot" against Buddhism was circulating among Southeast Asians. Piyananda went anyway. The dialogue group had originated in a chance encounter between a Catholic priest with the singular name of the Reverend Royale Vadakin and another Sri Lankan scholar-monk, the Venerable Havanapola Ratanasara, who had studied at Columbia University and the University of London before moving to Los Angeles. Their paths crossed at the post office one day in 1989; the two men stood out in their largely African American neighborhood—a white priest in a black suit and an Asian monk in a saffron robe. Vadakin politely asked if he might visit Ratanasara's temple; the monk reciprocated by inviting the priest for a celebration of Vesak, the Buddha's birthday. Vadakin, who at the time served as the archdiocese's chief ecumenical officer, sat cross-legged like his hosts, in the process developing a tremendous leg cramp. But they laid the groundwork for the dialogue group, as well as the friendships that would result from it.

For his part, Piyananda said the experience had increased his appreciation of Catholics, a response he shared publicly when he traveled to southeast Asia. He had spoken out on radio and television in his native Sri Lanka about the good relationships he had enjoyed. "I explain that when I go to any public meeting," he said. In the meantime, at least one of the Catholic participants had become close to Ratanasara. Mike Kerze, an adjunct professor in Loyola-Marymount University's theology department, had joined the group at the beginning and seen its discussions remain intellectually lively, while relationships between its members grew more relaxed and familiar. At eighty, Ratanasara became ill and, with his life ebbing, spent his time in a bedroom at Piyananda's monastery. Kerze went to visit, bringing fruit—mangoes and strawberries. Ratanasara reciprocated by engaging Kerze in a personal discussion, offering him advice on matters that Kerze incorporated into his private prayers. Of the experience of participating in the dialogue group, Kerze said, "I look at it as a grace in my life."

Positive relationships that cross religious lines are not to be taken lightly. One never knows where they will lead or what they may produce. There is, for example, Thich Nhat Hanh, the Vietnamese Zen monk who came to the United States in 1966 to seek American military withdrawal from his nation's war. Nhat Hanh, a longtime peace activist in Vietnam, was known for trying to create a "third way" for his nation, between Communism and dependence on the United States. He gained audiences with many people that year, including Secretary of Defense Robert McNamara. But his most important conversations may have been with the Reverend Dr. Martin Luther King, Jr. King, who increasingly turned his attention to speaking out against the Vietnam War, wrote a moving letter in January 1967 nominating Nhat Hanh for the Nobel Peace Prize. The civil rights leader referred to Nhat Hanh as his friend and also "a holy man." Many years later, when I interviewed Nhat Hanh, he remembered King as a friend—and something more. King had been a *bodhisattva*, Nhat Hanh said, using a term that describes an enlightened being who dedicates himself through many lifetimes to helping others reach a state of ultimate awakening. In one of his books, *Living Buddha, Living Christ,* Nhat Hanh—who eventually created a community in France—reflected on his early experiences in the United States, saying that King and other "active Christians" were "the Americans I found it easiest to communicate with."

Reading his words, it's easy to forget how far ahead of their times King and Nhat Hanh were. Formal discussions between Christians and Buddhists about religious matters didn't really get going until the 1980s. In organizing a Catholic–Buddhist dialogue group within the Los Angeles Archdiocese, Vadakin and Ratanasara were pioneers. "With Buddhism, it's a hard dialogue," Vadakin told me, meaning that Christians found themselves in a territory devoid of most basic shared reference points. This wasn't like speaking with Jews or Muslims, fellow monotheists. And for Buddhists, such a dialogue was no easier: How would they explain to a Christian the principle of dependent origination, in which everything in the universe depends on everything else for its existence, the uncreated creation? "With Buddhism, friendship is crucial," Vadakin said, echoing Piyananda. "When there is a difficulty with a community, it's not then that you want to call up someone that you don't know. You want to call up someone you do know."

At moments like this, after visiting and speaking with people so involved in these efforts at societal bridge building, I found myself asking two essential questions. Did all these various activities I encountered really represent a movement? The answer to that, for now, has to be somewhat ambiguous. On one hand, interreligious work in the United States lacks any sort of central organization, with a clearly identified leading figure—something like the Southern Christian Leadership Council in the civil rights era, for example. But at the same time, the interfaith ideal—that people may work together deliberately, peacefully, and productively across religious lines—has caught fire nationally and internationally. There are organizations that devote themselves to it part time or full time by the hundreds and more. They work at the grassroots level. Problem is, as Faroque Khan, the mosque president on Long Island, once said to me, few of them know what the others are doing. That is the price paid for such decentralization.

The other question, which may sound a bit harsh, is whether this movement is primarily about talking. Here, I would offer a measured yes. But what is important is that a great deal can flow from talk, provided it is accompanied by listening, too, among all parties. Then it becomes a conversation, with the opportunity for its participants to gain in knowledge and respect, develop friendships, and share in projects together. Jules Isaac, the elderly Jew on the run for his life from the Gestapo, talked and talked with the young Frenchwoman who sheltered him; their conversation certainly included the research for the book he was writing, *Jesus and Israel,* whose argument against Christian contempt for Judaism helped change Christian-Jewish relations in so much of the world. But then you have to believe that talk—human communication—can matter.

You can put this work in secular terms as an ultimately human project. To say that brings me round to someone I quoted earlier— Albert Camus, whom one would not describe as a religious man. In the articles he wrote late in 1946, collected under the title *Neither Victims nor Executioners,* he wrote about the ethical question of how one should live in a world so prone to violence and destruction, a theme that seems acutely related to religious differences now. His perspective was as a citizen of a continent nearly broken by Nazism and a world threatened by yet another war, between the United States and the Soviet Union. He wrote against killing, as he said, "To save what can be saved and leave ourselves a chance for the future—that is our motive and logic, our passion and sacrifice." In his final essay of the series, Camus calls for the defense of dialogue and universal communication. His tone is urgent—with a flicker of hope, but without a shred of sentimentality. He concludes with what seems now a remarkably prescient view toward the twenty-first century: "In the coming years an endless struggle will be waged across five continents, a struggle in which either violence or dialogue will prevail. Granted, the former has a thousand times the chances of the latter. But I have always thought that if the man who places hope in the human condition is a fool, then he who gives up hope in the face of circumstances is a coward. Henceforth, the only honor will lie in obstinately holding to a formidable gamble: that words are stronger than bullets."

Perhaps in a time of peace and security, were one to imagine such a thing, those words would sound merely interesting. But in these times, they hold the power of a charge given, a responsibility above all responsibilities entrusted to us. We have seen the wreckage—if not up close before our eyes, then broadcast to us—of shattered buildings, airplanes, Humvees, family cars, and, of course, human bodies. The wars around the globe into which religion is woven—violence that over the past two decades has sent many tens of thousands of men, women, and children to terrible deaths in the Balkans, Iraq, Afghanistan, Indonesia, India, Israel, the Palestinian territories, and the United States—deeply threaten what we have of a human society. Denouncing religion itself is futile. (You might as well try to stop the tide coming in, like the English King Canute in legend.) And such simple reactions badly miss the point. It is among the religious believers that the work must be done, within that overwhelming majority who would find common ground in being human and not wanting destruction, if only because their traditions are about so much more. Those traditions contain life-giving possibilities, even if the worst demagogues would try to twist dogma so hard as to wring poison from it.

As Camus said, to work at creating lines of communication that insist on recognizing human beings despite their differences means taking a fundamental risk. Building trust is a great enterprise but a great gamble, too. It entails having faith and acting on it, the faith one places in people to reciprocate, to work together, to believe that what they share—life itself, the miracle of being human—is a gift in any language, any tradition. Yes, it may sound foolish to some, particularly in an era mired in irony, cynicism, and outright fear. But Camus was right: There's honor in hope; the alternative may well be cowardice. In writing as I do now, reflecting on what I have seen, I realize there is one thing I have held back. A thought has nagged at me now for more than six years, since the moment I stepped from the *Times* building on the night of September 11. I have never given it voice. But it is this: Those millions of us who lived or worked directly within the 9/11's smoking shadows—the ruins of the Twin Towers and the crumpled walls of the Pentagon—did so under clouds we never expected to see, much less have to measure morally. Thousands of people were crushed and incinerated in our neighborhoods that day. Together, they belonged to a vast, radically diverse crowd, of many religions, many ethnicities and nationalities. What ultimately became of them? I mean, in this life, the life of the rest of us, who stood in terrified awe beneath those clouds. Did we the living breathe in their ashes as they floated invisibly to earth? And if we did, what do we owe those people? Surely, something more imaginative and more hopeful than a war on terror. They deserve a better monument, a monument dedicated to life and to hope.

"People ask, 'Why do you do this?' " said the Reverend Alexei Smith, one of the newer members of the Catholic-Buddhist dialogue group in Los Angeles. He had assumed Vadakin's old position (after several others had occupied it) of being the archdiocese's officer in charge of ecumenical and interreligious relations. A tall, lean man with a neatly trimmed white beard, Smith had grown up before the reforms of the Second Vatican Council truly took hold. "I was raised pretty strictly," he told me. "I remember the nuns when I was growing up telling me not to hang with Protestants and not to go to their services." Smith came to the priesthood as a second career. He had gone to the University of Southern California and studied international relations. But as a senior he needed a part-time job and ended up applying for a position in a funeral home. They assigned him front-office work, mainly answering the phone and escorting bereaved families into "the viewing room," where the dead were laid out. Management liked him and promoted him through the company; eventually, Smith became a vice president in the chain that owned the place where he first went to work. Along the way, a cultural change was taking place. Funeral homes that once catered exclusively to a single ethnic identity or religious faith were growing more expansive as old social barriers began to break down. New immigrants changed the rules, as they brought their faiths with them. The people with whom Smith dealt expanded. "We served absolutely everyone," he recalled. He learned about Islamic funerary practices—the washing and wrapping of the dead by relatives—and the expectation among Hindus that their deceased relatives would be cremated. "It was such an enlightening experience to me to see how people of different faiths faced death, which is something that confronts all of us," he said. So I ask him what he tells people who ask why he got involved in interreligious activities, why he would spend so much time with Buddhists, Hindus, Jews, and Muslims—whom the nuns might also have warned him about, had they thought of it. "I usually answer, if you read the Creation account of Genesis, all of humankind is created in the image of God," Smith said. "We have to recognize that we are created by the same Creator. And that's why we talk together. And that's why we try to understand one another. And if we do recognize the presence of God in one another, we won't be fighting with one another."

On one of the last occasions I saw Piyananda, he quoted the Buddha, using language that I thought offered some response to Camus's stark vision. The occasion happened to be in Los Angeles's Cathedral of Our Lady of the Angeles, the archdiocese's new cathedral, dedicated in 2002. It's a place with an appropriately multicultural feel to it. Long, smooth surfaces, an exterior distinguished by earth tones and clean, direct lines evoke traditional architecture of the region's Native American and Hispanic peoples. Outside the main entrance, beneath a statue of the crucified Christ, a cornerstone bears an inscription of a familiar verse from the Hebrew Bible, the words of the Prophet Isaiah, in which God promises, "My house will be called a house of prayer for all peoples." It is a radically inclusive statement, dealing directly with the question of whether the ancient Israelites may allow foreigners entrance to the Temple in Jerusalem for sacrifice to God. Here's the King James Version of the verse (56:7) "Even them will I bring to my holy mountain, and make them joyful in my house of prayer: their burnt offerings and their sacrifices shall be accepted upon mine altar; for mine house shall be called a house of prayer for all people."

When I saw Piyananda there, he stood at the sanctuary's front among a dozen or so Catholics and an equal number of Buddhist monks and nuns, whose saffron robes provided a visual counterpoint to the cathedral's muted interior. Buddhist tradition holds that the historical Buddha, after his enlightenment, spent forty-five years teaching the path to spiritual liberation. Late in life, he was visited by a royal emissary, who told him a local king planned to attack a group called the Vajjians. The Buddha advised against it. When Piyananda rose to speak, he took his text from that dialogue, within the Scripture called "The Long Discourses of the Buddha." In it, the Buddha speaks favorably of the Vajjians as a people "who meet in harmony, break up in harmony and carry on their business in harmony." They are people, he says, who can be expected to prosper and not decline.

Those were among the last words spoken by the Buddha. He died not long afterward, aged eighty. As he lay down on the earth, tradition tells it, the trees around him broke into bloom and shed their blossoms upon him.

After the service, I walked out from the cathedral into a warm, autumnal evening. The sun had long since gone down, but the darkness that would have enveloped downtown Los Angeles was being kept at bay by the lights that blazed on the city's streets and in its buildings. I seemed to have the sidewalk to myself. At a moment like that, one could almost think of oneself as alone, a single individual walking an illuminated grid that spreads out in all directions for miles. But then one realizes that one is not alone; millions of others are afoot or at the wheel, sitting over dinner at home or bent over desks in their offices. True, those millions there in Los Angeles—and their billions of counterparts in cities and towns and villages worldwide—do not share a common faith. But as Martin Buber said once, they have something in common, living as they do in "the situation, of anxiety and of expectation."

They—we—have our basic humanity in common. We share a world, but one threatened by violent fanaticism. Buber, in his essay, described genuine dialogue as that state in which "each of the participants has in mind the other or others in their present and particular being and turns to them with the intention of establishing a living mutual relationship between himself and them."

And so we have a choice, a possibility of community before us, and so much about which we can speak to one another. The stakes are very high.

Acknowledgments

There were many people to whom I turned for aid and advice in writing this book. None were more important than Constance H. Buchanan, senior program officer at the Ford Foundation. Connie's belief in the project's value proved crucial to my undertaking it. She deserves my thanks above all.

Robert Wuthnow, professor of sociology and director of the Center for the Study of Religion at Princeton University, provided me with a stimulating environment in which to begin my research. I benefited, too, from the unfailingly cheerful technical help given by the center's administrator, Anita Kline. At Syracuse University, I extend thanks to Cathryn R. Newton, dean of the College of Arts and Sciences, and David Rubin, dean of the university's S. I. Newhouse School of Public Communications. With the support of former provost Deborah Freund, and, more recently, Chancellor Nancy Cantor, they have given me an exciting intellectual location in which to complete this work.

Wendy Wolf at Viking provided powerfully thorough and exacting editorial guidance, of which most writers would surely be envious. I thank her, along with her former assistant, Hilary Redmon, and my agent, Kris Dahl, who encouraged me in this project from its start.

Several individuals graciously accepted my requests to read early chapter drafts and offered valuable criticism: Clyde F. Crews; Eugene J. Fisher; James L. Fredericks; R. Scott Hanson; Joseph C. Hough, Jr., Leon Klenicki; Martin E. Marty; Kusumita Pedersen; and John F. Wilson.

Finally, I owe an incalculable debt to my beloved wife, Margaret L. Usdansky, for her practical advice and incisive comments. Although she chose another profession, I believe her a born editor.

Notes

PREFACE

xi   **"Absolutism":** Reinhold Niebuhr, *Moral Man and Immoral Society* (New York: Charles Scribner's Sons, 1932, 1960), 199.

INTRODUCTION: ON DOUBT AND CONVERSION

xv   **"the nations and the religions together":** *New York Times,* September 23, 2000, 8.

xvi   **using rape as a systematic weapon:** *New York Times,* January 9, 1993, 1.

xvi   **a suicide bomber murdered:** *New York Times,* May 2, 1993, 1.

xvi   **nine people perished:** *New York Times,* October 24, 1993, 3.

xvi   **"a conversion":** Ibid.

xviii **"demoralizing and terrorizing communities":** *New York Times,* January 9, 1993, 1.

xix   **"difficult to belittle and kill":** Mark Juergensmeyer, *Terror in the Mind of God* (Berkeley and Los Angeles: University of California Press, 2000), 174.

xx   **"an inescapable network of mutuality":** Reverend Dr. Martin Luther King, Jr., Letter from a Birmingham Jail, http://www.stanford .edu/group/King/frequentdocs/birmingham.pdf, 1–2.

xx   **basic education about religions:** Stephen Prothero, *Religious Literacy: What Every American Needs to Know—and Doesn't* (New York: HarperCollins, 2007), 127.

xxii **described in detail:** Diana Eck, *A New Religious America* (New York: HarperCollins, 2001), 4.

xxviii **"world house":** Reverend Dr. Martin Luther King, Jr., *Chaos or Community?* (London: Hodder and Stoughton Ltd., 1968), 167.

xxix **Protestant theologian Paul Tillich:** F. Forrester Church, ed., *The Essential Tillich: An Anthology of the Writings of Paul Tillich* (Chicago: University of Chicago Press, 1999), 215–16.

xxix **Christians must think of their faith:** Right Reverend Rowan Williams, "Christian Identity and Religious Plurality," archbishop's address to the ninth meeting of the World Council of Churches, Porto Alegre, Brazil, February 17, 2006.

xxx **"the will-to-live and the will-to-power":** Reinhold Niebuhr, *Moral Man and Immoral Society*, op. cit., 63.

xxxi **"a very high form":** Reinhold Niebuhr, *The Children of Light and the Children of Darkness* (New York: Charles Scribner's Sons, 1944), 134.

xxxii **"If you are mindful":** *Washington Post*, September 28, 1993, C1.

xxxiii **"When I speak of love":** Reverend Dr. Martin Luther King, Jr., "Beyond Vietnam—A Time to Break the Silence," a speech delivered April 4, 1967, at Riverside Church, New York. Available at http:// www.americanrhetoric.com/speeches/mlkatimetobreakthesilence .htm.

xxxv **"mocking metaphor":** *Dallas Morning News*, November 12, 2006.

xxxv **"one with You":** Lawrence S. Cunningham, ed., *Thomas Merton: Spiritual Master* (Mahwah, NJ: Paulist Press, 1992), 237.

xxxvi **"the overcoming of doubt":** Ibid., 228.

xxxvii **"The only alternative to talking":** Donald W. Mitchell and James Wiseman, O.S.B., ed., *The Gethsemani Encounter* (New York: Continuum Publishing Co., 1999), 16.

ONE: UNDER THE PILLAR OF SMOKE

3 **"backlash after every major":** *New York Times*, September 18, 2001, B5.

3 **"doing this for my country":** *New York Times*, September 14, 2001, 14.

3 **another man died:** *New York Times*, September 18, 2001, op. cit.

3 **glass strewn:** *New York Times*, September 22, 2001, 11.

10 **"ring of protection":** *Sojourners*, January/February 2002, 34.

11 **"had experienced kindness":** *American Muslims One Year After 9–11*, (Washington, D.C.: Council on American-Islamic Relations Research Center), 16–17.

11 **"our arms around":** *New York Times*, September 15, 2001, B6.

13 **"were so divided":** James H. Hutson, *Religion and the Founding of the American Republic* (Washington, D.C.: Library of Congress, 1998), 77.

13 **"a multiplicity of sects":** Robert S. Alley, *James Madison on Religious Liberty* (Buffalo, NY: Prometheus Books, 1985), 191.

14 **77 percent of Americans:** *American Religious Identification Survey* (New York: City University of New York Graduate Center), Key Findings, http://www.gc.cuny.edu/faculty/research_briefs/aris/key_ findings.htm.

15   **nearly one quarter of Europe's Jewish population:** Hasia R. Diner, *The Jews of the United States* (Berkeley and Los Angeles: University of California Press, 2004), 74.

15   **Tocqueville once asked:** George Wilson Pierson, *Tocqueville and Beaumont in America* (New York: Oxford University Press, 1938), 220.

16   **African Americans registered to vote:** *The Effect of the Voting Rights Act,* (Washington, D.C.: United States Department of Justice, Civil Rights Division, Voting Section), http://www.usdoj.gov/crt/voting/intro/intro_c.htm.

17   **"people could see my yarmulke":** *New York Times,* May 1, 1997, 1.

17   **"not a revolutionary bill":** National Public Radio, *All Things Considered,* May 9, 2006.

18   **Asian Indians numbered nearly two million:** U.S. Census Bureau, "The Asian Population 2000" and "A Profile of the Nation's Foreign-Born Population from Asia (2000 Update)," census briefs issued February 2002.

18   **nearly 1,600 mosques:** *"Geographic Distribution of Religious Centers in the U.S.,"* The Pluralism Project at Harvard University (cited October 15, 2007) http://www.pluralism.org/resources/statistics/distribution.php.

19   **Built at a cost:** "Largest U.S. Mosque," *Christian Century,* September 20, 2005, 17.

20   **Arab descent rose by nearly 40 percent:** U.S. Census Bureau, "The Arab Population 2000," census brief issued December 2003.

20   **half of the mosques had joined with non-Muslims:** Ihsan Bagby, "A Portrait of Detroit Mosques: Muslim Views on Policy, Politics and Religion," research paper published by the Institute for Social Policy and Understanding, Clinton Township, MI, 2004, 55.

21   **Born in Karbala, Iraq:** Imam Qazwini's biography is available on the Web site of the Islamic Center of America, http://www.icofa.com/.

22   **"Dialogue is an art":** Appeal for Peace, international prayer for peace (Washington, D.C.: Georgetown University, 2006).

24   **"rejects nothing":** "Declaration on the Relation of the Church to Non-Christian Religions," *Nostra Aetate,* Proclaimed by His Holiness Pope Paul VI on October 28, 1965, http://www.vatican.va/archive/hist_councils/ii_vatican_council/documents/vat-ii_decl_19651028_nostra-aetate_en.html.

27   **"promote joint reflection":** Joel Beverluis, ed., *A Sourcebook for Earth's Community of Religions* (Grand Rapids, MI: CoNexus Press, 1995), 161.

28   **"reconciliation among people":** "Interfaith Relations and the Churches: A Policy Statement of the National Council of Churches of Christ in the U.S.A.," November 10, 1999, http://www.ncccusa.org/interfaith/ifr.html.

33   **to speak in Princeton Theological Seminary's chapel:** "For Such a Time as This," *InSpire*, Winter 2002, vol. 6, no. 2.

TWO: BEYOND TOLERATION

37   **"Go, bin Laden!":** The story of the burning of Gobind Sadan U.S.A.'s building, the trial and punishment of the perpetrators, along with their forgiveness by the Sikhs is told in the film *North of 49*, a 2003 documentary by Richard Breyer, a professor at the S. I. Newhouse School of Public Communications at Syracuse University, and David Coryell, a screenwriter and adjunct professor.

40   **"Can we all get along?":** King's plea, with full attribution to the speaker, was stripped across the cover of *Time* magazine's May 11, 1992, issue, across a photograph of Los Angeles law enforcement officials racing toward a fire.

41   **The scene provoked widespread outrage:** *New York Times*, April 30, 1992, 1.

42   **"intolerance and ignorance":** *Los Angeles Times*, May 3, 2004.

42   **support of the Wiesenthal Center:** *New York Times*, August 17, 2003, 1.

43   **fired the columnist:** *The Guardian*, March 22, 2002.

43   **"another man's point of view":** Arthur Gilbert, *The Vatican Council and the Jews* (Cleveland, OH: World Publishing Co., 1968), 80.

44   **called the faith:** *New York Times*, April 18, 2003, 310.

44   **a remark for which he later apologized:** *New York Times*, October 14, 2002, 9.

44   **to declare a right:** *Los Angeles Times*, April 10, 2006.

45   **"not gay friendly":** *New York Times*, July 31, 2003, 3.

45   **"If Christians are to be warned":** John Locke, *A Letter on Toleration* (London: Oxford University Press, 1968), 88–89.

47   **"no more that toleration is spoken of":** Washington's letter is available at Touro Synagogue's Web site, http://www.tourosynagogue.org/.

47   **two dozen refugees:** Martin E. Marty, *Pilgrims in Their Own Land* (New York: Penguin, 1984), 69.

49   **the *Globe* chose:** National Public Radio, *Morning Edition*, February 7, 2006.

50   **"through dialogue":** Charles Taylor, *Multiculturalism and the Politics of Recognition* (Princeton, NJ: Princeton University Press, 1992), 34.

51   **"I assured them":** National Public Radio, op. cit.

51   **"A multicultural society":** Amy Gutman, "Introduction," Taylor, op. cit., 22.

53   **"Freedom means":** Franklin D. Roosevelt's "Four Freedoms"

speech may be found at http://www.fdrlibrary.marist.edu/4free.html
and at other Web sites.

55   **"Yes, what we must fight":** Albert Camus, *Between Hell and Reason*
      (Hanover and London: Wesleyan University Press, 1991), 138.

56   **The Methodists delivered their check:** United Methodist News
      Service, "Jewish Congregation Sheds Tears of Joy for United Meth-
      odist Support," June 28,1999.

57   **Episcopalians who thought:** *New York Times,* February 4, 2003, B1.

THREE: AN IDEA REVIVED FOR THE BATTLEFIELD

60   **"influential advocate":** *The Guardian,* November 1, 2001.

61   **impact on Ayman al-Zawahiri:** Gilles Kepel, *The Roots of Radical
      Islam* (London: Saqi, 2005), 11–13. (The quotations from Qutb are
      from Kepel.)

65   **"Islam is a very good religion":** Eboo Patel, *Acts of Faith* (Boston:
      Beacon Press, 2007), 96.

66   **"We have inherited":** King, *Chaos or Community?,* op. cit., 167.

67   **"It is not good to say":** *Selections from the Gospel of Sri Ramakrishna,
      Annotated and Explained* (Woodstock, VT: SkyLight Paths Publishing,
      2002), 90.

68   **"seemed to become absent-minded":** Ibid., 9.

68   **Interfaith Alliance:** Information on both the alliance and the World
      Conference on Religions for Peace may be found at their Web
      sites, http://www.theinterfaithalliance.org and http://www.wcrp
      .org/, respectively.

70   **"faiths may speak":** Reverend John Henry Barrows, ed., *The
      World's Parliament of Religions* (Chicago: Parliament Publishing Co.,
      1893), vol. 1, 72.

71   **"to respect their sincerity and zeal":** Charles Bonney, "The
      Genesis of the World's Religious Congresses of 1893," *New-Church
      Review,* January 1894, vol. 1, 78.

72   **"filled the earth with violence":** Swami Chetanananda, *Vive-
      kananda: East Meets West* (St. Louis: Vedanta Society, 1995).

73   **"the chain of the Ferris Wheel":** Ibid., 48.

74   **"be glad to learn":** Barrows, op. cit., 75.

75   **"a little ugly black image":** Kim Knott, *Hinduism: A Very Short Intro-
      duction* (Oxford and New York: Oxford University Press, 1998), 55.

75   **"how foolish":** Chetanananda, op. cit., 59.

76   **"flaming heart of the world":** Reverend Marcus Braybrooke,
      Pilgrimage of Hope: One Hundred Years of Interfaith Discovery (Norwich,
      England: SCM Press, 1991), 64.

77   **"If we are each":** Wayne Teasdale and George F. Cairns, eds., *The
      Community of Religions: Voices and Images of the World's Parliament of Re-*

ligions (New York: Continuum International Publishing Group, 1996), 19.

79 **an estimated eleven million Spaniards:** *New York Times,* March 13, 2004, 1

79 **"Under no circumstances":** BBC News, March 13, 2004.

79 **"to kill your own kind":** *USA Today,* March 17, 2004.

82 **Bunting-Meyerhoff Interfaith:** information comes from the chaplain's space within Johns Hopkins University's Web site (http://www .jhu.edu/~chaplain), accessed on December 10, 2007. It showed that a survey of nearly three quarters of the university's 4,273 registered students in the class of 2009 indicated 38 separate religious identities among that group, from African Methodist Episcopal to Zoroastrian. Of the 38 (which included students listing themselves as "other" and "none"), 20 identities fell under the broad umbrella of evangelical and mainline Protestantism. But the largest groups were Roman Catholics (29 percent), Jews (13 percent), no religion (12 percent), Presbyterians (7 percent), nondenominational evangelicals (6 percent), and Baptists and Hindus (5 percent each). Muslim students made up 2.4 percent of the total, close behind Lutherans. A similar survey, taken of the class of 2006, yielded similar results.

83 **"I sure hope":** Eboo Patel, *Acts of Faith* (Boston: Beacon Press, 2007), 163.

FOUR: HOSPITALITY

85 **"until the Holy Spirit moved someone":** Thomas Merton, *The Seven Storey Mountain* (New York: Harcourt Brace, 1998), 13.

86 **outside the mosque:** *New York Times, Long Island Weekly,* October 15, 2006, 1.

87 **Atique Sharifi:** BBC News, August 3, 2005.

88 **"a Londoner and British":** Ibid.

88 **"This terrorism":** National Public Radio, *Morning Edition,* May 17, 2007.

89 **7 percent:** Hartford Institute for Religion Research, "A Quick Question: Has Interfaith Worship Increased Since 9/11?," http://hirr .hartsem.edu/research/quick_question46.html (Web site summary of findings taken from institute's publication "Faith Communities Today, 2005").

92 **"a monstrosity":** *The Guardian,* February 19, 1996, quoted by Human Rights Watch, "Bosnia and Herzegovina," http://www.hrw .org/reports/1997/bosnia/Bosnia-02.htm.

95 **a place run by extremists:** *New York Times, Long Island Weekly,* op. cit.

97 **"many more Muslims":** *New York Times,* December 21, 2006.

97 **"many different faiths":** Ibid.

97   **"Sir, prove to me":** The videotape showing the segment of the interview has been posted on Youtube.com.

98   **should "show solidarity":** *Washington Post,* December 21, 2006, B5.

98   **what might be acceptable:** *New York Times,* June 10, 2007, Week in Review, 1.

99   **two-thirds immigrant:** Pew Research Center, "American Muslims: Middle Class and Mostly Mainstream," May 22, 2007.

101   **"those who claim":** Ingrid Mattson, "A Call for Moral Leadership: Imagining a New Heroism," an online article at the Duncan Black MacDonald Center for the Study of Islam and Christian-Muslim Relations, Hartford Seminary, http://macdonald.hartsem.edu/mattsonart7.htm.

102   **"Different Religions Week":** State of Tennessee, proclamation by Governor Phil Bredesen, signed July 1, 2003.

102   **"become more aware of our temple":** *The Tennessean,* September 14, 2003.

103   **"Open Mosque Day":** *Los Angeles Times,* August 22, 2005, B1.

104   **"the religiosity of Muslims":** Pope John Paul II, *Crossing the Threshold of Hope* (New York: Knopf, 1995), 93.

105   **"The pilgrims should pray together":** Donald W. Mitchell and James A. Wiseman, eds., *The Gethsemani Encounter: A Dialogue on the Spiritual Life by Buddhist and Christian Monastics* (New York: Continuum, 1999), 49.

107   **"a great many stereotypes":** Omar Safi, ed., *Progressive Muslims: On Justice, Gender, and Pluralism* (Oxford: One World, 2003), 267.

109   **incidents of verbal harassment:** *Washington Post,* November 16, 1992, 1.

111   **"introduced to learning":** Shakunthala Jagannathan and Nanditha Krishna, *Ganesha: The Auspicious . . . the Beginning* (Bombay: Vakils, Feffer and Simonds, Ltd., 1995), 3.

111   **concept called** *darshan:* Diana L. Eck, *Darsan: Seeing the Divine Image In India* (New York: Columbia University Press, 1998), 3.

112   **a violent encounter:** *New York Times,* September 25, 2002, 8.

114   **"religious liberty is not an act of charity":** Mehran Kamrava, ed., *The New Voices of Islam* (Berkeley and Los Angeles: University of California Press, 2006), 117.

116   **"The raving Quakers":** Rufus M. Jones, *The Quakers in the American Colonies* (New York: W. W. Norton, 1923), 218, 225.

116   **Flushing Remonstrance:** R. Ward Harrington, *Speaking Scripture: The Flushing Remonstrance of 1657* (Friends Historical Association), pamphlet available at Quaker Meeting House, Flushing, NY.

117   **"Let everyone remain free":** Jones, op. cit., 228.

120   **merely manifestations:** Horst Georg Pohlmann, *Encounters with Hinduism* (New York: SCM Press, 1996), 37–38.

120   **a registered Republican:** *New York Times,* November 3, 2000, B2.

121   **experience of encounters:** Harold Coward, ed., *Modern Indian Responses to Religious Pluralism* (New York: State University of New York Press, 1988), 11.

FIVE: AN ERA OF CONVERSATION

124   **"The door opened":** Primo Levi, *Survival in Auschwitz* (New York: Macmillan, 1978).

124   **"*Shoah* took place in Europe":** Vatican Commission for Religious Relations with the Jews, *"We Remember: A Reflection on the Shoah,"* March 16, 1998, 3.

125   **"condemnation of anti-Semitism":** Pope John Paul II, "Address to Jewish Leaders," Strasbourg, France, October 9, 1988. (The phrase is quoted in *"We Remember."*)

127   **"Remember, one God speaks to us all":** International Conference of Christians and Jews, "Reports and Recommendations of the Emergency Conference on Anti-Semitism" (Geneva: The International Conference of Christians and Jews, 1947), 13.

127   **The Jews were branches:** Mary C. Boys, *Has God Only One Blessing?* (Mahwah, NJ: Paulist Press, 2000), 55–56.

130   **"a common action":** Charles Taylor, *Philosophical Arguments* (Cambridge and London: Harvard University Press, 1995), 189–90.

132   **"our *religious* prejudices":** Thomas Kennedy, quoted in *Sketch of Proceedings of the Legislature of Maryland, December Session, 1818, on What Is Commonly Called the Jew Bill,* 15.

137   **"reams of documents":** Boys, op. cit., 248.

137   **"Grieving the complicity":** Evangelical Lutheran Church in America, "Declaration of the Evangelical Lutheran Church in America to the Jewish Community," April 18, 1994.

137   **"The madness":** Alliance of Baptists, "A Statement on Jewish-Christian Relations from the Alliance of Baptists," March 4, 1995.

138   **"called by God":** Consultation of the National Council of Synagogues and the Bishops' Committee for Ecumenical and Interreligious Affairs, USCCB, "Reflections on Covenant and Mission," August 12, 2002.

139   **to show each other mutual respect:** *Los Angeles Times,* August 20, 2005, 1.

140   **Jewish organizations . . . expressed outrage:** Anti-Defamation League, "ADL Outraged by Southern Baptist Statements Rooting

Jewish Conversion Appeals in Theology," press release, September 28, 1999.

140   **first-century Judaism:** Amy-Jill Levine, "Misusing Jesus," *Christian Century,* December 26, 2006, 20–25.

144   **"Let us pray":** Gilbert, op. cit., 30.

145   **"have conscripted Jews":** Right Reverend Rowan Williams, *Writing in the Dust* (Grand Rapids, MI, and Cambridge, England: William B. Eerdmans Publishing Co., 2002), 63.

146   **"For what Christians received":** Jules Isaac, *Jesus and Israel* (New York: Holt, Reinhart and Winston, 1971), 386.

147   **The distraught husband:** Michael Phayer and Eva Fleishner, *Cries in the Night: Women Who Challenged the Holocaust* (Kansas City, MO: Sheed & Ward, 1997), 104.

147   **"the two of us":** Ibid., 106–7.

148   **"the major lesson":** Isaac, op. cit., 400.

149   **Christians must remember:** International Council of Christians and Jews, op. cit., 14–16.

149   **"are beloved for the fathers' sake":** Ibid., 16.

150   **"its persistence and growth":** Ibid., 3.

152   **"God holds the Jews most dear":** Declaration on the Relation of the Church to Non-Christian Religions, op. cit.

152   **"to my brothers and sisters":** Pope Benedict XVI, mass for the inauguration of the pontificate of Pope Benedict XVI, "Homily of His Holiness Benedict XVI," April 24, 2005.

152   **"genuine religious conversations":** Martin Buber, *Between Man and Man* (New York and London: Routledge, 1947), 7–8.

153   **he felt compelled:** Phayer and Fleischner, op. cit., 106.

153   **"The struggle against anti-Semitism":** The National Conference of Christians and Jews, *The Seelisberg Conference, August 1947,* Human Relations Pamphlet No. 13, 3.

154   **"The restoration of honor":** Ibid.

158   **"There are few Jews":** Thomas Kennedy, *"Sketch of Proceedings,"* 31, 34, 38.

158   **He died six years later:** *Baltimore Sun,* March 19, 1972, 89.

SIX: GATEKEEPERS

160   **"In Louisville":** Lawrence S. Cunningham, ed., *Thomas Merton: Spiritual Master* (Mahwah, NJ: Paulist Press, 1992), 144.

162   **"waking from a dream of separateness":** Ibid., 145.

173   **Catholics dedicated their own building:** Clyde F. Crews, ed., *Hallowed Ground: Louisville's Historic Cathedral of the Assumption* (Louisville, KY: Archdiocese of Louisville, 2002), 17–27.

176 **"in comparison with"**: *New York Times Magazine,* March 17, 1997, 42.

178 **"how Christians should understand others"**: W. Eugene March, *The Wide, Wide Circle of Divine Love* (Louisville, KY: Westminster/ John Knox Press), 104.

179 **the Dalai Lama called Merton:** Thomas Merton, *The Asian Journals of Thomas Merton* (New York: New Directions Books, 1975), 125.

179 **"I was suddenly"**: Ibid., 233–35.

180 **"I will be a better Catholic"**: Cunningham, op. cit., 133.

181 **"my attitude toward Christianity"**: Mitchell and Wiseman, op. cit., 48.

CONCLUSION: WORDS OVER BULLETS

187 **his Buddhist identity:** Bhante Walpola Piyananda, *Saffron Days in L.A.* (Boston and London: Shambhala, 2001), 101.

187 **a book claiming:** Lecture by Piyananda quoted in Daniel A. Reinke, "Buddhist-Roman Catholic Dialogue in Southern California: An Historical Overview" (unpublished master's thesis for the Department of Theological Studies, Loyola-Marymount University, 2001), 113.

190 **"To save what can be saved"**: Camus, op. cit., 138, 140.

195 **"each of the participants"**: Buber, op. cit.

Bibliography

I. DECLARATIONS, SERMONS, SPEECHES, AND OTHER
STATEMENTS

Alliance of Baptists, "A Statement on Jewish-Christian Relations from the Alliance of Baptists," Washington, D.C., March 4, 1995.

Anti-Defamation League, "ADL Outraged by Southern Baptist Statements Rooting Jewish Conversion Appeals in Theology," press release, September 28, 1999.

"Appeal for Peace," International Prayer for Peace, Washington, D.C., Georgetown University, April 2006. Events sponsored by: Communità di Sant'Egidio, Rome; Roman Catholic Archdiocese of Washington, D.C.; Georgetown University; and the Catholic University of America.

Pope Benedict XVI, mass for the inauguration of the pontificate of Pope Benedict XVI, "Homily of His Holiness Benedict XVI," April 24, 2005.

Consultation of the National Council of Synagogues and the Bishops' Committee for Ecumenical and Interreligious Affairs, USCCB, "Reflections on Covenant and Mission," August 12, 2002.

"Declaration on the Relation of the Church to non-Christian Religions" (Nostra Aetate), Proclaimed by His Holiness Pope Paul VI, October 28, 1965.

"Different Religions Week": State of Tennessee, Proclamation by the Governor, signed by Gov. Phil Bredesen, July 1, 2003.

Evangelical Lutheran Church in America, "Declaration of the Evangelical Lutheran Church in America to the Jewish Community," April 18, 1994.

Roosevelt, Franklin D., "Annual Address to Congress," January 6, 1941 (also known as "The Four Freedoms Speech") http://www.fdrlibrary .marist.edu/4free.html and at other sites.

"Interfaith Relations and the Churches: A Policy Statement of the National Council of Churches of Christ in the U.S.A." November 10, 1999.

Pope John Paul II, "Address to Jewish Leaders" Strasbourg, France, October 9, 1988.

King Jr., Rev. Dr. Martin Luther, Letter from a Birmingham Jail, April 16, 1963, http://www.stanford.edu/group/King/frequentdocs/birmingham.pdf and other sites.

Mattson, Ingrid,"A Call for Moral Leadership: Imagining a New Heroism," May 25, 2007, online article at the Duncan Black MacDonald Center for the Study of Islam and Christian-Muslim Relations, Hartford Seminary http://macdonald.hartsem.edu/mattsonart7.htm.

Vatican Commission for Religious Relations with the Jews, "*We Remember: A Reflection on the Shoah,*" March 16, 1998.

Williams, Rt. Rev. Rowan, Archbishop of Canterbury, "Christian Identity and Religious Plurality," Archbishop's address to the ninth meeting of the World Council of Churches, Porto Alegre, Brazil, Feb. 17, 2006.

II. NEWSPAPERS AND MAGAZINES

The Baltimore Sun
The Christian Century
The Dallas Morning News
The Guardian
Inspire (Princeton Theological Seminary)
The Los Angeles Times
The New-Church Review
The New York Times
The New York Times Magazine
Sojourners
The Tennessean
Time
USA Today
The Washington Post

III. PAMPHLETS, RESEARCH PAPERS AND PUBLISHED SURVEYS

American Muslims One Year After 9–11, Council on American-Islamic Relations Research Center, Washington D.C., 2002, 16–17.

American Religious Identification Survey (New York: City University of New York Graduate Center, 2001), Key Findings, available at http://www.gc.cuny.edu/faculty/research_briefs/aris/key_findings.htm.

"Effect of the Voting Rights Act, The," U.S. Department of Justice, Civil Rights Division, Voting Section, 2005, available at http://www.usdoj.gov/crt/voting/intro/intro_c.htm.

"Geographic Distribution of Religious Centers in the U.S.," the Pluralism Project at Harvard University (cited October 15, 2007), 2005, available at http://www.pluralism.org/resources/statistics/distribution.php.

Harrington, R. Ward, *Speaking Scripture: The Flushing Remonstrance of 1657* (Friends Historical Association), undated pamphlet available at Quaker Meeting House, Flushing, N.Y.

Hartford Institute for Religion Research, *A Quick Question: Has Interfaith Worship Increased Since 9/11?* (summary of some findings in institute's "Faith Communities Today 2005" survey, published 2006), available at http://hirr.hartsem.edu/research/quick_question46.html.

International Conference of Christians and Jews, "Reports and Recommendations of the Emergency Conference on Anti-Semitism" (Geneva: The International Conference of Christians and Jews, 1947).

National Conference of Christians and Jews, *The Seelisberg Conference, August 1947,* Human Relations Pamphlet No. 13.

Piyananda, Walpola. "Love in Buddhism" (Los Angeles: Dharma Vijaya Buddhist Vihara, 1990).

Daniel A. Reinke, "Buddhist-Roman Catholic Dialogue in Southern California: An Historical Overview" (unpublished master's thesis for the Department of Theological Studies, Loyola-Marymount University, 2001).

"Sketch of Proceedings of the Legislature of Maryland, December Session, 1818, on What Is Commonly Called the Jew Bill."

III. RADIO AND TELEVISION BROADCASTS

BBC News, heard on http://www.bbc.co.uk.

CNN (clip on YouTube.com)

National Public Radio, *All Things Considered* and *Morning Edition*

National Public Radio, *Morning Edition*

IV. BOOKS

Alley, Robert S., *James Madison on Religious Liberty* (Buffalo: Prometheus Books, 1985).

Barrows, John Henry, ed., *The World's Parliament of Religions* (Chicago: Parliament Publishing Co., 1893), v. 1.

Beverluis, Joel, ed., *A Sourcebook for Earth's Community of Religions* (Grand Rapids, Mich.: CoNexus Press, 1995).

Boys, Mary C., *Has God Only One Blessing?* (Mahwah, N.J.: Paulist Press, 2000).

Braybrooke, Rev. Marcus, *Pilgrimage of Hope: One Hundred Years of Interfaith Discovery* (New York: Crossroad Publishing Co., 1992).

Bruteau, Beatrice, *Merton and Judaism: Holiness in Words* (Louisville: Fons Vitae, 2003).

Buber, Martin, *Between Man and Man* (New York and London: Routledge, 1947).

Camus, Albert, *Between Hell and Reason* (Hanover and London: Wesleyan University Press, 1991).

Chetanananda, Swami, *Vivekananda: East Meets West* (St. Louis: Vedanta Society, 1995).

Church, F. Forrester, ed., *The Essential Tillich: An Anthology of the Writings of Paul Tillich* (Chicago: University of Chicago Press, 1987).

Coward, Harold, ed., *Modern Indian Responses to Religious Pluralism* (New York: State University of New York Press, 1988).

Crews, Rev. Clyde F., ed., *Hallowed Ground: Louisville's Historic Cathedral of the Assumption* (Archdiocese of Louisville, 2002).

Cunningham, Lawrence S., ed., *Thomas Merton: Spiritual Master* (Mahwah, N.J.: Paulist Press, 1992).

Eck, Diana, *A New Religious America* (New York: HarperCollins, 2001).

————, *Darsan: Seeing the Divine Image in India* (New York: Columbia University Press, 1998).

Fredericks, James L., *Buddhists and Christians: Through Comparative Theology to Solidarity* (Maryknoll, N.Y.: Orbis Books, 2004).

Gilbert, Arthur, *The Vatican Council and the Jews* (Cleveland: World Publishing Co., 1968).

Hutson, James H., *Religion and the Founding of the American Republic* (Washington: Library of Congress, 1998).

Isaac, Jules, *Jesus and Israel* (New York: Holt, Reinhart and Winston, 1971).

Jagannathan, Shakunthala, and Nanditha Krishna, *Ganesha: The Auspicious . . . The Beginning* (Bombay: Vakils, Feffer and Simonds, Ltd., 1995).

John Paul II, Pope, *Crossing the Threshold of Hope* (New York: Knopf, 1995).

Jones, Rufus M., *The Quakers in the American Colonies* (New York: Norton and Co., 1923), 218, 225.

Juergensmeyer, Mark, *Terror in the Mind of God* (Berkeley and Los Angeles: University of California Press, 2000).

Kamrava, Mehran, ed., *The New Voices of Islam* (Berkeley and Los Angeles: University of California Press, 2006), 117.

Kepel, Gilles, *The Roots of Radical Islam* (London: Saqi, 2005).

King, Rev. Martin Luther, Jr., *Chaos or Community?* (London: Hodder and Stoughton Ltd., 1968).

Knitter, Paul F., *Introducing Theologies of Religion* (Maryknoll, N.Y.: Orbis Books, 2002).

Knott, Kim, *Hinduism: A Very Short Introduction* (Oxford and New York: Oxford University Press, 1998).

Levi, Primo, *Survival in Auschwitz* (New York: Macmillan Publishing Co., 1978).

Locke, John, *A Letter on Toleration* (London: Oxford University Press, 1968).

M., a disciple of the master, *Selections from the Gospel of Sri Ramakrishna, Annotated and Explained* (Woodstock, Vt.: SkyLight Paths Publishing, 2002).

McLeod, Hew, *Sikhism* (London: Penguin Books, 1997).

March, W. Eugene, *The Wide, Wide Circle of Divine Love* (Louisville: Westminster/John Knox Press).

Marty, Martin E., *Pilgrims in Their Own Land* (New York: Penguin, 1984).

Merton, Thomas, *The Asian Journals of Thomas Merton* (New York: New Directions Books, 1975).

Mitchell, Donald W., and James A. Wiseman, eds., *The Gethsemani Encounter: A Dialogue on the Spiritual Life by Buddhist and Christian Monastics* (New York: Continuum, 1999).

Niebuhr, Reinhold, *The Children of Light and The Children of Darkness* (New York: Charles Scribner's Sons, 1944).

———, *Moral Man and Immoral Society* (New York: Charles Scribner's Sons, 1932, 1960).

Patel, Eboo, *Acts of Faith* (Boston: Beacon Press, 2007).

Phayer, Michael, and Eva Fleishner, *Cries in the Night: Women Who Challenged the Holocaust* (Kansas City, MO: Sheed & Ward, 1997).

Pierson, George Wilson, *Tocqueville and Beaumont in America* (New York: Oxford University Press, 1938).

Piyananda, Bhante Walpola, *Saffron Days in L.A.* (Boston and London: Shambhala, 2001).

Pohlmann, Horst Georg, *Encounters with Hinduism* (New York: SCM Press, 1996).

Prothero, Stephen, *Religious Literacy: What Every American Needs to Know—And Doesn't* (New York: HarperCollins, 2007).

Safi, Omar, ed., *Progressive Muslims: On Justice, Gender, and Pluralism* (Oxford: One World, 2003).

Taylor, Charles, *Multiculturalism and the Politics of Recognition* (Princeton, NJ: Princeton University Press, 1992).

———, *Philosophical Arguments* (Cambridge and London: Harvard University Press, 1995).

Teasdale, Wayne, and George F. Cairns, eds., *The Community of Religions: Voices and Images of the World's Parliament of Religions* (New York: Continuum International Publishing Group, 1996).

Tocqueville, Alexis de, *Journey to America* (New Haven and London: Yale University Press, 1959).

Williams, Right Reverend Rowan, Archbishop of Canterbury, *Writing in the Dust* (Grand Rapids and Cambridge, U.K.: William B. Eerdmans Publishing Co., 2002), 63.

Index